COLONY AND EMPIRE

DEVELOPMENT OF WESTERN RESOURCES

The Development of Western Resources is an interdisciplinary series focusing on the use and misuse of resources in the American West. Written for a broad readership of humanists, social scientists, and resource specialists, the books in this series emphasize both historical and contemporary perspectives as they explore the interplay between resource exploitation and economic, social, and political experiences.

John G. Clark, University of Kansas, Founding Editor
Hal K. Rothman, University of Nevada, Las Vegas, Series Editor

COLONY AND EMPIRE

The Capitalist Transformation
of the American West

William G. Robbins

 University Press of Kansas

Published by the University Press of Kansas (Lawrence, Kansas 66049), which was organized by the Kansas Board of Regents and is operated and funded by Emporia State University, Fort Hays State University, Kansas State University, Pittsburg State University, the University of Kansas, and Wichita State University

Library of Congress Cataloging-in-Publication Data

Robbins, William G., 1935–
    Colony and empire : the capitalist transformation of the American
West / William G. Robbins.
       p.   cm. — (Development of western resources)
    Includes index.
    ISBN 0-7006-0645-9 (alk. paper)
    1. Capitalism—West (U.S.)—History.   2. West (U.S.)—Economic
conditions.   3. Mexican-American Border Region—Economic conditions.
4. Canada, Western—Economic conditions.   5. United States—Economic
conditions—Regional disparities.   I. Title.   II. Series.
HC107.A17H63   1994   94-11029

British Library Cataloguing in Publication Data is available.

Printed in the United States of America

10 9 8 7 6 5 4 3 2 1

The paper used in this publication meets the minimum requirements of the American National Standard for Permanence of Paper for Printed Library Materials Z39.48-1984.

With great affection for their friendship and politics,
this book is dedicated to
the Thanksgiving Day Crowd

CONTENTS

PREFACE

We must not delude ourselves with an idea that the past is recoverable. We are chained and pinioned in our moment. . . . What we recover from the past is an image of ourselves, and very likely our search sets out to find nothing other than just that.

—*Bernard DeVoto*[1]

This study of the American West is an inquiry into the dynamics of change for a particular place: the dramatic demographic decline in the Native American population and the equally significant resettlement by a variety of ethnic groups; the repeated introduction of new modes of production; stunning advances in the technology of production; great alterations to the natural landscape; the emergence of imposing new centers of power and influence; the construction and perpetual reconstruction of economic life and social associations; and the continued evolution of new sets of relationships between a relatively well-defined geographical region and the rest of the world. In it, I posit the argument that inquiries into political economy and systems of power and dependency are central to understanding historical change. There is no convincing alternative, I believe, to the encounter with ideology, with the politics and economics of social and class relations and their myriad contradictions, and with the all-embracing influence of capital as an agent of change. Those dynamics are part of the revolutionary world that is modern capitalism.

This book is an inquiry into plausible causation, the search for a general model to explain, over time, material/historical change and related phenomena for a particular place. Too often, in my view, scholars mask their explanations for change in the modern world by rhetorical euphemism and subterfuge, devices that address shadow rather than substance, symptoms rather than primary causes, and strategies that ignore fundamental facets of the material world. The more plausible and enduring explanations for historical change, I believe, rest in the material world: in the economic relationships among people; in the ever-changing dynamics of particular economies;[2] and in the set of values and assumptions, the mode(s) of production, inherent in what we call capitalism, the basic organizing principle for much of the global economy from the onset of the Industrial Revolution to the present. The cluster of suppositions and motives to human action associated with capitalism provides the most coherent, the most useful, and the most productive strategy and framework for discussing change in the modern world.

The chapters in this book are really a series of discrete essays, each addressing questions that are important to understanding the process and direction of change in the American West during the last century and a half. Mindful of the manner in which past narrative has conditioned the historiography of the region, I explore the comparative differences in transnational historical conventions (Canada and Mexico) to explain the special influence of powerful myths on both popular and scholarly writing about the North American West. But the theme that I attempt to pursue most consistently is the association between capitalism (and the capitalist ethos and all that it entails) and its revolutionary consequences for a particular place.

The physical region covered in this book encompasses the area from the ninety-eighth meridian (the Dakotas, Nebraska, Kansas, Oklahoma, and Texas) west to the Pacific, exclusive of Alaska and Hawaii. Because capital knows no national boundaries, the Mexican and Canadian borderland areas also figure in the analysis. It is this West that has undergone such spectacular change in the last 150 years or so. Until the great California gold rush of the mid-nineteenth century, most of the region was beyond the reach—or at best on the periphery—of the immense market-induced cultural, economic, and ecological changes that were occurring in the eastern half of the continent and in western Europe. The conquest of the Native Americans, their confinement to preserves, and the subsequent resettlement of western North America by others, therefore, are recent events, extending back in time little more than a century and a half. Indeed, what is striking about this relatively brief period in human history is the dramatic scope and the rapid pace of change over extensive areas in a brief span of time.

In his magnificent work *The Corporate Reconstruction of American Capitalism, 1890–1916* (one of the most significant pieces of historical literature published during the 1980s), Martin J. Sklar restates the proposition that capitalism is much more than pure economics: "[It is] a system of social relations expressed in characteristic class structures, modes of consciousness, patterns of authority, and relations of power." Capitalism, he emphasizes, is economics and much more: "It is property relations; it is class relations; it is a sociopolitical mode of control over economics and over a broad field of social behavior besides; it is a system of law and governance; it is ideology."[3]

As social formations that change over time, capitalism and the capitalist class are associated with values, objectives, principles, and interests. Thus we ignore at great risk material social relations, their associated institutions (i.e., the world of the corporation, the law, and so on), and the "widespread restructuring of economics, politics, and society."[4] Capitalists (and capitalism) have a history whose critical discourses—economic, political, and legal—are intertwined in complex and intricate ways. It is important to recognize that the imposition of capitalist property relations explains both the appropriation and the allocation of resources in the societies it has influenced. And pertinent to the region discussed in this book and its treasure house of resources, it should be emphasized that for the United States the direction and character of exploiting natural resources, the interpretation of great constitutional principles, and alterations in property law over time together reflect the constantly changing network of capitalist relations.[5]

Explanations of the transformation of the American West—from the world of pastoral hunter-gatherers to the amalgam of extractive, industrial, and engineered production forces of the late twentieth century—should be informed by some understanding of the ever-expanding boundaries and the constantly changing parameters of capitalism, especially in its national and international contexts. The fur trade, the settler movement, the mineral rushes that occurred everywhere across the region, and the transportation revolution were manifestations of the influence of global capitalism. As a flexible and transformable form of wealth, the movement and the dynamics of capital as it played itself out on the western landscape will reveal more about the modern West than discussions about the clash of cultures, economic development, or the disingenuous language associated with modernization and the achievements of the region as a pacesetter for the rest of the nation.

With some qualification as to aridity, distance, and ruggedness of landscape, there are serious weaknesses to exclusively essentialist arguments about the West or, for that matter, for any other region of North America. Events in the West were always inextricably linked to wider phenomena, to the dynamics of demography, to expanding and collapsing empires, and to an evermore expansive market system, itself in a state of incessant change. To understand the region properly, then, is to examine natural conditions such as aridity as well as the human institutions and effects brought to bear on a common place. Aridity itself explains nothing; how human cultures have adapted to, manipulated, created, and reshaped their surroundings tells us much more.[6] Prevailing over all other explanations for change were the biological exchanges, the enormous movement of people across vast distances, and the expanding sphere of market capitalism that provided the impetus, the direction, and the scope of the transformation in question.

This is not a study in economic history, nor do I view this effort as an economic interpretation of a particular place. To see it thus is to misconstrue the meaning inherent in capitalism as a set of values, a collection of assumptions and motives to human action, the comprehensive way that people view their world. My late friend and colleague, William Appleman Williams, preferred the descriptive term *Weltanschauung* (borrowed from Dilthey), in which economic decisions and political acts were components of a larger scheme (for Williams, this meant capitalism) that involved a particular perception of reality by which people conducted their daily affairs.[7] Capitalism, according to Fernand Braudel, "is of necessity a reality of the social order, a reality of the political order, and even a reality of civilization" itself.[8] In this special sense, capitalism provides structure, coherent organization, and a unifying theme for discussing change in the American West during the last two centuries.

The extension of the market economy to the most remote corners of the American West in the years following the Civil War illustrates still other characteristics of capitalism: its propensity to expand, its persistent drive toward accumulation, and its inclination to repeated technological change. In the process of extending its reach across the trans-Mississippi West, capitalism destroyed as it created. In its early market-resource form it destroyed the native subsistence economy and created in its place rudimentary market-exchange mechanisms; it destroyed Native American Indian communal landholding practices and replaced them with complex legal arrangements that granted primacy to private property rights in land. Eventually, through its proclivity for systems of large-scale production and its disposition to favor urban centers, it destroyed much of the rural West that it had created in an earlier time under a different set of capitalist relations.

The historical moment addressed in this book embraces a century or more of incredible change: the forced subjugation and colonization of the original occupants of the land, stupendous feats of human accomplishment and technological achievement, and equally significant evidence of human failure and suffering. This is a study in unrelenting change, a world perpetually in the process of becoming, of reforming, and seemingly of functioning (at times) on the edge of chaos. As the nineteenth century waned, the emerging industrial world, with its expanding network of national and international market and investment programs, increasingly influenced life in the region. That new and ever-changing set of relations—in which the West served as the vital raw-material reservoir for industrializing sectors in the eastern United States and in western Europe—institutionalized economic instability and further restricted the region's already limited autonomy.

There is little harmony and accord in the telling of this story. The celebrated freedom and autonomy of the West, to the extent that it existed, was the province of the few, of those individuals with power and influence and especially of those with capital. In contrast, dependent relationships abounded and in a variety of contexts: between wage worker and employer, between hinterland and metropolis, between marginalized subsistence communities on the one hand and the private sector and government agencies on the other, between small businesses and local contractors on one side and national corporations on the other, and between a capital-poor region and distant centers of capital savings. It is also important to understand that none of those entities represents static categories; rather, they were in a continual state of flux, reflecting changing configurations of power and similar alterations in capitalist property and market relations.[9]

There is yet another important caveat to add: as one system of production evolved into another, as one form of technology replaced another, the consequent processes of economic restructuring created winners and losers, and for the latter, pain and suffering. The Okie migration to the Far West, in brief, had much more to do with agricultural mechanization and shifting modes of production than with a Dust Bowl exodus. Indeed, the West abounds with similar examples in virtually all its major extractive industries: mining, agriculture, logging and lumbering, fishing. Among the revolutionary effects of mechanization were benefits for the few, not the many, greater power and influence for the metropolis, the marginalization and depopulation of the countryside, and the further centralizing and concentration of economic (and political) power.

If capitalism is an inherently revolutionary and volatile system, forever in the process of change, then the argument detailed in the following chapters provides an appropriate script. The spectacular urban growth in the region following World War II, the installation of new and innovative manufacturing facilities, and the explosive expansion of the high-tech sector brought both economic blight to the countryside and, in time, produced growing urban and suburban poverty. The present development of a new rural West—centered in the information revolution and the reverse movement of middle- and upper-class people from metropolitan areas to the remote corners of the West—reflects a continuum of those postwar conditions. Hence, the drumbeat of incessant change continues. To view the history of the region from the vantage outlined in these chapters, therefore, is to engage in the telling of one segment of the proverbial never-ending story.

ACKNOWLEDGMENTS

The route to the publication of *Colony and Empire* has its beginning in file folders of articles, book reviews, newspaper clippings, and "idea" notes that date to the early 1980s. Segments of chapters have appeared in *Environmental History Review, Montana: The Magazine of Western History,* and *The Western Historical Quarterly.* The accumulated debts for this book, then, are many. They include the formal comments and insights of scholars at several professional conferences; those who have given generously of their time and support in my pursuit of fellowships and travel grants; public and private funding agencies and institutions; and the casual exchanges with colleagues at Oregon State University and beyond that helped shape the particular direction of the study. The following grants and fellowships have supported this work: James J. Hill Research Grant (1987); Herbert Hoover Library Association Research Award (1987); Rockefeller University Grant (1988); DeGolyer Fellowship, Southern Methodist University (1988); Center for the Humanities Fellowship, Oregon State University (1989); Wayne Aspinall Lectureship, Mesa State College (1990); and a Bradley Senior Fellowship, Montana Historical Society (1991).

Because this book is largely derivative, my greatest debts are to the following people for the provocative ideas in their writing, for their questions, criticisms, and wit in shredding some of my off-beat notions, and for their generosity of spirit and friendship: Carl Abbott (for his incisive reading of the entire manuscript but especially the "Country and City" chapter); Judy Austin; "Bing" Bingham (for friendship and wise counsel); Richard Maxwell Brown (for the best of institutional friendships); Bob Bunting (for being a faster runner); Dan Cornford; Bill Cronon; Ed Craypol (for the "Maker's Mark"); Ivan Doig; Dick Etulain; Steve Haycox (for his enthusiasm about "doing" history); Norris Hundley; Maryanne Keddington and Bill Lang (for special friendships); Patty Limerick (for failing to list the words "Canada" or "capitalism" in the index to *Legacy* and thereby giving me something to write about); Richard Lowitt; Mike Malone; Clyde Milner; Spencer Olin (for his theoretical explanations and insights to the modern West), Earl Pomeroy, Chuck Rankin; Henry Sayre (a friend and great idea person); Carlos Schwantes (for the Amtrak traveling seminars); Marty Sklar; Elliott West; Richard White (who once accused me of attempting to burn the house down rather than repair the roof); Tom White; and Don Worster (especially for the long conversations en route to the Oregon coast).

Among my colleagues at Oregon State University, special thanks to Bess Beatty for her reading of the chapter on the South and West; to Bill Husband for his incisive critique of the preface; to David LaFrance for his perceptive review of the "United States—Mexico Borderlands" chapter; and to Paul Farber for his friendship, support, and the stimulating intellectual presence he has brought to the History Department. The always supportive office staff over the past few years—Marilyn Bethman, Julia Bruce, Sharon Johnson, and Barbara Morikawa—helped bring this work to conclusion. And the undergraduate and graduate students who have matriculated through my American West class during the last decade have contributed more than they can guess; a special note of thanks to Laurie Arnold, Karyle Butcher, Nancy Garcia, Ron Gregory, Tripp Hartigan, Lindon Hylton, Robert Self, Paul Snowbeck, Craig Wilkinson, and Don Wolf.

And finally to Karla, Kelly, and Aubrey for keeping me in the real world of family, school, and recreative activities; for tolerating my periodic trips away from home; and for appreciating the T-shirts and sweatshirts that I hauled home from strange and exotic places like Austin, Boise, Butte, Dallas, Grand Junction, Helena, Iowa City, Laramie, St. Paul, San Francisco, State College (Pennsylvania), Tacoma, and Tarrytown.

PART ONE

Western Myth,
Western Reality

CHAPTER ONE

Ideology and the Way West

From my point of view, any . . . history that ignores or treats lightly the pervasive power of the capitalist system finds itself working on secondary or minor themes.

—Norman Best[1]

It is appropriate that this book begin with Herbert Hoover, a graduate of Stanford University and the first true westerner to become president of the United States. The Iowa-born Quaker's rise from humble beginnings to positions of wealth and global influence—even before his election to the presidency—provides an appropriate symbol for the American West at the turn of the century. The story of the youthful mining engineer who journeyed to Australia in 1898 in the employ of the British firm Bewick, Moreing, and Company sharply challenges the notion that the western United States functioned as an isolated backwater of an emerging world power. Even Hoover's education suggests the influence of the region's major industry on university training—in his case, mining. His professional engineering experiences, first in Australia and later in China, also point to the revolutionary effects of capital in simultaneously reshaping landscapes and economies in various parts of the globe.[2] The movement of capital from points of accumulation to points of investment triggered mass migrations and disrupted indigenous populations worldwide, circumstances that reflect the totality of the modernizing forces that must properly be called "global capitalism."

The fact that the West Coast should be the focal point for American relations with other Pacific Rim countries should come as no surprise. From the beginning of the sea-otter trade along the northern Pacific Coast at the close of the eighteenth century through the years of the California gold rush, the Pacific slope was tied to oceanic routes for travel, for trade, and to a significant degree—particularly in the case of San Francisco—for sources of investment capital. For more than two centuries, then, Pacific and Asian ties have been a geopolitical reality for the Far West.[3] The transcontinental rail links that began to span North America during the last thirty years of the nineteenth century firmed and further integrated eastern ties to an area that could truly be seen as an increasingly international web of cultures, economies, and regions.[4] It is

3

proper, therefore, that Herbert Hoover, who was educated in the West and whose early career took him to the western edge of the Pacific Rim, should be acclaimed as America's first international citizen.

The American West always has been important for its oceanic links to distant places, peoples, and cultures and for its borderland ties to Mexico and Canada. Until recently, however, that historic connectedness to reciprocal continental and transoceanic associations has been little more than a sideshow to most scholarly enterprise.[5] In lieu of those broader geographical and cultural relations, historians have focused their attention on the evolution and expansion of the nation-state and on the positioning of the West within an insular ideological context. Henry Nash Smith attributed the problem to the agrarian tradition, so evident in Frederick Jackson Turner's writing, which "made it difficult for Americans to think of themselves as members of a world community because it affirmed that the destiny of this country leads her away from Europe toward the agricultural interior of the continent."[6]

Looking west across the landscape in linear and chronological sequence—from the colonial period along the eastern seaboard to the forging of a continental empire in the mid-nineteenth century—has been a powerful and seductive habit for historians.[7] In a wonderful essay, "The Idea of the West," Loren Baritz has singled out the commanding influence on American historical scholarship of the fascinating and mythical world that lay beyond "the point where the sun crossed the horizon," the place where "earthly glory and power tended." The consequences of that collective effort, Baritz argues, suggested a unilinear progression to ever-higher stages of civilization and presented the West as a land of promise, "the last refuge for man and God," an environment "where woe and wail would be no more." As the decades of the twentieth century have advanced, scholars have increasingly questioned those exceptionalist verities (as did Baritz), arguing that they are fraught with error and tend toward the ahistorical. In a farewell note to his profession, William Appleman Williams underscored the problem, strongly hinting that the exceptionalist view posed real difficulties for American historians: "We seem to be driven by a kind of compulsion to prove professionally as well as politically and socially, that we have been right from beginning to end."[8]

That exceptionalist tendency has led historians to praise national behavior in the interests of the state and to sacrifice the larger search for truths. Like other empires before it, the United States has generated a series of legitimizing myths to sanction its push to the western sea. Frances FitzGerald made that charge explicit in her study of the United States and Vietnam: "Americans see history as a straight line and themselves standing at the cutting edge of it as representatives for all mankind."[9] Although scholars have questioned and challenged the exceptionalist theme in recent years, it still holds great persuasive power, especially in the wake of the collapse of the Soviet Union and the eastern-bloc nations. The consequence of that power is found in a body of literature that praises the virtues, the social values, and the accomplishments of those people who came to dominate the continent.

From the Puritans through the writings of Charles Beard, David W. Noble contends, American historians have interpreted their culture as if it were standing apart, independent and unique from the experience of other nations. That observation is borne out by the remark of a former president of the American Historical Association, who suggested in 1986 that a basic operating assumption of Americans is that they differ "in some important ways from the people of other nations."[10] Hence, although the scholarship of the last few years shows that a blanket indictment of the profession is wide of the mark, the exceptionalist version lingers both in the academy and in the world beyond.

The controversy in spring 1991 over a Smithsonian exhibit at the National Museum of American Art, "The West as America: Reinterpreting Images of the Frontier, 1820-1920," is a case in point. Although on one level it illustrates the pressures that prominent political figures exercise over our collective memory, on a more significant level the reaction reveals the power of myth in our national culture. For too long, the great legends of the American West—discovery, exploration, and settlement—have controlled historical narrative, turning the story into metaphors and symbols that serve to explain and justify a society's essential rectitude. As exhibit director William Truettner has pointed out, "West as America" suggests the way myth has functioned "to control history, to shape it . . . as an ordained sequence of events."[11]

The media's reaction to the exhibit strongly confirmed Truettner's point, suggesting that those mythical visions still find considerable support within the academy just as they do from the general public. Daniel Boorstin, historian and former Librarian of Congress, wrote in the guest book at the exhibit hall that "West as America" was "a perverse, historically inaccurate, destructive exhibit. No credit to the Smithsonian."[12] Journalists and art critics also leaped into the fray, charging that the exhibit falsified the past, distorted the historical record, and demeaned the achievements of westward expansion. *New York Magazine* writer Kay Larson complained about the "carping tone" in the exhibit's story line, and *New York Times* art critic Michael Kimmelman chastised the show for its "simplistic" and "forced analysis."[13]

Despite the notoriety and the media attention it brought to the field, the current debate over "West as America" should be instructive for students of western history. The critics of the Smithsonian exhibit neglect the profound way that dominant cultures and their accompanying ideologies forge memory, shape perceptions and values, and otherwise become preoccupied with national virtue. It is not surprising, then, that both conservative politicians and some academics would heap abuse on those individuals who challenge the prevailing ideology, who offer different perspectives about the course of western history.

Accusations that the recent revisionist interpretations in western history and art are political represent little more than attempts to discredit the new scholarship because it questions protocols of objectivity in the more conventional stories. A considerable volume of the new work, according to Martin Ridge, is an angry story that emphasizes resource exploitation and the retelling of efforts by underclass groups in the West to regain control of their own destiny. "It is a history," he charges, "where ideology is too often substituted for evidence." Such criticisms, however, ignore the fact that *all* interpretations are political in their potential for shaping myth. Donald Worster has pointed to the irony of becoming an ideologue, "a dreaded label which often is applied to any historian who doesn't take the dominant or official ideology for granted." I would argue that scholars in the past who wrote about the "drama" of western settlement were as ideological as today's critics of those same processes.[14] There is a simple candor to Barrington Moore's remark of three decades ago: "Truthful analyses are bound to seem like exposures rather than objective statements."[15]

Although the exceptionalist theme is recurrent in studies of American history, it is especially and most glaringly obvious in interpretations of the American West. In the older, conventional view, the West was opportunity, a lotusland and haven, a refuge for the discontented and outcast, a place of perpetual youth where life could begin over and over again. But in what has become the great American myth, it was above all the *promise* of the West that loomed largest; for it was there that people would find the answer to their quest for a better life. Reality, in that special sense, was less important than the symbols through which people perceived a larger design; indeed, in that scheme, symbol and myth passed for reality. In an approach that has been called a "triumphalist literature," the easy virtues of drama served as a substitute for explanation and interpretation.[16]

To the degree that the West became the archetype for the triumphalist and exceptionalist ideology of the nation-state, it marked a retreat from history, a focus on a narrow exclusiveness, a lack of an appropriate context within a wider world, an escape from the material base of things. That descriptive tendency, despite its obvious flaws, has from time to time exercised a commanding influence on scholarly work because it better fits the national mythology. Such a mood is consistent with the consensus interpretations of the years following World War II and with the periodic calls for new syntheses in historical writing. Works in the latter category, Eric Monkkonen has warned, especially lend themselves to vacuous references to exceptionalism and the American character. A region, after all, is more than national history replicating its political, economic, and cultural self across the land; rather, it is a distinct part of that larger aggregate.[17] The argument tendered in this book suggests that we turn from the easy and comfortable designs of triumphalism and success and look more closely at alternative approaches to understanding the West, especially examining the structural role of capitalism in our national culture.

In its less pretentious forms, the study of history involves inquiries into power and change. Expressions of those two elements manifest themselves at several levels in ascending order from the personal and family to the village and community, then to the larger political and geographic realms—territorial, state, and regional—and finally to national and global influences. The aspects of change and the components of power to be discussed in this book embrace major transitions in productive relations from the pastoral to subsistence agricultural to the industrial and postindustrial, with each successive transformation reflecting evermore distant influences—the regional, national, and international. I also argue—with neither apology nor regret—that capitalism is the common factor essential to understanding power, influence, and change in the American West from the onset of the fur trade to the present.

A more inclusive understanding of western America rests in the ability to grasp the full meaning of capitalism: the set of values and perceptions associated with that phenomenon, its structural framework as expressed in social and political relations, and its pervasive reach through American life (what Donald Worster calls our "complex economic culture"). Scholars would be wise to read again Fernand Braudel's suggestion that capitalism provides an identifying theme for studying "the basic problems and realities" of the modern world. It provides "structure," an organized way for examining relatively fixed relationships between reality and society.[18] Because charges of intellectual flaccidity have been especially conspicuous in the field of western history, its practitioners need to be particularly sensitive to issues of political economy in the larger arena of world affairs—the interrelationships between political and economic activity and the alterations in those relations over time. To grasp the larger meaning of the transformation of the American West during the past two centuries requires a search for more compelling approaches to historical analysis, approaches that confront directly the broader meaning of capitalism, the system that has so persistently and continuously revolutionized our social order.

The history of the United States reveals the evolution of a market society, a society representing a particularly complex social-cultural construct, the "money-market system." As such, the United States, according to Martin Sklar, has been a "political society (or group of political societies) undergoing continuous evolutionary change." Its history exemplifies a culture centered in change, or better yet, "addicted to change." The United States also has been a nation of intersecting and interrelated regions, with differing modes of production extant in different regions at the same moment. Sklar points out that those divergent modes of production go far to explain interregional conflict.[19] It is important to recognize, too, that in terms of tradition and institutional restrictions acting to restrain market practices during the late nineteenth century, the United States (with the exception of the South) stood virtually alone among the industrializing nations of the world in the absence of such constraints.[20]

Woodrow Wilson—a public figure never confused as a revolutionary in the political sense of the word—understood the vital link between changes in the economic realm and "questions of the very structure and operation of society itself, of which government is only the instrument." In his inaugural address as governor of New Jersey in 1911, Wilson acknowledged that "the whole world has changed within the lifetime of men not yet in their thirties; the world of business, and therefore the world of society and the world of politics."[21] Though his assessment is narrowly centered on an economic analysis of American society, Wilson understood the larger relationship between economic and political culture.

Despite the reputation of the United States as the leading capitalist nation of the modern age, historians generally have been reluctant to pursue lines of inquiry focusing on the broader influence of capitalism on the country's historical development. The failure to reckon with capitalism indicates, in part, an unwillingness to confront significant power and influence in our culture, a tendency that is widespread, especially so in the study of the American West. Most historians do assume the existence of capitalism; the problem rests in the inclination to disregard its imperatives, its broader implications for society, the nature of the economy, and politics.[22] Even the innovative social and environmental histories of recent years evade central issues of power, politics, and the relationship of those elements to the essentials of the world of capitalism. The new social history, Herbert Gutman has charged, describes with some precision, but it fails to explain within the context of the broader workings of our cultural world.[23] In essence, history written "from the bottom up" is limited when it ignores larger constellations of power.

Elizabeth Fox-Genovese and Eugene Genovese have chided social historians for failing to acknowledge real power and for attempting "to deflect attention to the bedrooms, bathrooms, and kitchens of each one's favorite victim." Although that glib assertion may be too inclusive, if recent books and articles are an indication, evidence exists that the issues of political economy often do not inform investigations of gender, of class and race relations, and of family life. Those works may not be in the "neoantiquarian swamp," as the Genoveses claim, but they do ignore the material base that is the essence of the historical process.[24] The tendency to depoliticize is apparent in social histories of the American West as well, where the imperatives of capitalism are often muted or ignored. To the degree that politics, power, class relations, and other expressions of capitalism do not inform our work, scholarship is more readily susceptible to being trapped in the exceptionalist quagmire.

If, as Gene Gressley remarked at the 1987 meeting of the Western History Association, "our contemporary world requires illusion," then there is still a considerable body of scholarship on the American West—with the notable exception of some of the work published in the last fifteen years or so—to feed that world of myth and fantasy.[25] Thus is that world sustained, at least in the sense that scholars of western America fail to confront essential questions of political economy and the basic organizing structures that move cultures to behave in certain ways. There is a danger, I believe, that in our regional conferences and in the increasing volume of scholarly literature on the West, we could pass through this life unaware of the fundamental and transforming influence of capitalism in shaping the course of history.

Panel discussions at the 1987 meeting of the Western History Association provide a case in point. In one set of exchanges, "The Twentieth-Century West: A Retrospective Panel Discussion," there was virtually no mention of the broader themes associated with capitalism although the panelists (Gene Gressley, Gerald Nash, Robert Hine, and Howard Lamar) addressed problems of "insecurity" in the field, the search for synthesis, issues of federalism, the new social and intellectual methodologies, and continuity in western history. Howard Lamar, for one, disagreed with the charges that "gloom and failure" persisted among its practitioners and applauded the contributions of recent scholarship. But in that wide-ranging discussion no one mentioned such fundamental and divisive issues as class, poverty, inequality, or the historically marked differences among the subregions of the West. Nor did the panelists reckon with Samuel Hays's admonition to the profession, in the face of recent work in society and politics, that historians need to confront "persistent inequality as a central concept around which American history is to be organized."[26]

A second panel on environmental history (William Cronon,

Stephen Pyne, Susan Schrepfer, Richard White, and Donald Worster) raised more probing questions about the West: as a place to study human interaction with the landscape, as a prototype for examining adaptation or nonadaptation, as an environment for looking at different modes of production, and as a forum for the study of federal influences, especially in land ownership. In considering the West as the most "land centered" region, William Cronon suggested the need to view it as an aspect of an expanding European metropolitan community; rural change, he argued, begins in urban centers. Put simply, the pull of the market economy has had far-reaching implications. Most of the panelists agreed with the claim that the major influence on the western environment was the capitalist revolution and the consequent extension of industrialism to the region.[27]

Thus, although there is lively promise in the field, an inclination to avoid discussions of the hegemony of capitalism still exists, a propensity that neglects important questions in western history. In *Dust Bowl*, which won the Bancroft prize, Donald Worster warns that those scholars who avoid the word "may also ignore the fact," a common tendency in much of our historical literature. The words associated with capitalism, he adds, offer clues to its wider meaning: "private property, business, laissez-faire, profit motive, the pursuit of self-interest, free enterprise, an open marketplace, the bourgeoisie." Robert Heilbroner once thought he could avoid the difficulties associated with the term, relegate it to the netherworld, and concentrate instead on the "particulars of the business system." More recently he has realized that it was impossible to skirt the issue by resorting to "less contentious terms such as the business world or modern industrial society"; scholars would do well to learn from Heilbroner's experience.[28]

In the search for a more compelling interpretive model, it is important to begin with Karl Marx, whose historic achievement was to show the tremendous productive powers generated by capitalism and how those forces revolutionized life, first in the industrial core nations and then progressively around the globe. Among the anti-Marxists who pose significant questions is Peter Berger, who argues in *The Capitalist Revolution* that capitalism "has radically changed every material, social, political, and cultural facet of the societies it has touched, *and* it continues to do so." Understanding its cataclysmic and revolutionary impact, Berger cautions, "is a formidable . . . task."[29] But such a step is necessary to provide greater theoretical clarity and a broader intellectual scope to western American history.

Because the mode of production associated with capitalism is perpetually in a state of flux and constantly imposing new conditions on the societies it influences, understanding its complexities is important for the study of western North America. The penetration of market forces in the late eighteenth and early nineteenth centuries, the subjugation and colonization of native people between 1840 and 1890, the resettlement of western lands during that same period, and the progressive integration of the West into national and international exchange relationships provide the essential framework for broad historical analysis. Those forces, the prime movers in shaping (and reshaping) both the western environment and the emergent political economy, have been of peripheral concern to the academy, despite the proliferation in recent years of methodologies that have added new dimensions to our understanding of western history.[30] The structuring and restructuring of economic life and social relations in the American outback, after all, are expressions of the changing character of capitalism.

Both Frederick Jackson Turner and Walter Prescott Webb circumvented the issue through evasive language, albeit unintentionally. Turner thought only "an understanding of the rise and progress of the forces which have made it what it is" could assist in comprehending the United States of his day. Although he mentioned that the transformation of the country was "long in preparation" and was "the result of worldwide forces of reorganization," he did not specifically associate that transformation as part of the evolution of modern capitalism. Alan Trachtenberg has argued that Turner's thesis was "as much an invention of *cultural belief* as genuine historical fact." In a provocative essay, William Cronon attributes part of the problem to Turner's poetic and "fuzzy" language that gave the "illusion of great analytical power" to otherwise broad and ill-defined terminology. Ultimately, and Cronon emphasizes the point, Turner paid little attention to the eastern institutions that dominated life in the West, including the corporation.[31]

Webb's concept of the Great Frontier came closer to identifying capitalism as the central issue in western development. Formulated late in his career, Webb's notion of the Great Frontier was the land beyond the Metropolis (western Europe) at the time of the Columbian voyage. The opening of those distant places to European exploitation meant a series of windfalls that brought great riches to the Metropolis. Webb's frontier was an Eden, a "vast body of wealth without proprietors," and it was closely associated with the development of an emergent world capitalism.[32] Yet Webb failed to carry his analysis further; he saw the Great Frontier in its epic windfall stage coming to an end by the mid-nineteenth century.

Those grand masters of western history did not pay sufficient attention to political economy. Moreover, the dramatic alterations to the western American landscape of the nineteenth century—the human and cultural genocide waged against its indigenous population, the extension of

capitalism to the land beyond the Mississippi, and the exploitive and turbulent nature of its many economies—did not end with the close of that
century. And therein lies part of the problem: with the exception of some
recent and evocative work, scholars have yet to forge an analytical tool, a
comprehensive thesis to explain the transformation of the American
West from an area dominated by preindustrial societies to a region that is
an integrated segment of a modern world capitalist system.[33]

Changing power relationships and lines of dependency and authority have accompanied those revolutionary forces. As the United States
slowly broke the British and European mercantile hold over North
America in the years after independence, centers of influence shifted
from London and its metropolitan counterparts on the Continent to
emergent command posts on America's Atlantic Coast. In a complex web
of relationships those centers in turn spawned subsidiary trading liai-
sons in the interior as the market system worked relentlessly westward.
New Orleans, St. Louis, and by the 1830s and 1840s, Chicago provided
connective links between eastern metropolitan hubs and the Indian
trade that was entwining the native population and its subsistence base
within the market nexus.[34]

Then came the gold rush, an entrepreneur's dream and a great spur
to capital accumulation. For the shrewd, the tactful, the risk takers, and
those with access to credit, the world lay before them. It brought venture
capital from all corners *and* all at once. Many came, especially to San
Francisco, the growing imperial center of a sprawling web of investment
and finance that touched the tiniest outpost on the Pacific slope. Still
others ventured to the hinterland, to find sources of raw material or to
establish subsidiary houses in the growing western settlements that paid
homage to San Francisco. In truth, this was market capitalism at the moment of its most expansive growth.

In that sense, the gold rush exemplifies the most remarkable feature
of the revolutionary conditions that existed between 1825 and 1875, a
feature that historians sometimes overlook: the striking rapidity with
which the transformation took place.[35] By the time the first transcontinental railroad had provided a commercial artery across the continent,
the turbulent forces of an expanding capitalist economic system had
wrought a vast continental empire whose productive capacity—for a
time—would astonish the world. The construction of the remaining
transcontinental lines, the settlement of the interior, and the opening up
to commercial exploitation of its great mineral wealth were, in effect, a
kind of mopping up in establishing the contours of that new, spacious,
but still colonial West.

Until well into the twentieth century the colonial paradigm provided
convincing explanation for western development. Popularized in the

writings of Bernard DeVoto and others in the years just before World War II, this view described the region as little more than a geographical extension of eastern capital, a western outpost for Wall Street bankers to fleece.[36] But that interpretation lost currency in the explanations for the boom period after 1945 when it became fashionable to describe the West as a full and equal partner in the national political economy. The war, Gerald Nash contends, brought a "social and cultural transformation" of major proportions. Most important, it led to a diversified economic life, gave the region a new self-confidence, and left westerners with the perception "that now they were no longer colonials."[37] Both paradigms, however—the colonial model and that of the more recently liberated West—omit vital relationships, especially the continuity of much of western history in the age of modern capitalism.[38]

During the course of the twentieth century, the financial hold of the East upon the West has become increasingly more complex. As Donald Meinig pointed out more than twenty years ago, the heyday of the financial influence of the East, "the essentially 'colonial' relationship between the old, rich, powerful, industrial workshop and the new, money-short, vulnerable, raw material producer," had passed. In place of the old and long-resented imperial influence of the East, a modern, "insidious and relentless imperialism" had emerged, a phenomenon that extended from new centers of power in Texas and California.[39]

In lieu of the inadequacies of the simplistic colonial model, William Cronon and Richard White, among others, have suggested that dependency or world-systems theory would appear to offer a more fruitful way to explain change and relationships of power in the West. Cronon believes it would be productive to examine core and peripheral relations as a means of assessing differences in the "frontier experience." The dynamic and expanding capitalist economy of the United States, he argues, provides a necessary larger framework for evaluating that difference and diversity. In his study of dependency among the Choctaws, Pawnees, and Navajos, White advises that the examination of an interrelated set of phenomena is the best approach to understanding relationships of power: "the extent to which economic activities within a region . . . reflect factors essentially controlled outside the area; the lack of economic diversification and choice; and domestic distortions—social and political, as well as economic—within affected societies."[40]

Until the last ten years or so historians of the region showed ˙˙tle interest in such modeling as a structural forum for studying thᴇ West. References to the theoretical work of Immanuel Ѵ Fernand Braudel, and other early proponents of world-sysᵗ pendency approaches were customarily relegated to an obᴶ note—if they were mentioned at all. This is not to suggesᵗ should adopt some of the problematic directives of the dependency school; Wallerstein, for instance, ignores the dynamics of those internal class relations that have contributed to the changing faces of capitalism. There is, however, more than a germ of suggestive ideas in world-systems analysis—in its sharp criticisms of capitalism—and in other, leftist critiques of capitalism sufficient to provide a framework for examining the workings of that system in the American West.[41]

Taking a broader perspective of the ever-changing influence of capitalist structures in the West might also offer insights into the turbulent nature of much of the regional economy. Success and failure in the American West, after all, were components of larger processes in the expansion and development of worldwide capitalism. Because its conquest and resettlement coincided with the great period of industrialization, the trans-Mississippi West has been closely tied to volatile swings in the network of investment, exchange, and trade relationships that linked Great Britain, Europe, North America, and increasingly other parts of the globe in a world economy.[42] Indeed, if there is continuity to western history, especially to the story of its hinterland regions, it rests in the perpetually unstable nature of the region's material and economic base and its relations with the rest of the world.

During the last century, those conditions have brought periodic crises to western populations: shifting modes of production, mercurial fluctuations in the prices of mineral resources and agricultural products, the introduction of new technologies, and uneven development within the region as new and influential concentrations of power have emerged.[43] Moreover, an interconnectedness links those crises, one that rested with the revolutionary and transforming agency of the internal and external class relations of capitalism as it shaped and directed the course of western development. At least until World War II, there were few autonomous actors in the West.[44] Instead, most of the population in the region was linked to a system that perpetually forced people to the edge of change: to shift occupations, to move toward the setting sun, or to fall into a *lumpen* underclass of wage laborers.

That turbulent world has always produced winners and losers. Raymond Williams has recognized the relationship in his reference to country and city, "changing historical realities, both in themselves and in their interrelations." The actions of oil and mining companies in our present age, he argues, are similar to those of landlords in bygone days. In that process, the needs of locales and communities are often ruthlessly overridden.[45] And so it is with the hinterland West where capital has migrated from one region to the next, from one sector to another in its incessant quest for ever-higher profit taking. New modes of production—mechanization, new technologies, and the use of chemicals for a variety of purposes—invariably have benefited the few, not the many.

The migration of capital within as well as beyond the borders of advanced industrial nations is not a new phenomenon, however. Although capital investment in the agricultural sector has disrupted rural life in every region of the United States, it has had its greatest impact in the twentieth-century South as the institutional obstacles to investment were removed. During the 1930s and 1940s, the changing nature of federal policies and interregional labor markets transformed a low-wage, labor-based agricultural system into capital-intensive activities that involved base and extractive industries such as textiles, steel, forest products, mining, and, later, electronics production. Those revolutionary changes in the rural South enriched the landowning class while it crippled the tenants.[46]

The dramatic changes that came to the South beginning with the Great Depression and that continued through and after World War II were linked to conditions in the American West in profound ways. Huge federal subsidies to reclaim arid lands and heavy capital investment to put those lands to agricultural production, especially the growing of cotton in California's Central Valley, helped speed the demise of the labor-intensive system in the South. Following World War II, with record sales of mechanical pickers of all kinds, California was en route to becoming the prototype for new forms of productive relations in agriculture. External relationships were essential to that capital-intensive mode of production: marketing arrangements, credit houses, tax lawyers, and other institutional privileges available to the corporate few.[47]

The division between development and underdevelopment, between center and periphery, between the colonizer and the colonized is therefore complex, existing at several levels: national, regional, local; within segments of the local population itself; and in both intra- and interclass relations. Critical to understanding new bursts in economic growth is a recognition of the evolving dialectic between changes in world capitalism and local economies.[48] Hence, there are obvious social and regional contradictions in the development of the United States, conditions, Andre Gorz has argued, that resemble the relationship between an imperial center and a dominated periphery. The evolution of the American economy, he observes, proceeded from urban centers in the East: "Not until oil was discovered in Texas and sources of private accumulation were created by public finance (i.e., the creation of war industries in California) did other large industrial and financial centers emerge at the other end of the country."[49]

Yet the growing number of metropolitan centers in the twentieth-century West—Los Angeles, Denver, Seattle, Phoenix—did little to stabilize the region's economy, despite claims to the contrary.[50] In the land beyond those metropoles, communities continued to sway to the tune of financial pipers in places far removed. Mining, lumbering, and agriculture persisted as the most volatile sectors of economic life in the region. Dependent on often depressed and distant markets, those industries provided little security or stability for the producing classes, who were forced to sell their labor in the marketplace. In his study of the timber-dependent community of Everett, Washington, Norman Clark puts the case clearly for the resident work force: "[This] was not and could not be a humane system." His assessment fits the turbulent employment conditions in the mining towns of the Intermountain region as well as the agricultural communities scattered throughout the West.[51]

In truth, the great hinterland of the West remained as an integral, albeit extractive, appendage of urban finance—even though the power brokers were sometimes closer at hand as the century advanced.[52] In a provocative account of the New West, *Empires in the Sun*, Peter Wiley and Robert Gottlieb argue that the election of Ronald Reagan signified "further integration of the new western power centers, especially California," into the national political economy. They conclude, however, that the old pattern of relationships has persisted: the riches gleaned through the exploitation of the region's natural wealth and the profits garnered through the processing and manufacturing of the West's primary resources continued to wend their way into the hands of corporate financiers. Yet those conditions are not unique to the West; in the Appalachian coal country, one of the most depressed regions in the United States, more than two decades of federal assistance have done little to bring parity with more prosperous areas nearby. A recent study blamed "political and economic power configurations" and nonresident ownership for the region's problems.[53]

The juxtaposition of development and underdevelopment is both a western and a transnational problem. The dynamics of modern capitalism in Canada and Mexico, immediate borderland neighbors to the western states, have exhibited similar tendencies. Over the long course of economic development in British Columbia and Alberta, cycles of boom and bust in mining, lumbering, and agriculture have been the standard, with much of that cyclical activity following similar patterns south of the forty-ninth parallel. For their part, Canadian scholars have recognized the special character of the resource-based economy in the western provinces. The sociologist Patricia Marchak has noted the congruence between private activity and public policy in the development of Canada's hinterland regions, especially in rail construction. By the late nineteenth century western Canada was exporting lumber, wheat, minerals, and other raw materials in exchange for American manufactured goods—the classic form of reciprocity, according to Marchak, between an industrial center or metropolitan region and an exploited periphery or hinterland region.[54]

There is a striking degree of continuity—a strange dialectic of sorts—to the story of economic activity in western North America, but most scholars have been slow to acknowledge it. For much of the history of western America during the last 200 years, the real and effective cutting edge of change resided in the great centers of financial and political power in London, Paris, Berlin, and subsequently, in New York, Boston, Philadelphia, and their financial satellites in the interior of the continent. Although those centers have become more dispersed in the twentieth century, they are no less influential—whether they are in Mexico City or in Vancouver or Victoria—in determining the viability of communities in the surrounding countryside. And they are all of a piece, linked in a variety of ways to each other through the complex interstices of modern capitalism.[55] The rationale and the justification for the historic shifts in investment capital, I submit, will reveal more about the American West than idyllic notions about frontier exceptionalism or the habit in recent years of describing the region as a pacesetter for the modern age.[56]

In what I believe is one of the more important essays to appear in the last two decades, William Cronon asks why core and peripheral American regions have experienced such different developments. The various parts of the continent, he reflects, had evolved as part of "a larger system of political and economic relationships . . . all within the framework of an expanding capitalist economy."[57] It should be added that the major feature of capitalist relations in the American West and in its borderland countries, the point of origin of the capital notwithstanding, has been one of unequal exchange. Since the turn of the century, the metropolis has increasingly solidified its control over the hinterland, a development that has become particularly obvious in the years since World War II.

Although certain sectors within the metropolitan economy have waxed fat on defense and silicon-related industrial activity, that prosperity has not been evenly shared, as any casual drive through the hinterland West (or through urban centers, for that matter) will reveal. Rather, in the eyes of some observers, a dual economy has emerged, with a growing cultural and political division between rural and urban areas, a phenomenon especially noticeable in the more resource-dependent states. But even centers of power in southern California and in the Silicon Valley, despite their space-age, high-tech industries, harbor large work forces of unskilled, low-income, and unorganized laborers.[58] A careful look at the dynamics of class relations, therefore, reveals the complexity of the issues involved, both in the metropolis and in the countryside. Add another complication: with the onset of the 1990s and the end of the cold war, California is confronting the unraveling of its aerospace and defense-related economy.

Is there a qualitative difference, then, between the early and turbulent world of corporate exploitation in the extractive industries and the present conditions in many parts of the West? To be sure, some observers have pointed to the beneficence of the advanced capitalist class in the development of the West, and more recently, the ameliorative policies of welfare capitalism have muted the worst forms of suffering for the victims of economic catastrophe. Still, capital has retained its ability to shift from declining to rising sectors to meet the corporate need for profits.[59] And for many western communities, a new and even more threatening prospect is now emerging. The old extractive, primary-products economy, according to Peter Drucker, has come uncoupled from the rest of the industrial economy; whereas that sector was once central to the life of developed countries, it is now marginal.[60] Those circumstances already are wreaking havoc to communities in the hinterland West.

During the last decade, the daily newspapers continued to press on the public the most recent crises in agriculture. Less noticeable but no less ominous, according to Michael Malone, were parallel developments in metal mining, once a staple of western industrial activity. "With what seems incredible abruptness," he points out, the early 1980s "witnessed the utter devastation of the West's oldest industry." From western Montana through northern Idaho, Utah and Colorado and to Ajo, Arizona, energy conglomerates that had purchased the old metal-mining firms during the 1970s began closing them down. "Foreign competition," Malone argues, "has devastated western metal mining." The demise of mining, he suggests, "is part of a greater whole"; it marked the progressive "integration of the western economy into the global economy."[61]

Malone's assessment of the mining industry also fits the restructuring of the forest-products sector as well as the changing world of agriculture. After overseeing a sharp decline in union membership in the 1980s and the corresponding flight of capital to more lucrative arenas of investment, one state labor official offered an explanation: "What I think has to be understood is that the . . . multinational corporations have no national loyalties. Certainly they don't have any state loyalties, but they don't have any national loyalties either."[62] Hence, the contemporary West continues in a state of flux; from the oil fields of Oklahoma to the wheat fields of Washington, basic industry is languishing, victim to world economic changes. The journalist Michael Zielenziger put it succinctly: "Lacking in diversity, dependent on foreign trade and natural resources, the West's economy is unraveling." Current prospects, he observes, suggest the ushering in of a "dark, new West," one with islands of urban prosperity surrounded by an impoverished hinterland.[63]

Now that time (and power) is shifting beyond Henry Luce's "American Century" to westerly points across the Pacific, it is incumbent that in our scholarly endeavors we pay greater attention to our economic culture, the ever-changing and turbulent world it has produced, and the way it has worked its will on our common history. Many years ago Lewis Mumford pointed to the unceasing ability of capitalism "to revolutionize the means of production," to promote population shifts, and to allow room for some to "take advantage of the speculative disorder." The stability achieved under those arrangements, according to Mumford, was akin to the "equilibrium of chaos."[64] That description fits the pattern of uneven and incessantly changing economic activity described here, a system that brought dramatic and persistently destabilizing influences to major sectors of western American life.

Without a feudal past, the history of the American West is at one with the great transformations associated with modern capitalism. Because capitalism is a powerful, integrating, and homogenizing force, it diffuses differences, erodes contrasts, and undermines regional identity. Cynics may scoff, then, and ask, "Why the importance of western history?" That is not the point because the American West does provide a unique arena for scholarly work with its divergent resource base, its recent large-scale settlement patterns, the excessive volatility of much of its economic activity, and the persisting claims to colonialism in the region. To recognize that capitalism dissolves some elements of regional distinctiveness is not to suggest that we discard the study of western history, a conceptual trap that can lead only to sterile and circular debate. It would be better, I submit, to look at the American West as a prototype for modern capitalism.

As an underlying theme for making sense of western history, capitalism has been the centerpiece for precious little scholarly work. That neglect is a measure of the way we have ignored primary and hegemonic features of our collective history. In an address to the Organization of American Historians in March 1988, Donald Meinig urged his listeners to free themselves from the "crippling insularity" of their field, "the overweening exceptionalism of the American case, the rigidities of the assumption of the nation-state as the highest form in the political division of earth space." To question the idea of exceptionalism in the story of the West, therefore, is simply to recognize the revolutionary and transforming influence of capitalism as it has affected the region. "History," William Appleman Williams reminded the profession, "is dialogue, not consensus."[65] To strive toward a better understanding of the West, both in its national and international contexts, we should indulge less in celebration and in a quest for uniqueness and engage in a dialogue about the material structure of its history, an approach that will lead us closer to the realities of the region.

Lest I complain too loudly about the present state of affairs, it should be made clear that the lively debates of the last few years have invigorated and enlivened western history. The recent discussions have added new elements to the debate about the region, questions that revolve around the influence of capitalism, corporate leverage in manipulating natural resources, and the changing place of the region in the global economy. One consequence of these sharp and lively exchanges, discussions that encompass both empirical and theoretical formulations, is that scholars of the American West are beginning to vie with those from other regions in framing discourse about the national culture and its relationship to larger global phenomena. Richard White, who has raised some of the more fundamental questions, believes that the dialogue has reinvigorated and will continue to stimulate, sharpen, and deepen the study of western history. The current recognition of the strategic importance of the Pacific Rim, he points out, has placed the West at the physical center of events in the larger realm of national affairs.[66] The heyday of southern history, once the preeminent field for the most progressive and exciting endeavors in American historiography, has passed. If the impressive vitality of the current literature on the West is any indication, the new geographical setting for the most engaging scholarly discourse is America beyond the Mississippi. As the long American Century draws to a close, the West may be the most appropriate regional forum for that discussion.

And the stakes are high. If law represents the power to order the contemporary world, then broadly interpretive and widely accepted historical explanation represents the power to define a national culture. Certainly that is true of the Turner thesis, which, at least until the onset of the Great Depression, provided a seemingly convincing approach to explaining the growth and development of the United States. Indeed it was an argument that fit the prevailing mentalité of the patriarchal, Anglo-Saxon-dominated world of the early twentieth century. It also posited a thesis that the American frontier was a unique and independent agent, little influenced by outside forces and therefore a powerful environmental determinant in shaping human inhabitants to accord with its own requirements. With its strident emphasis on positivism and the exceptionalism of the American condition, Turner's thesis offered an explanatory model that was largely unchallenged until the spiraling unemployment and economic crisis of the Great Depression.[67]

But the Turner myth, spurred on by American global hegemony im-

mediately following World War II, lived on in lecture halls and public forums, despite the early admonishments of Frederick Shannon, Henry
Nash Smith, Earl Pomeroy, and a host of other critics.[68] Even though historical scholarship on the West was little affected at the time, the exceptionalist theme began to erode in the wake of events both distant and domestic—the Vietnam War and the civil strife of the 1960s—when scholars
began to take a less celebratory, more tragic view of the American past.[69]
William Howarth put the case well in a review essay in 1987: "After Dallas and Vietnam it was hard to admire gunfighters or new frontiers. . . .
The old landscape of hope has faded: Today the western news is of
dying farms and toxic dumps, the latest detonation at Ground Zero." Or
as Peter Shrag of the *Sacramento Bee* has observed: long before the October 1989 earthquake and the collapse of the Nimitz Freeway, the story of
the once Golden West had "turned toward the dark side of things."[70]

It is appropriate to point out that the true West, or the new interpretative work of the last few years, had its origins in the graduate acade-
mies of the late 1960s and the 1970s. European scholarship—especially
that associated with social history, world systems, and dependency
modeling—and other academic disciplines have infused the new history
with fresh insights and novel formulations and methodologies. The old
themes associated with the frontier, Elliott West argues, are now only
components of "a longer, more complex, and more interesting story"
that embrace cultural disruption, dramatic environmental change, and
economic abuse. The end result, according to West, is that "the prevailing view of the western past has changed more in the last ten years than
in the previous ninety."[71]

CHAPTER TWO

The U.S.-Mexico Borderlands: Tradition versus Modernization

Ez fer war, I call it murder,—
   There you hev it plain an' flat;
They may tolk o' Freedom's airy
   Tell they're pupple in the face,—
It's a grand gret cemetary
   Fer the barthrights of our race;
They just want this Californy
   So's to lug new slave-states in
To abuse ye, an' to scorn ye,
   An' to plunder ye like sin.
                 —*James Russell Lowell*[1]

The astonishing global expansion of capitalism during the third quarter of the nineteenth century included its spread to the largely agrarian countries of Latin America, nations ruled by oligarchies that had hitherto been beyond the reach of modern industrial capitalism. The integration of the old Spanish and Portuguese empire into the expanding and modernizing network of capitalist relations involved various degrees of direct interference by the industrializing world, including acts of open aggression, the most notable being the American seizure of vast territories in Mexico between 1846 and 1848. Beginning in the 1870s and with increasing momentum in the succeeding decades investors from distant places began funding the development of a continental infrastructure to serve the requirements of the industrializing world (the need for markets and raw materials).[2] Both the northern territories of the old Mexican empire (now part of the United States) and Mexico itself were included in that transformation.

The Mexican-American War, despite pretensions to the contrary, was a war of aggression, perhaps even as its harshest critics charged, a cynical, greedy offensive move against a nation incapable of defending itself. The Treaty of Guadalupe Hidalgo, which boldly proclaimed a new political geography, severed the expansive northern territories from the old Mexican empire, deprived its Indian residents of citizenship rights, and made the United States a vast continental political unit. The boundary between the two nations, drawn across lands cartographers and politicians called "empty country," actually cut directly through the hunting and gathering grounds of native peoples. But even the settlement of 1848 proved unsatisfactory to American interests, who soon pressed for a cession of additional territory to provide a more convenient route for a Pacific railroad. There were also rumors, according to one source, that the area south of the Gila River was rich with mineral deposits. In any event, the Gadsden Purchase concluded in 1853 subsequently embraced some of the richest copper deposits in the United States.[3]

The legacy of that new political reckoning profoundly redefined geopolitical realities between the United States and Mexico, a dynamic relationship that has been far more turbulent and less stable than many Americans would like to believe. Moreover, the results of the war made it glaringly apparent to the old imperial powers of Europe that the new continental empire in North America was not to be trifled with. The British journal *Spectator* recognized the significance of the push to the Pacific: the United States had become "a power of the first class, a nation which it is very dangerous to offend and almost impossible to attack."[4]

"Borders are volatile areas," according to historians Linda B. Hall and Don M. Coever, because they embrace expanses of territory that reflect cultural, social, and economic influences coming from different directions. For the U.S.-Mexican border, one of the longest unfortified boundaries anywhere in the world, the larger borderland represented a social and cultural world through which people of Mexican descent moved with little effort between two nation-states. Carey McWilliams once observed that "nothing like this zone of interlocking economic, social and cultural interests can be found along any other border of comparable length in the world." In the realm of historical scholarship, the borderlands region has always represented the antithesis of the conventional story of the American West because its racial and ethnic complexities did not match the prevailing Turnerian notions of an Anglo-American frontier.[5]

The dynamics of the Hispanic communities that were once part of the Mexican empire have much to reveal about culture, commerce, class structure, and patterns of migration across national sovereignties. To inquire into the influences of investment capital on traditional subsistence cultures and to examine the enormous economic transformation that has occurred in the old Hispanic borderlands is to open a window on the tricultural histories of Indian, Hispanic, and Anglo-American struggles for domination and control in the boundary region.[6] The United States was verging toward core status among the nations of the world in the mid-nineteenth century, and its burgeoning economy emerged as the most influential factor in Mexican affairs during the 1890s, a circumstance that subsequently would foster revolutionary conditions in Mexico. But the boundary itself was a chimera, a fiction in the sense that it had little relevance to the persistent transborder movement of both capital and people.

From the perspective of the 1990s, the U.S.-Mexican border is a study in paradox and contrast between two cultures, two economies that extend along the 2,000-mile boundary from Brownsville and Matamoros in the east to San Diego and Tijuana in the west. The international border-crossing between Tijuana and San Diego, an area where encounters between the two cultures are more recent, represents a contrast to the border country farther to the east, where interaction between people along the boundary is much older. The sociologist Jorge Bustamante points out that the border areas of the two countries pose sharp contrasts to their national economies:

> With the exception of California, the United States border with Mexico is one of the less economically developed areas. In contrast, Mexico's border with the United States is one of the more developed areas, with most economic indicators above the Mexican national average.[7]

This peculiar legacy rests in the unique historical circumstances that accompanied the social and economic transformation of the American Southwest, including the capitalist development of the Mexican border states of Sonora, Chihuahua, Coahuila, Nuevo Leon, and Tamaulipas.

Library shelves across the land are lined with unexamined and unquestioned narratives, boastful, celebratory, and heavy with meaning, of the westward expansion of the United States. The more conventional of those stories treat vast borderland areas—embracing adjacent continental and oceanic peoples, cultures, and nation-states; distant Pacific island constellations; the densely populated nations of the Orient; and Canada to the north and Mexico to the south—as subservient to the primary theater of action, the United States proper. The border with Mexico, a political boundary established through conquest and purchase, fits this prescription well and provides the thematic setting for some of the more celebrated and patriotic accounts of the American nation-state.[8] But in the last decade or so the borderlands area has also been the subject of some of the more innovative scholarly work on western America. The element of violent conquest, the persisting issues of race, caste, and class, and the special tensions associated with the labor question in the last half of the twentieth century have stimulated a thriving field of scholarship.

The now-sizable population centers located in one of the most arid regions of North America and the persistent northward movement of Hispanic peoples unquestionably have contributed to the attractiveness of the borderlands region as an arena for historical inquiry. A perusal of the scholarship indicates that historians of the region have little interest in the great mythologies that have so profoundly influenced the writing of western American history. The presence of Mexico, still relatively underdeveloped and a peripheral nation in the world capitalist system for much of its existence, looms large in any analysis of the borderlands region. Mexico, Donald Meinig reminds us, is more than simply "a coloration on the map."[9] It has reality as a place, a neighbor from whom the United States has extracted territory, wealth in mineral and petroleum riches, and a continuing stream of cheap labor.

Unlike their American counterparts, Mexican historians have never crafted a national success story for their homeland. David Weber, one of the foremost borderlands scholars of the moment, points to one of the ironies in comparing Mexican and U.S. history: "[In Mexico] there has been no counterpart to the American idealization of frontier life. No myth about the salubrious impact of the frontier exists on which a Mexican Turner might construct a credible intellectual edifice."[10] From the perspective north of the border, Weber argues, two factors have influenced traditional Anglo-American views of the Hispanic borderlands region: (1) racism—Anglos met a predominantly mestizo population in the vast reaches of the continent from Texas to California; and (2) Hispanophobia—Hispanic people presented an obstacle to the ambitions of the Anglos. History matters a great deal in this analysis because following the conquest of 1848 the victors controlled not only the newly annexed territories but also the writing of its history.[11]

The American Southwest is linked—decidedly more so than the northern West—to traditions of violence and cultural and ethnic oppression, circumstances that still persist.[12] Early in the nineteenth century, various American adventurers had been involved in Spanish and subsequently in Mexican affairs. The conquest of 1848, which halved the Mexican nation, marked the emergence of a robust continental empire well on its way to becoming one of the foremost industrial powers in the world. Although the Mexican War resulted in impressive victories and added vast and now familiar territories to the United States, Mexican scholars remember the encounter as the "intervention" that cost Mexico half its territory. Moreover, Mexican fears about additional territorial designs persisted, with good reason, into the twentieth century. The historical consequences of the intervention, the loss of a vast territory, and the persisting worries about further aggressions helped forge modern Mexican nationalism.[13]

The conquest, which meant the arbitrary drawing of lines across the physical landscape irrespective of political and cultural preferences, has turned the international boundary with Mexico into one of "the world's great cultural borderlands," a meeting ground for diverse peoples, cultures, and economies. For Jorge Bustamante, who grew up in the northern Mexican state of Chihuahua, the border represented sharp cultural and economic contradictions and an arena for the working out of accommodations between the two.[14] But the borderlands of the American Southwest were significant in other ways as well. With the completion of two transcontinental railroads through New Mexico and Arizona in the early 1880s, the region became an important reservoir of raw materials for the expanding production of the industrial sectors of the U.S. economy. Despite its wealth in natural resources, the capital-poor southwestern-borderlands region remained marginal and far removed from arenas of power and decisionmaking.

As the twentieth century has advanced, the border separating the United States and Mexico continues to capture public attention; it remains, as it has for more than a century, the meeting place of two dramatically different nation-states, the one the most powerful and advanced world capitalist power for much of the twentieth century, the other the only Third World nation in the northern hemisphere to have a common border with a modern industrial nation.[15] The background to the contemporary borderlands story involves issues of conquest, continued economic domination, and cultural and racial oppression. It also includes the forcible imposition of capitalist legal relations and contests over landownership that accompanied the transition from subsistence living to the integration of indigenous people into the modern wage-labor force. Yet for the burgeoning enterprises of a modernizing capitalist system, the political boundary between the United States and Mexico did not present an imposing barrier, nor does it in the late twentieth century.

During winter 1989–1990 both the Berlin Wall and the Iron Curtain crumbled in the midst of the dramatic events that triggered the political transformation of Eastern Europe and subsequently of the old Soviet Union. At that same time, and an ocean removed from those European events, the borderland between the United States and Mexico was seemingly moving in the opposite direction. American critics of drug smuggling and illegal crossings by Mexican nationals into the United States were proposing a variety of water-moat barriers and "taco curtains" to fortify the border between the two countries. For a deficit-ridden nation, the construction costs involved in those proposals were as mind-boggling as the earlier effort by the administration of Richard Nixon to seal hermetically the 1,933 miles of border to drug traffickers in 1969. Known as Project Intercept, that aborted effort accomplished little more than to underscore the administration's ignorance of borderland geography.[16] It also indicated the futility of attempting to make the border an impassable barrier.

The establishment of the U.S.-Mexican boundary in Spanish-speaking and Indian homelands placed some restrictions on travel and transborder social and cultural life. Yet it did nothing to inhibit the flow of capital through the region, nor did it unduly restrict cross-border business development and exchanges. The conquest did dramatically increase the pace of change, however; it unleashed the Anglo penetration of the Southwest, first in the extension of existing trading networks and then—with the arrival of the railroads—in the appropriation of the region's resources by distant capital. Sociologist Thomas D. Hall argues that until 1848 the influences of the outside world in the region that was to become the American Southwest were relatively limited. But the conquest "brought several major changes in quick succession," all of them linked in some way to the forces of the industrial revolution. These changes included the extraction of the region's resources and the transfer of those resources and the wealth gleaned through their appropriation elsewhere. The conditions for the relative underdevelopment of much of the Southwest, Hall contends, were established early on through "unfavorable economic relations."[17]

Those conditions are apparent on the upper Rio Grande today in one of the more distinctive historical-cultural regions in the United States. First colonized in a series of Spanish settlements in the 1600s, the Rio Arriba as it became known served as a unique ethnic and rural homeland that has persisted to the present despite an aggressive and dynamic Anglo-American economic system. Practicing subsistence forms of agriculture through the 1930s, the Spanish-American population of the area remained outside the mainstream of the modernizing world of capitalist agriculture while its growing population provided a marginalized and seasonal labor force for the larger commercial farms beyond the Rio Arriba.[18] Indeed, one study found that by 1900 the area was the point of origin for most Spanish-Americans living in Colorado.[19] Hence, one can conclude that fifty years removed from the conquest of 1848 the Rio Arriba people were subject colonials on lands they had occupied for more than three centuries.

Along with its isolation from primary channels of communication and commerce, its internal conditions and the lack of markets contributed to the region's historic marginalization. Through the first thirty years of the twentieth century, farmers in the Rio Arriba sold modest surpluses of apples, wild pinon nuts, and hay, and vendors from the area traveled to Albuquerque and Santa Fe to sell chili peppers, fruit, and woolen blankets. With the growing influence and importance of a cash economy, however, the residents of Rio Arriba had relatively little means to obtain currency other than through the sale of their labor outside the district. By the time of the Great Depression, low farm incomes and small land units situated in overpopulated microbasins characterized the Rio Arriba. "The Spanish Americans' self-reliant practices," according to geographer Alvar Carlson, "have led to endemic poverty and dependency upon government assistance programs" that have persisted to the present.[20]

Today the integrative and homogenizing influence of modern capitalism is apparent everywhere in the Rio Arriba, resulting in a declining percentage of Spanish Americans in the area and its erosion as a distinctive cultural region. Since the 1970s the takeover of the land base by non–Spanish Americans has accelerated, and the number of people farming small acreages has continued to drop. The values of market capitalism now thoroughly permeate the Rio Arriba as it becomes increasingly the focal point of Anglo-American speculative interest. With its arid climate and spectacular mountain scenery the region is being rapidly commodified as an attractive investment arena for venture capitalists interested in recreative, tourist, and retirement projects.[21]

But the Rio Arriba represents only a microcosm of changes that were taking place everywhere in the greater Hispanic Southwest, where tradition and subsistance living gave way to the attractions of wage labor and the inroads of market capitalism. Both push and pull factors were involved in the breakdown and destruction of traditional society. The widespread privatization and the federal withdrawal of lands that formerly had been used as commons grazing lands restricted the size of village sheep and cattle herds. The rules and regulations of the federal agencies favored the larger commercial grazing operations and discriminated against family and cooperative village units that had been using the lands for generations. John Nichols's *Milagro Beanfield War*, a fictional account of the regional conflict between Hispanic villagers and the appropriative influences of commercial agriculture and development interests, captures the spirit of the struggle. Overpopulation in many of the settlements also appears to have created additional pressures on a limited arable land base. The result was a shift to urban centers, especially among younger people, a phenomenon Richard Nostrand calls "village depopulation." A traditional and rural Hispanic society, he notes, "was rather quickly transformed to an industrial and more Anglo-oriented society."[22]

Perhaps the most clearly delineated study of the intrusive and pervasive influence of market capitalism on the Southwest is Sarah

Deutsch's *No Separate Refuge,* an inquiry into a regional community of Hispanics in northern New Mexico and southern Colorado. The thrust of her investigation is the gradual erosion of the community's autonomy as its residents were gradually drawn into the network of market and wage relations over an extended period of time. Despite the inroads of industrial capital in the form of railroad enterprises, commercial stockmen, timber interests, mineral companies, and friendly federal agencies to do their bidding, Hispanic villagers had maintained a modicum of autonomy into the twentieth century through seasonal migration from their communities to participate in the growing regional wage-labor economy. The larger regional Hispanic community survived only to the extent that the dominant Anglos had no vested interest in appropriating the fledgling commercial life of the villages.[23]

Deutsch offers a persuasive argument, one that employs gender as a category of analysis and that fully integrates corresponding issues of culture, class, and market and wage relations as she focuses on the meeting point of Hispanic and Anglo worlds. Although women conducted subsistence activities in several villages in northern New Mexico and southern Colorado, the Hispanics adopted only those elements of Anglo culture that suited their needs. Yet with the emergence of corporate units such as the Colorado Fuel and Iron Company, the autonomy of the regional Hispanic community and its village system began to erode. Finally, when Hispanic women increasingly entered the Anglo-dominated wage-earning work force as the twentieth century advanced, the villages found themselves "isolated and peripheral for the first time."[24] The communities Deutsch studied are similar to those in the Rio Arriba in that they illustrate the increasing marginalization of their constituents over time. Hence, the story of the Hispanic villagers counters the positivist tendencies of American historical writing that presents those communities as progressively integrated and assimilated into the Anglo world as the twentieth century advanced.

The same market forces that propelled the course of events in the northern reaches of the old Mexican empire unleashed strikingly similar influences in Texas, especially after its annexation to the United States in 1845. A commercial Spanish-Mexican society with aristocratic, even feudal ideas about land and labor was rent asunder in the ensuing decades. The first significant commercial ties linking Texas to the expanding industrial centers in the United States were the great cattle drives of the post–Civil War era.[25] The coming of the railroads and the ranching bonanza of the 1870s and 1880s accelerated the pace of change, especially the onset of a massive transfer in land titles—with all of the customary forms of chicanery and outright violence—from Mexican to Anglo ownership. David Montejano's *Anglos and Mexicans in the Making of Texas,* the

best account yet of the borderlands area in Texas, strips away the romantic and legendary aspects of that story and portrays a world in which the
displaced Mexicans, who had formerly worked on the great landed estates, were reduced to wage laborers.[26]

The capitalist transformation of southern Texas, in Montejano's
view, created a world where cowboys were wage workers and indebted
servants, where the coming of barbed wire represented an enclosure
movement that displaced people and left them landless, and where the
great cattle trails became routes that linked the region to national and international markets. For Mexicans in Texas, the nineteenth century was
characterized by the loss of their land base and the twentieth century by
the "organization of Mexican wage labor" to satisfy the needs of capitalist agriculture. Most of that revolutionary change in the regional economy occurred between 1900 and 1910 with the increasing commercialization of agriculture and the replacing of the old order with the new.
Outside promoters and speculative schemes disrupted the remnants of
the old Mexican-dominated ranch economy as agricultural production
grew apace, the end result being the conversion of ranch to farm and the
displacement of Mexican vaqueros and peons. At the outset of the 1920s
Mexicans were reduced, "except in a few border counties, to the status of
landless and dependent wage laborers."[27] Montejano's book and studies
of its kind go far to reclaim voices absent from the conventional western
success story. They also remind us that the capitalist transformation in
the United States involved both the agricultural countryside as well as
the industrializing metropolis.

The racial violence that accompanied those wrenching changes, including widespread executions and lynchings, indicates that the transformation of south Texas involved heavy doses of racial and class conflict. Although an abundance of statistical evidence and historical work
on the brutalities committed against blacks in the American South is
available, the racial atrocities that occurred in south Texas are less well
known. The long revolutionary decade in Mexico (1910–1920) and World
War I aided and abetted tensions in the region. At the peak of the violence, thousands of people left south Texas, Mexicans going to Mexico
and Anglos to Corpus Christi or San Antonio. Montejano estimates that
as many as 5,000 Mexicans may have been killed during those years,
whereas sixty-two Anglo citizens and sixty-four U.S. soldiers lost their
lives. Most of the violence took place in four counties, precisely the areas
where the commercialization of agriculture was having its greatest impact.[28]

Because of the large indigenous Mexican and Indian population in
the southern borderland area at the time of the conquest, more violence
accompanied the contest for land there than in other regions of the

American West.[29] Genocide, intimidation, and the removal of native people characterized the migration to California in the 1850s and 1860s; similar sharp reductions in the native population, albeit not in the hundreds of thousands as in California, occurred in Oregon and Washington and on the northern and southern plains.[30] But with the possible exception of the ongoing Indian struggle over treaty-guaranteed rights everywhere in the West, the contest for land in the Southwest was more protracted and intense.

Montejano and other borderland revisionists portray a version of southwestern history that is something less than a triumphal narrative. Although Montejano's story is not one of total and unmitigated tragedy and failure, it presents a sobering picture of a struggle for space and against cultural and economic oppression. In every respect a thoroughly researched work, *Anglos and Mexicans* provides a new way to envision and analyze western history. Montejano places the south Texas, Mexican-border area in the larger context of continental and world affairs; he is aware of the integrating forces of the market mechanism and the complexities of international relations. In that context, the conquest of 1848 reflected new political realities; it did not mean a permanent separation of cultures, economies, and peoples.

If there are monuments to capitalist expansion in the nineteenth century, the great railroad systems that increasingly criss-crossed the land masses of the earth would be the most representative example. The railroad, the revolutionary new technology that Karl Marx called the crowning achievement of industrial capitalism, opened several transportation corridors through the American West during the 1880s.[31] The coming of railroads marked the onset of the economic, social, and cultural transformation of the Hispanic borderlands and the linking of the broader region with the world's expanding capitalist economy, and in the process sowing the seeds for revolutionary discord in Mexico. The dark side to the dazzling achievement of railroad building, according to Ramon Ruiz, was the dismantling of "traditional society while cementing in place a new capitalist edifice."[32]

Unquestionably the most significant regional power center to emerge along the U.S.-Mexican border in the late nineteenth century was the city of El Paso. Located in a low pass along the Rio Grande River—known to Mexicans as Paso del Norte—El Paso and its counterpart, Ciudad Juarez, on the Mexican side of the river, occupied a strategic geographic area with a long history of serving as a crossroads of communication and travel. Like other areas in the interior West, distant from links to global centers of industry and capital, El Paso underwent a dramatic transformation with the arrival of the transportation infrastructure so vital to capitalist expansion. Between 1881 and 1883 three lines converged in El Paso: the Southern Pacific from the west; the Atchison-Topeka-Santa Fe from the north; and the Texas-Pacific and the Galveston-Harrisburg-San Antonio from the east. As one scholar remarked, "Capital flowed immediately into El Paso." When a southerly route into the Mexican heartland was completed in 1884, El Paso solidified its position as a regional urban power.[33]

Capital followed the steel rails to El Paso and its extensive, resource-rich hinterland. The coming of the new transportation spurred the development of copper mining and the extraction of other minerals on both sides of the border but especially the rich lodes in southern Arizona, New Mexico, and the Mexican states of Chihuahua and Sonora. Although the extensive rail system served as the catalyst for entrepreneurial activity, mining was the centerpiece for economic growth: it encouraged investment in cattle raising and other forms of agriculture (on both sides of the border) to feed the growing number of mine workers; it led to the establishment of machinery and goods-distribution houses in El Paso; and it convinced several mining-supply firms to locate in the growing city.[34]

Because of its historic location on the borderland between different cultural worlds and its relative isolation from major population centers, El Paso exhibited features common to similar environments where stratification by class and race were obvious. As a strategic crossing point on the U.S.-Mexican border, El Paso developed as an entrepôt and marketplace for unskilled and cheap labor. During the years of dramatic industrial growth, entrepreneurs looked south of the border to satisfy much of their labor needs for the railroads, in the mines and smelters, and for agricultural production. Mexican immigration into the north, Mario Garcia contends, must be placed within the context of the unique economic infrastructure that developed in the Southwest with a recognition of the consequences that American investments in Mexico had upon that nation's resident population. The growth of capitalist agriculture in Mexico, financed by foreign investment, forced people off the land and sent them trooping north where they served as a source of cheap labor.[35]

Within this isolated, regional metropolitan core and in the hinterland beyond, distinct and obvious class and racial divisions developed. The agent managers, professional and technical staff, and other skilled workers were mostly white Americans, and Mexicans constituted the great majority of blue-collar labor. Whether they were longtime residents of the area or newly arrived from south of the border, Mexican people found that El Paso's agricultural and extractive economy offered little in the way of social advancement. Indeed El Paso was but a microcosm of the larger region in which Mexican workers provided the essential backbone for most forms of productive activity. Patricia Nelson Limerick's comparison of the South and the Southwest is apt: "As the economy of the South rested for decades on the availability of black people's labor, so that of the Southwest depended on Mexican labor."[36] It is important to emphasize that although the metropolis historically may have dominated and dictated the terms of its relationship with the countryside, it is a mistake to describe that dialectic in terms of a simple imperial/colonial relationship. One was relatively more powerful than the other, but both were divided along class lines and, in the case of the American South and Southwest, along racial lines as well.

Elsewhere in the Southwest the influence of the railroad and the capitalist transformation was equally apparent. Albuquerque, Tucson, and Phoenix, old Spanish towns established in the seventeenth and eighteenth centuries on the northern limits of New Spain, joined El Paso in gaining rail connections to a wider world in the early 1880s. Each of those river cities, in Bradford Luckingham's words, served as "spearheads of desert development," linking vast, sparsely populated but resource-rich areas to distant centers of investment capital and industry. Although the Santa Fe railroad made Albuquerque "the metropolis of New Mexico" with direct routes to the gulf ports of Houston and Galveston, the city also had taken on much of the character of a company town by 1910. As the Santa Fe's most important terminal point between Topeka and Los Angeles, Albuquerque was home to the railroad's huge regional shops, office facilities, and switching yards, and nearly 2,000 of its 11,000 residents worked directly for the railroad.[37]

The desert country of southern Arizona was integrated into the revolutionary world of industrial capitalism when both the Southern Pacific and the Santa Fe lines were extended through the area between 1878 and 1881. As in many of the mining areas in the West, a silver boom set off the initial rush to Tombstone in the southeastern corner of the territory. Despite that much celebrated phenomenon, it was copper mining—with the emergence of camps such as Bisbee, Globe, Jerome, and Morenci— that quickly moved to the forefront to dominate the economic and political order in Arizona Territory. The Guggenheim and Phelps-Dodge families were active both in the territory and in the northern Mexican state of Sonora. Eventually Phelps-Dodge acquired Guggenheim's Sonoran properties and controlled a vast copper empire in the Southwest by the early twentieth century. The firm's investments brought industrial activity to the spare, arid country of eastern Arizona and western New Mexico and created a wage-earning labor force to work the area's mines and smelters. By the turn of the century more people were employed in mining than in any other enterprise in the territories of Arizona and New Mexico.[38]

Meanwhile, politics and geography conspired to place the mining districts of northern Mexico within the expanding sphere of dynamic American capitalists. Weak and financially strapped central governments and the barrier of the Sierra Madre Occidental, which made north-south travel difficult, left the rich copper fields of the north (less than 100 miles from the border) within easy striking distance of American capital. Although northern Mexico was isolated from the nation's heartland, one scholar has noted that it was easily accessible "to the dynamic transport and economic systems of the United States—at a time when American financiers had been granted a carte blanche for investment in Mexico." The result was early rail construction that linked northern Mexico to continental lines north of the border; none of the early railroads tied the north to the interior of the country.[39]

Although ranching, agriculture, and mining provided the basis for the regional economy on the American side of the border, local entrepreneurs in western Texas, New Mexico, and Arizona also took advantage of the amenities of climate to boost the region. Physicians elsewhere in the country began advising wealthy patients to spend their winters in the land of perpetual sunshine in New Mexico and Arizona. A local booster in El Paso declared that "the dry refined air of the region is a luxury to breathe." Some individuals who came to recover their health stayed on. Dwight Heard, a successful Chicago businessman, came to Phoenix in 1897 and made the small desert metropolis his home. Representing the opening wedge for Chicago capitalists, Heard and his cohorts specialized in a variety of real estate and development projects.[40] But whether they were developing smelters in places such as El Paso or investing in resort hotels such as the Santa Rita in Tucson and the Adams in Phoenix, the combination of those external forces brought constant and persistent change in the Southwest.

As several recent studies have illustrated, changes in the larger world of global capitalism influenced settlements on both sides of the U.S.-Mexican border; hence, the persisting and defining historical themes for the greater Hispanic borderlands remain the influx of outside capital to the region, the Mexican revolution, and the migration of Mexican people to the north. This migration should be placed firmly in the larger context of geopolitics, its most significant features being foreign investments in Mexico during the rule of Porfirio Diaz and the socioeconomic dislocations that followed.[41] The transforming influences of industrial capitalism (and capitalist agriculture) on both sides of the border weighed heavily in laying the groundwork for the revolutionary turmoil that ravaged Mexico and spilled across its northern border in the second decade of the twentieth century.

Modern Mexican history begins with the liberation from French rule in 1867 and the ensuing policies that permitted foreign investments in railroad construction, land purchases, and a variety of mineral- and oil-leasing arrangements. Under Porfirio Diaz (1876–1911) the Mexican government pursued a modernization policy that encouraged foreign-capital investment in the development of an infrastructure that would invite further ventures in other sectors of the economy (silver, copper, tin, oil, lead, rubber, and coffee). That strategy brought tremendous change to the Mexican countryside, especially in the northern states of Chihuahua and Sonora. Communal Indian lands passed into individual holdings, thereby transforming land into a marketable commodity. There was also a proliferation of individually owned farms or ranchos, accompanied by a great concentration of landed property, much of it in the hands of Americans. New incentives for capitalist agricultural production, especially for the export market, made land more valuable and thus brought on those wrenching changes in the control of land. John Mason Hart points out that those forms of government-sponsored foreign investment "reached an unprecedented magnitude, especially in the far north." The Porfirian achievement, in brief, readily embraced "foreign domination [largely American] of economic life and public policy."[42]

The capitalist transformation taking place in Chihuahua and Sonora after 1880 mirrored the changes occurring simultaneously north of the border.[43] The same venture capitalists who invested in railroad, mining, and agricultural enterprises in the border states of Texas, New Mexico, and Arizona also appear in the stock-and-bond ledgers of the foreign corporations that were in the process of transforming the Mexican countryside. The list of financial backers of the four great trunk lines linking the Mexican heartland with U.S. entrepôts at Nogales, El Paso, Eagle Pass, and Laredo included the leading American capitalists of the late nineteenth century: E. H. Harriman, Jay Gould, Russell Sage, J. P. Morgan, John D. and William Rockefeller, Meyer and Daniel Guggenheim, Grenville Dodge, and Southern Pacific's Colis P. Huntington. The Mexican government made huge land grants to the groups involved in the financing and building of the railroad system, concessions that eventually emerged as key factors in the nationalist revolution that began in 1910.[44]

On both sides of the border, places relatively self-contained and distant from centers of capital were drawn in as extractive, raw-materials producers for the world economy. The scenario played out in the Rio Arriba, in the lower Rio Grande Valley, and elsewhere throughout the sparsely populated precapitalist American side of the border was repeated in the Mexican states of Chihuahua and Sonora. For arid and isolated Chihuahua, the infusions of foreign capital magnified and accelerated concentrations in landownership and in the possession of wealth and placed the state's economic welfare in concert with the cyclical moods of global capitalism. The foreign-controlled mining industry, key to Chihuahua's export economy, ultimately destabilized traditional social relations and contributed to profound social disruption.[45]

In the special case of Sonora, foreign (United States) capital built the railroads, the critical infrastructure for exporting raw materials and importing manufactured goods. Because the state's industrial livelihood was linked to mining, especially silver and then copper, the volatile swings of world mineral prices determined whether Mexicans had jobs.[46] The building of railroads and the industrialization of Sonora, albeit largely in a single extractive industry, were revolutionary instruments in the sense that they brought jobs in agriculture, mining, and commerce. The effect of copper mining in the state, according to Ramon Ruiz, was the erosion of traditional culture and the erection of a capitalist infrastructure. Mining provided income for state coffers that financed the building of public schools and other aspects of cultural life, and it brought a level of dependency apparent to all Sonorans, even to those who benefited from the system. Such as it was, the mining boom was relatively short-lived. A drop in the international price of silver and the opening of new copper mines in Chile cut into mining profits even before the escalating violence and disruptions associated with the revolution began. And beyond the realm of mining, Sonora had no industry.[47] When the mines closed down or the ores ran out, the state was left with a marginalized and itinerant labor force ready to move across the border in search of work or to join in revolutionary activity against the Mexican government.

Although the American side of the border was absent the great violence that occurred in Sonora and Chihuahua, the years between 1910 and 1920 were turbulent: New Mexico and Arizona gained statehood; conflicts over the labor question, especially in Arizona, were strewn with violence and the gross violation of basic civil liberties; and an agricultural revolution occurred in the lower Rio Grande Valley that brought a new, modernizing commercial farm system, replacing and dispossessing the old Mexican rancho society. The events in the Rio Grande Valley best illustrate the dynamic effects of local conditions—racial animosity, economic change, and an irredentist movement—seen in the context of international tensions that involved revolution in Mexico and war in Europe.[48]

The insurrection that scorched the Rio Grande Valley between 1915 and 1917 centered on an irredentist program, the Plan de San Diego, that called for the old Mexican provinces (now part of the United States) to proclaim their independence from Yankee tyranny. Mexican and Mexican-American raids in south Texas during the twelve-month period that began on July 15, 1915, brought conditions of hysteria in south Texas, twenty-one American deaths, and reprisals against Mexicans that included the execution of at least 300 Mexicans without trial. "The armed insurrection of Texas Mexicans and its brutal suppression by Texas Rangers," according to David Montejano, "turned the Valley into a virtual war zone."[49]

At its roots, the threatened race war reflected currents deeper than merely a local manifestation of national and international events and circumstances. The border violence marked the transition from an older, paternal ranch society to a thoroughly commercialized farm society heavily dependent on wage labor. Most of the disorder occurred in counties where the commercialization of agriculture was most advanced, and crudely put, the opposing armies were made up of displaced Texas Mexicans and the Texas Rangers.[50] The disruptions of 1915–1917 and the mass exodus from the lower Rio Grande Valley left a bitter residue of hatred, suspicion, and animosity in the region that only the passage of time has begun to lessen.

Through the nationalist forces unleashed by its revolution, Mexico regained control of its land base and subsurface mineral rights from the intruding foreign investors (even in Sonora) and moved toward an open society that emphasized mobility and competitiveness. Yet in a larger sense, according to John Mason Hart, "the still powerful foreign element prospers through the global financial structure and a commitment to advanced technology," a role conceded to it by Mexico's bourgeois elite, the true victors of the revolution. And in certain sectors of the economy, as in mining, foreign-based corporations such as Anaconda and American Smelting and Refining Company (ASARCO) still prevail with an active staff of corporate experts who are Americans.[51]

On the northern side of the border, Arizona and New Mexico were increasingly integrated into and linked with corporate and governmental structures beyond the region. The New Mexico Bureau of Immigration, for example, published a series of booklets to promote the economic expansion of the territory. In *The Mines of New Mexico*, the bureau extolled the potential riches of the region, citing its "inexhaustible deposits . . . unequaled in any state or territory." The bureau also promoted Santa Fe County as a place of settlement for the "Sight Seeker, the Health Seeker, and the Wealth Seeker and Home Seeker." And in *Ho! To The Land of Sunshine*, the agency provided information attractive to immigrant homeseekers. With the development of rail connections to outside markets, agricultural production grew apace in New Mexico after 1910. The population of the territory increased by 68 percent in the first decade of the twentieth century as the number of farms tripled and vast acreages of land were put to the plow, some of it with federal subsidies for irrigation development. With the onset of World War I and rising prices for beef, wool, wheat, and mineral ores, circumstances beyond New Mexico continued to fuel the economic advance, but the great boom ended just as abruptly in the wake of depressed conditions in agriculture and mining.[52]

In the adjacent territory of Arizona, with its thoroughly integrated ties to distant corporate investors and world economic forces, the production of copper ruled supreme. Although its population did not surpass that of New Mexico's until World War II, Arizona's economy more clearly reflected the colonial relationship between the region and the outside world. Although cattle and sheep raising and irrigation agriculture had made considerable advances by the 1920s, until World War II the copper industry provided Arizona's most important source of personal income and tax revenue. And if economic power represents political power, Arizona's copper magnates have been good examples, ruling their fiefdoms with a mixture of paternalism and the occasional use of the mailed fist. Isolated Bisbee, controlled for most of its history by the Phelps-Dodge Corporation and the most striking example of resource-dependency on Arizona's southern border, had extensive ties to a larger world of corporate investment, and ultimately, disinvestment. In the case of Bisbee and its companion towns—Jerome, Globe, Ajo, Clifton, Morenci, and Douglas in Arizona, and Santa Rita in New Mexico—local developments can best be understood in the context of national and global economic relations.[53]

Until World War II, manufacturing was nonexistant in both Arizona and New Mexico; thus the two economies remained dependent on the mineral prices and on an often-glutted market for agricultural goods. Arizona's copper economy, moving with the rhythms of international pricing arrangements, experienced the conventional boom-and-bust characteristics of single-industry communities. Yet even in the best of times, few of the rewards trickled down to the workers who operated the mines, the smelters, and the transport and supply systems; those conditions fostered strikes, violence, and ultimately the state's open and repressive use of force on behalf of the companies.[54]

The new sets of economic relations that were firmly fixed along both sides of border—in the Mexican states of Chihuahua and Sonora and on the U.S. side in Arizona and New Mexico—shared much in common. The four states were integrated into the industrial infrastructure of world capitalism at approximately the same time, and common actors in the world economy dictated their relative prosperity. Chihuahua and Sonora may have been somewhat better off compared with other states in developing Mexico, but both states paralleled early twentieth-century New

Mexico and Arizona in the larger constellations of financial power. Similar circumstances prevailed along the Texas-Mexican border. The commercialization of agriculture on the U.S. side of the Rio Grande converted the area to a wage-labor system for Mexican workers, and across the international boundary, the Mexican states of Coahuila, Nuevo Leon, and Tamaulipas underwent a comparable transformation.

Although the huge infusions of federal investment during World War II dramatically altered conditions on the U.S. side of the border, certain common features of dependency remained: for Arizona and New Mexico an infrastructure heavily infused with federal defense and reclamation subsidies emerged, and on the Mexican side a tradition of continued dependency persisted in the form of the Border Industrial Program, a corporate-supported arrangement between the United States and Mexico enabling American-based businesses to take advantage of cheap labor on the Mexican side for purposes of manufacturing, assembly plants, and the like. And despite their successes, the Mexican bourgeoisie, the managerial classes, did not control their own destiny. Every Mexican player, Ramon Ruiz concludes, "took his marching orders from capitalists and markets 'on the other side.' "[55]

CHAPTER THREE

The American and Canadian Wests:
Two Nations, Two Cultures

> Americans routinely perceive and accept Canada itself as a borderland and
> take for granted the easy transnational movement of people, goods, money,
> and ideas—all the while quite blind to the fact that Canadians may have a
> rather different view of that boundary and what it means to live within the
> towering shadow of a world power.
>
> —*Donald W. Meinig*[1]

Bob Brooks celebrated the 1992 Toronto Blue Jays' World Series victory
over the Atlanta Braves at the Double Overtime Sports Grill in Vancouver, British Columbia. Brooks, who joined with other fans in festivities
that took place everywhere across the "great white north," enjoyed a
moment rich in irony for all Canadians: "Canada's team" defeating
"America's team," in a game billed as America's national pastime. Referring to an incident that took place in the second game of the series in Atlanta when the U.S. Marine color guard displayed the Canadian flag bot-
tom-side up, Brooks remarked, "They turned our flag upside down—we
turned their world upside down." There was an additional point of
pride concerning the partying and carousing that followed the victory in
the Blue Jays' hometown: police reported little crime.[2]

The fact that the Canadian people would be euphoric should come
as no surprise—the Blue Jays were, after all, the first major league base-
ball team outside the United States to win the World Series—but the Canadian celebration represented far more than the ritual merrymaking following a World Series victory. It also resonated with feelings of
vindication, apprehension, resentment, and envy. It is important for
Americans to remember, as Donald Meinig points out, "that the bedrock
of Canadian nationalism is the determination not to be American." The
larger meaning of the Toronto victory pointed to still another irony: although Canadians have always taken a great deal of interest in American
politics and sports, Americans have shown little interest in matters having to do with Canada.[3]

More than twenty years ago, Sen. Everett Dirksen of Illinois described the 5,524-mile-long U.S.-Canadian border as an "unfortified,
heart-warming symbol of trust, co-operation and friendship—the sym-

40

bol of a bond." Dirksen's remark is indisputably "American" in its implication that Canada should be taken for granted, a widely shared view
that has a long and honorable tradition in the United States. In contrast
to their relations with Mexico, Americans are virtually oblivious of matters having to do with their northern neighbor. Canada, for many Americans, is vacationland, a source of wood fiber, the point of origin for the
ubiquitous weather patterns that vex the eastern half of the country—
and the birthplace of Gordon Lightfoot, Bryan Adams, Monty Hall, and
Peter Jennings. Americans, according to Canadian historian Kenneth
Coates, "seemingly give little thought to the influence of Canada" in
their lives.[4]

Although that temperament is pervasive in American popular culture, it also extends to historical studies of relations between Canada and
the United States. Donald Worster drew attention to the problem in a
summary address at a 1988 conference celebrating the statehood an-
niversaries of the northern-tier states:

> In comparison to the southern borderland shared by the United
> States and Mexico, this northern one has gotten little attention from
> historians, though both have had a similar past of imperial struggles
> between European powers, of declarations of independence and na-
> tionality, of confrontations over sovereignty, of migration back and
> forth. We have no real school of northern borderlands history, no
> Herbert Bolton or John Francis Bannon for these parts.[5]

And yet, as Meinig argues, Canada, which sprawls across the continent from the Atlantic to the Pacific, "is one of the great facts of American life." The historical evolution and the political structures of the two
nations, he suggests, provide a comparative context for the study of Indian and European relations, "immigration and assimilation, industrialization and urbanization, and an array of questions relating to nationalism, federalism, regionalism, [and] pluralism." And there is an
additional element, one often lost on Americans: If Mexicans have been
fearful of their proximity to the United States—a point recognized in virtually all borderland studies—then it is not surprising that Canadians
should attach special meaning to "continentalism," the persistent fear
that the infinitely more powerful United States might devour its northern neighbor. Grasping that special reality, Meinig suggests, can help us
understand the American impact on modern-day Canada.[6] The problem
also holds the potential for generating cross-border historical analyses
and comparisons.

The two great borderland regions separating the United States from
its northern and southern neighbors also reflect fundamental historical

and cultural differences. Despite the aggressive designs of the United States, especially in the nineteenth century, the Canadian-American boundary was established through negotiation rather than by naked conquest. But that veneer of accommodation and sense of common purpose masks more than it discloses because there are notable differences separating the two countries. Canada and the United States celebrate different traditions and conventions; each has inherited unique and distinctive historical legacies. Markedly disparate mythologies, cultural attributes, and accumulated traits distinguish the two nation-states. In contrast to the great myths of the American nation, especially in its western regions, in Canadian literature, as Seymour Martin Lipset points out, "the frontiersman has never been a figure for special glorification."[7]

In the boundary regions separating the United States and Mexico, issues of race and class are too obvious to ignore, matters that are much less apparent along the U.S.-Canadian border. Population centers along the northern border, Raul Fernandez points out, do not share the same historic conditions that prevailed among their southern counterparts. Moreover, in our public discourse even the references carry different meanings: the "boundary" divides the United States and Canada, but the "border" separates the United States and Mexico. The larger meaning of "border" and its corollary "border town," according to Fernandez, "has negative connotations which imply conditions of unsettlement and hostility."[8] That particular sense of enmity and malevolence has never prevailed in the U.S.-Canadian borderlands.

When one views entire national populations, the demarcation among cultures and societies is even more distinct between the United States and Mexico. To begin with, the disparities in class are infinitely greater between the United States and Mexico than they are between the United States and Canada, but on the U.S. side of that southern border, the picture is less distinct. The great numbers of Spanish-speaking people (and increasingly those of other cultural and language groups) in California and the Southwest confuse the clear delineation of race and class, of cultures and societies. Historically such conditions have never prevailed along the U.S. border with Canada. And at least for the twentieth century, there has been no mass movement of Canadians to the western United States that compares with the Mexican migration into the American Southwest.

Those long-standing historical circumstances along the two western borders of the United States have profoundly influenced the direction of historical studies. If it is true that historical scholarship tends to seek out points of social tension in our contemporary world, then it follows that the southern borderland simply may provide a more attractive arena of research for many scholars. The region's special circumstances inviting inquiry include the shattering and building of empires, the economic colonization of one nation by another, and the complex dynamics of race and class. Freed from the mental constraints of the grand national mythologies associated with the westward movement, students of southwestern history and culture have more readily adopted newer methodologies and theoretical models in their work.

Because of the expanding scope and complexity of scholarly inquiry on Mexican/American, border/borderland issues, historical research on the continental perimeters of the western United States has fallen victim to a conceptual trap of sorts. Indeed, such is the prolific discourse on Hispanic-American affairs that historians have come to see the borderlands of the North American West exclusively in terms of the Southwest. In her provocative and widely acclaimed book, *The Legacy of Conquest*, Patricia Nelson Limerick adds to the fashion of seeing the western United States in terms of a unilinear physical boundary that seemingly extends about its full perimeter: "Beyond its national role, Western America has its own regional significance. Remoteness from New York and Washington, D.C.; the presence of most of the nation's Indian reservations; [and] proximity to Mexico."[9] The index to *Legacy* indicates that matters pertaining to U.S.-Mexican border issues are addressed on several pages. The name Canada does not appear in the index.

While public attention and most academic discourse has focused on the economic, political, and cultural implications of the transborder movement of peoples in the Southwest, there has been little inquiry into the impressive demographic shifts, the repeated introduction of new technologies, the common transformation of landscapes, and the evolution of industrial and capitalist relations along the Canadian-American border. Indeed, the transborder movement of people and ideas along the forty-ninth parallel is a largely unexplored topic. The U.S. and Canadian Wests were both scenes of the dramatic population decline and removal of native peoples, the large-scale resettlement of those landscapes by aggressive, acquisitive-minded newcomers, and the reshaping and management of those settings to suit the production and marketing needs of the newly dominant population. As some writers have suggested, the obvious route to fresh perspective and insight into Canadian-American borderland peoples and cultures is the removal of nationalistic blinders and a concomitant increase in intellectual border-crossings.[10]

Thus we shall focus on the different national traditions in Canada and the United States (with the emphasis on the former) and on the influence of those historical legacies on a common western border. I am particularly interested in narrative expression and how it reflects themes of dominance and conquest in the western expanses of both countries. Although the westward push of Euro-Americans appears to be as much a divine mandate to Canadians as to Americans, the former seem to have couched their ambitions in less provocative rhetoric. And there are additional observations: in the process of resettlement and economic development Canadians moved with greater prudence and caution, with some attention to matters of social conscience, while their American counterparts were faster off the mark, more aggressive and innovative, and never looked back.[11]

The groundwork for the emerging mythology of the northern West originated in the economic culture—the set of ideological conventions—brought by several invading groups: (1) the early European seafarers who ventured along the North Pacific coast in search of sea otter in the late eighteenth century; (2) their compatriot overland voyageurs who carried the lucrative fur business through the passes of the Rocky Mountains in the early nineteenth century; and (3) the myriad adventurers, official explorers, missionaries, farmers—the foot soldiers of the American and Canadian advance to the Pacific.[12] Collectively, those groups produced a literature that embraced essential elements defining human character, human conduct, and human attitudes toward the natural world—the building blocks of legend and mythology.

This brief review begins with the British sea captains, James Cook and George Vancouver, who saw material bounty and bright prospects on every hand when they visited the Northwest Coast between 1778 and 1794. Cook's *Voyages*, published in 1784 and subsequently advertised among merchant circles in England, drew attention to the great commodity value in furs and timber along the Northwest Coast. The fur of the sea otter, the report concluded, was "softer and finer than that of any others we know of; and therefore the discovery of this part of the continent . . . where so valuable an article of commerce may be met with, cannot be a matter of indifference."[13] *Voyages* hinted to a larger audience about the bright market prospects in the region, a potential that could be realized only through the domination of native peoples and their economies. The commercial objectives of the discovery also emphasized the fact that expansion was metropolitan-based and reflected metropolitan desires and objectives.

Vancouver followed suit in his great reconnaissance expedition for Great Britain in 1792, a direct consequence of metropolitan-based pressure on the British government. The controversial and domineering captain looked with favor on the lush greenery of Puget Sound; visiting Protection Island in May, he found the landscape "almost as enchantingly beautiful as the most elegantly finished pleasure grounds in Europe." Finally, ashore at Tulalip on Sunday, June 4, Vancouver took "formal possession of all the countries we had lately been employed in exploring, in the name, of, and for His Britannic Majesty, his heirs and successors."

By virtue of that act, according to Barry Gough, the Northwest Coast was now "a dominion, a future sphere of empire." Those individuals who followed, he concludes, "brought with them their morals, ideologies, knowledge, technology, plants, and animals. They also brought diseases, rum, and guns. They brought with them powers to build and powers to destroy."[14] And, it should be added, they possessed the power to create their own version of reality.

Yet it is the land-based newcomers to the northern West who have left the most coherent body of writing about the land and its native peoples. The values and meaning associated with the words in that corpus of literature have contributed mightily to shaping the mythical story of the West at large. For the "place" under examination here, the proper sources to consider first are the journals of Lewis and Clark, a collective reportage that is at once instrumentalist, descriptive, scientific, commercial, even clinical in its detail. The potential of the western country is noted, especially for its commodity prospects (furs) and for the great wealth to be made in expanding the Indian trade. Through the descriptive power of the journals, Lewis and Clark influenced ideas and molded lasting images about the northern West.[15] When the expedition completed its tour in September 1806, it moved from Jeffersonian enterprise into the national mythology; hence, as explorers in the pantheon of American mythmakers pointing the way toward new lands, Lewis and Clark rank with Columbus and Daniel Boone.

The captains' observations, then, have carried great weight in a variety of scholarly fields but especially in their accounting of native people. Despite some initial promise, the end result of that assessment is a darker judgment, one that followed familiar ideological, racial, and cultural contours. In his provocative study, *Lewis and Clark among the Indians*, James Ronda acknowledges that the captains were unable to overcome deeply embedded stereotypes; I would take that observation one step further and suggest that Lewis and Clark, because of their influence in the shaping of western myths, contributed to a hardening of those conventional perceptions, a temper that has fixed firmly in our historical literature fundamental aspects of conquest and domination.[16]

The *Journals* are equally significant for what they reveal about the western environment, its climates, its contours, its flora and fauna, and its potential in other resources. According to John Logan Allen, the literary contributions of Lewis and Clark were important "as acceptors, modifiers, and shapers of geographical lore and images;" they reaffirmed "the iridescent vision of an agricultural paradise in the West" because the descriptions of the route of travel did not appreciably challenge or dispel existing assumptions about the western landscape. Though the journals described a region geographically more complex and multifaceted, they still represented to readers an objective confirmation of the pastoral image, albeit a bit more restrained.[17]

As the corps waited at Fort Mandan for the ice to clear from the Missouri before resuming their upriver trek, Lewis described the surrounding countryside in a letter to his mother. "This immense river," he wrote, "waters one of the fairest portions of the globe," an area of open prairie "fertile in the extreme, the soil . . . consisting of a fine black loam." Game was abundant, he noted, "and seems to increase as we progress." In his September 1806 report to President Jefferson, Lewis emphasized practical, instrumentalist findings, especially the rich fur resource of the Missouri and its tributaries. He cited the navigability of both the Missouri and Columbia rivers to points well upstream, and although the Rocky Mountains were a "formidable barrier," they could be breached easily during the summer months with horses obtained "for the most trivial consideration from the natives."[18]

Lewis advised that the northern West and the Columbia River country should be part of a larger global-marketing strategy. Furs from the Missouri River and the Rocky Mountain region "may be conveyed to the mouth of the Columbia . . . and from thence be shiped to and arrive at Canton earlier than the furs which are annually shiped from Montreal arrive in England." With limited government aid, he continued, "we shall soon derive the benifits of a most lucrative trade." Above all, he warned, "if we are to regard the trade of the missouri as an object of importance to the U. States," the moves of the Northwest Company toward the Missouri "must be vigelently watched."[19] The by-line for this argument subsequently became a central tenet of economic development policy: (1) nature is capital; (2) these resources are economic assets that should be realized and maximized; and (3) the culture should encourage such activity.

Clearly the Lewis and Clark expedition stimulated American interest in a larger continental context. It excited the youthful imaginations of would-be empire builders such as John Quincy Adams and Thomas Hart Benton, among others.[20] But the immediate influence of the expedition—and the point of attraction for the entrepreneurial minded—focused on the resources of the region: the *Baltimore Federal Gazette*, in what future events would prove an understatement, reported that the publication of the captains' journal "will no doubt be . . . importantly interesting to us all"; an item in the *Philadelphia Register* noted that "one of the hands" recently returned disclosed that the Indians on the Columbia were "peaceable" and the "winter was very mild"; the *National Intelligencer* informed its readers that Captain Lewis "speaks of the whole country furnishing valuable furs"; and the *New York Gazette*, acknowledging the fur resource, added that the Columbia and its tributaries "abound in salmon. The timber is pine, maple, ash, poplar, and oak."[21]

Those who followed Lewis and Clark through the northern West did not appreciably depart from the captains' narrative descriptions with the result that the familiar imagery about native people and the western landscape was firmly fixed. The journals of Ross Cox, Astorian and subsequently Northwest Company operative, reveal a common theme in descriptions of the region and its people: lower Columbia River natives were "ugly specimens of morality, . . . [who] were thorough-bred hypocrites and liars." Still, like the captains before him, when Cox turned to observations of the physical environment, he reported "with pleasure" on the "productions of the country, amongst the most wonderful of which are the fir-trees." The climate in the Willamette Valley, he remarked, was "remarkably mild . . . [and the valley] possesses a rich and luxuriant soil, which yields an abundance of fruits and roots." He urged missionary societies to extend "their exertions to the northwest coast of America" to assist the native people who were "still buried in deepest ignorance."[22] In reiterating the inferior status of these people, Cox and others perpetuated old stereotypes in their cultural repertoire and laid the groundwork for common attitudes in historical narrative toward native peoples in the Northwest. Those premises included a clear sense of superiority and the identification of Anglo-Saxon values with values in general.[23]

Alexander Henry and David Thompson, the Montreal-based Northwest Company adventurers who traveled through the northern West, recorded similar observations about Indians and their places of habitation. The people of the lower Columbia, according to Henry, lived in houses "exceedinly filthy. . . . the men seemed brutes, and the women devoid of shame or decency." Henry reported late in December 1815 of word from the Willamette River where the "beavers are numerous, but the natives, who are also very numerous, will not hunt them" but spend their time digging roots and "stealing beavers from [our] traps." Henry was obviously disgruntled and frustrated at the unwillingness of the valley Indians to participate in the company's commercial ventures. For mindsets like his, the motives of "the other" were always negative; when Indians in the vicinity of the mid-Columbia rapids were friendly, he remarked, "This shows them to be treacherous."[24]

Just the American Robert Gray took possession of the lower Columbia River on behalf of the United States, so did David Thompson claim that portion above the confluence with the Snake River for the British government. By right of "discovery," Thompson proclaimed on July 9, 1811: "Know hereby that this country is claimed by Great Britain as part of its Territories, & that the N W Company of Merchants from Canada, finding the Factory for this People inconvenient to them, do hereby intend to erect a factory in this Place for the Commerce of the Country around." In addition to recognizing his discovery of the upper Columbia River country, historians usually pay tribute to Thompson's other "contributions," especially his trove of cartographic information.[25] Yet they fail to indicate that ethnographic knowledge was considered irrelevant as an end in itself; its sole function was to serve the purposes of expanding the Northwest Company's trading empire.

John McLoughlin, the chief factor for the Hudson's Bay Company's Columbia District, is generally credited with a sense of fairness toward Indians, an attribute accorded to few others in the fur trade. Yet, as some writers have indicated, McLoughlin was a calculating man, cruel and ruthless on occasion, and given to shrewd manipulation of Indian and trader alike to promote the interests of the company. McLoughlin directed trading activity with the objective of maintaining the company's "influence over Indians," of doing everything possible to keep native people faithful to the company's trading network (even if it meant using liquor, a tactic he generally opposed), and of trapping out the Snake River country to discourage the Americans (to the point that the beaver were "getting nearly exhausted"). McLoughlin was candid with company directors when the potential of an area did not "prove-up" as was the case with Peter Skeene Ogden's excursion to California; Ogden reported a country the "poorest in Furs that he had hitherto explored."[26]

But no entrepreneur was more alive to the potential for profit taking in western North America than McLoughlin's boss, George Simpson, field chief for the Hudson's Bay Company and the architect of Great Britain's imperial dominion over much of Canada. Perhaps even more so than his American counterparts, Simpson was alert to the broad range of commodity value to be realized across the vast reaches of the West. Though the resources of the country were "abundant," the natives in his view were "excessively indolent," despite what he viewed as the opportunities before them.[27] It was his responsibility, Simpson believed, to engineer mechanisms for bringing natives under the control of the Hudson's Bay Company and thereby within the embrace of the market system.

In his travels through the Columbia River country in 1824 Simpson described the bounty of salmon in the Arrow Lakes area; he took note of the fertile soil and "salubrious" climate further downriver and observed several places where "a trading Establishment properly managed ought to live in the midst of plenty." He cited the strategic advantages in selecting the site for Fort Vancouver, the company's trading center on the great Columbia system:

The place we have selected is beautiful as may be inferred from its Name and the Country so open that from the Establishment there is good travelling on Horseback to any part of the interior; a Farm to any extent may be made there, the pasture is good and innumerable herds of swine can fatten.

While the peripatetic Simpson was setting in motion the subsequent domination of Columbia River trade, he complained that earlier Northwest Company and Bay Company traders had failed to gather "useful information" about the lower river.[28]

And what purpose might that "useful information" serve? Simpson's journal provides a clear answer. The large number of Indian lodges on the lower river and the great waterway's bounty in fish impressed the practical-minded trader. The river afforded its permanent residents "an abundant provision at little trouble for a great part of the year," he observed; moreover, during the fish runs "the whole of the interior population flock to its banks." Ever mindful of advancing the business interests of the company, Simpson saw advantage in those circumstances: because of their sedentary habits, the natives could "be civilized and instructed in morality and Religion at . . . a moderate expence"; at the same moment, the river afforded "ample provision and the Earth yields spontaneously nutricious Roots in abundance."[29]

But Simpson's thinking included more than the mere propagation of Christianity: the conversion of the Indians would have a salutary effect because they would become accustomed to European products, manner, and dress, and ultimately, "they might likewise be employed . . . as runners Boatsmen &c and their services in other respects turned to profitable account." Religion, in that sense, would serve Simpson's larger purpose of promoting the interests of the Hudson's Bay Company and of linking native people to its business activities. In his widely acclaimed book, *Roots of Dependency*, Richard White points out that the one common thread among Indian people in the postcontact era resulted from "the persistent effort of whites to integrate Indian, land, labor, and resources into the market."[30] George Simpson, for one, grasped well the fundamentals of that relationship.

Because of the Bay Company's ties to global market networks, Simpson wanted to turn to its advantage the immense stands of timber west of the Cascade Range. Shortly after the company began operating a water-powered sawmill a short distance upriver from Fort Vancouver, Simpson observed that the timber trade with the Hawaiian Islands "has the potential to yield us large profits." He advised John McLoughlin to keep the mill constantly at work "as I expect that fully as much advantage will be derived from the timber as from the Coasting Fur Trade." And if its location hampered production, he suggested a move to the falls of the Willamette River where company officials "can attend to the Mill, watch the Fur and Salmon trade, and take care of a Stock of cattle."[31]

With a command infrastructure extending from London and Montreal, the Hudson's Bay Company was in the process of introducing vast changes to the northern West and its resident people. As its key administrator, George Simpson was the exemplar and master of market integration on a continental scale. And the interlopers who followed—missionaries, miners, farmers, and promoters and developers—righteously heralded their work in providential terms as the inevitable wave of progress. More significantly, the expansion and successes of the intruding system have come to dominate historical narrative and have been fundamental elements in the forging of regional and national mythologies. But the necessary basis for the accomplishments of the Euro-Americans was the merciless destruction of the native people's traditional world. The end result: domination for one group and dependency for the other.

Irrespective of national rivalries, those people who followed the Corps of Discovery and the fur traders further elaborated and built upon the now familiar themes of progress, development, the civilizing of native people, and the conquest of nature. The literature that emerged by the 1830s and 1840s extolled the virtues and successes of those earlier individuals and promoted and embellished myths associated with conquest and civilization.[32] Whether they were temporary sojourners in the northern West, actual residents of the region, or writing from afar, the literature they produced marched to rhythms of optimism and progress about the future; the element of tragedy in stories about the West arose in the efforts of later writers and chiefly in works of fiction.[33]

Artists and illustrators, through powerful visual images, confirmed in the popular mind the interpretations of the explorers, fur traders, and others who journeyed through the northern West. Paul Kane, the itinerant artist who traveled across western North America between 1845 and 1848, offered both written and visual assessments of the places he visited. He praised the Hudson's Bay Company for its "just and strict course," for providing assistance "in times of scarcity," and for furnishing medicine to the sick. Kane's sketches of Bay Company outposts, according to one expert, represented them as "squat bastions in the wilderness spaces [that] spelled safety and comfort when travellers saw them from a distance." The American-settler movement westward also stirred his imagination, as evidenced in his paintings of Oregon City, of mission posts, and of a fledgling settlement on Puget Sound.[34]

Although Kane's work includes many paintings and sketches of native people, the substance of his art was the representation of civilization in the wilderness, and thus was he at one with other artists of western America who extolled the elements of progress and civilization. Moreover, Kane influenced one authority to portray the wandering artist in the heroic mode usually reserved for explorers and trappers themselves. J. Russell Harper, editor and compiler of Kane's materials, described the artist as an intrepid, even mythical figure:

> He covered many thousands of miles, through high mountain passes in icy weather and across deserts in the blazing sun, hungry and thirsty; he descended torrents in frail canoes; he worked constantly among not always friendly native people.[35]

Such assessments perpetuate and enhance myth; they do not promote understanding. Harper simply lacked critical insight, both in appraising his subject and in comprehending works of art as cultural symbols; he did not understand that pictures of western settlement were themselves image creating, that the author's selection of materials usually represented the story of winners in the contest for supremacy over place. Elizabeth Johns has grasped the essence of the mythical imagery in nineteenth-century western art, a rendition that portrayed a social world filled with promise where settlers flourished and "energy and hard work were rewarded."[36]

So much a part of the writing of quixotic individuals such as Hall Jackson Kelley, dreamer and would-be emissary of Christian colonies along the shores of the Columbia, that heroic vision took on an equally exaggerated form in political rhetoric.[37] The writing and speeches of Thomas Hart Benton, the longtime senator from Missouri and tireless promoter of U.S. expansion to the Pacific, provide insight into the shaping of the myth. For Benton, "the great event of carrying the Anglo-Saxon race to the shore of the Pacific Ocean" began with the emigrant trek to the Oregon country in the early 1840s. The accomplishment was heroic in the extreme because it was not "an act of the government leading the people" but the people going forward "and compelling the government to follow." To Benton, the 1843 pilgrimage was of epic proportions: more than 1,000 Americans made the long trip overland "with their wives and children, their flocks and herds, their implements of husbandry." Those "bold adventurers" faced six months "filled with hardships, beset by dangers from savage hostility."[38]

Like most of his fellow lawmakers, Benton was certain of the essential rectitude in dispossessing others of their homeland. Grants of land to prospective settlers "were the grand attractive feature to the emigrants"; no one would make the trip to Oregon, he said in support of a bill before the Senate, "without the inducement of land." In more general terms, Benton argued that the white race was justified in possessing the land of the Missouri and Columbia "because they used it according to the intentions of the Creator." The great valley of the Columbia was vast and open: "It is ours and our people are beginning to go upon it. They go under the expectation of getting land; and that expectation must be confirmed."[39]

The boundary settlement of 1846 between Great Britain and the United States and the enactment of the Oregon Donation Land Law in 1850 give Benton's earlier statements the ring of preemptive strike. Yet for the developing mythology of the northern West those remarks embody in crude form notions that permeate much of the historical literature, especially the descriptive writings from south of the international border. Even the more recent assessments of the Donation Land Law center on the legislation as democratic, embracing the Jeffersonian ideals of promoting the interests of common people, and as progressive, because women could hold legal title to land under the act.[40] American scholars have been less successful than their Canadian counterparts in penetrating that veil of peaceful appropriation, perhaps because there is a darker hue to Indian relations in the Oregon country.

Much of the literature on Indian-white relations on the American side of the border ignores the fact of massive dispossession of native people and, in more than one instance, the commitment of outright genocide. In contrast, in the Canadian West neither the British government nor the incoming settlers turned to policies of genocide to clear Indians from the land. Although whites introduced devastating diseases and brought disruptive cultural change, there was, according to Paul Tennant, "no armed conquest, no widespread displacing of villages, and relatively little forced admixing of differing communities. The aboriginal past was not cut off."[41] Events to the south, however, were a different matter. In the wake of the violence that took place in Oregon's Rogue River country between 1851 and 1856 and in eastern Washington during 1855 and 1856, the Bay Company's James Douglas thought the Americans would eventually "glut their revenge upon the wretched Indian, although from their want of discipline and means, it will require a length of time to effect the work of destruction." Even U.S. army officer Phillip Sheridan called the killing of innocent Indians in eastern Washington the work of "inordinate hatred."[42]

The resolution of the boundary issue between Great Britain and the United States formalized the westward extension to the Pacific of two continental empires. From that point forward two fairly distinct societies evolved north and south of the forty-ninth parallel, each reflecting the traditions, values, and behavioral norms of their polities. For the Canadian West, the ever-present fear of American penetration of the region and the consequent threat of annexation to the United States were the critical factors influencing the course of events. With its decision to remove the authority of the Hudson's Bay Company in far western Canada during the Fraser River gold rush, the British government formally extended its imperial control to the Pacific. In the words of Canadian geographer Barry Gough, that action provided a "structured unity" with a relatively strong and centralized legal authority to maintain the civil peace.[43]

In effect, the British government's decision to extend its civil authority west, ahead of the advancing tide of Euro-American settlement, had far-reaching consequences, especially in the greater respect for civil law and in the evolution of a less violent society. Charles Wilson, a member of the Royal Engineers and secretary to the British Boundary Commission, referred to the obvious differences emerging on the opposite sides of the boundary as "the rule of law, on the one hand, and violence and lawlessness, on the other." According to Seymour Martin Lipset, the movement into the Canadian West of the Northwest Mounted Police, often in advance of white settlement, undermined the rampant individualism and disrespect for authority that existed in the western United States. In his comparative study of Seattle and Vancouver, Norbert MacDonald quotes one contemporary who observed that the British Columbia metropolis "was never like Seattle": There was no "rowdyism, no revolvering, no instance or need of lynch law."[44]

Differing national traditions between Canada and the United States also have contributed to contrasting literary conventions, particularly with respect to the linguistic play given to themes of dominance and conquest across the western expanses of both countries. Because of the particular nature of Canada's historical development, the inclination toward rhetorical chauvinism and ethnocentrism has been muted in Canadian literature. Put simply, there may be some truth to Seymour Martin Lipset's seemingly whimsical quip: "Americans are descended from winners, Canadians . . . from losers." Lipset grounds his argument on the fact that the American nation was forged in a successful revolution, Canadian nationhood in counterrevolution. Though writers have crafted Canadian representations of the triumphal narrative, the tensions central to the traditions of British-Canadian and French-Canadian historiography have made suspect grand myths of conquest and settlement. "Canadians," one scholar remarked, "lack the revolutionary tradition that encourages the idea of American exceptionalism and superiority." As in the case of Mexico, there is no Canadian counterpart to Frederick Jackson Turner.[45]

That mood of skeptical inquiry into the process of settlement is a dominant theme in some of the recent interpretive work in western Canadian history, in which scholars have grounded part of their argument on the importance of the Indian response to European intrusion.[46] But even the earlier histories of western Canada are less bombastic, less prone to journalistic praise for the settlement process than is the American approach. George F. G. Stanley, who authored in 1936 the conventional interpretation of the Riel uprisings, described them as a manifestation of the frontier, "the clash between primitive and civilized peoples," a phenomenon that occurred in all parts of the world where white settlements intruded on land occupied by native people. Stanley linked those tragic conflicts to two events: (1) the removal of the Hudson's Bay Company as the ruling force in western Canada, and (2) the final construction phase of the Canadian Pacific Railway. He viewed the last of the rebellions in 1885 as an effort to "withstand the inexorable advance of white civilization."[47]

Stanley ultimately placed the Riel rebellions in the context of an earlier, essential premise of Canadian national history: unity. Because all the provinces had contributed to the suppression of the 1885 rebellion, that coordinated effort had the effect of promoting Canadian nationhood. But he acknowledged that the latter crisis had involved both politics and race, the most serious such clash in early Canadian history. And the problem lingered to the time of his writing in the form of racial and cultural clashes, with the British arguing "for the punishment of the 'rebels' and the French for the pardon of the 'patriots.'"[48] Stanley's work clearly illustrates the factors that have complicated historical interpretation in Canada: (1) ambivalence and division about the notion of conquest; and (2) the French and British-Canadian struggle for autonomy and national survival. Those circumstances, which reveal tragedy and friction rather than triumphal union, are even more apparent in the recent writing on western Canada.

In the most important synthesis yet of the Canadian prairie, Gerald Friesen cites the attractive aspects of prairie society, "a relatively peaceful and comfortable home to immigrants from around the world" that has "given its children a hopeful future." But he balances that positive vision with the tragic reality of the region's history: "The single most important challenge to this optimistic assessment is the status of native people." The fur trade and its links to international capital initiated the disruption of traditional patterns of native life; a general equality prevailed between the two cultures until about 1840, but in the half century that followed, the relationship "was challenged and destroyed." Subsequently, "Indian reserves, the square survey, the railway—imposed a new order on the land."[49]

The removal of the means of subsistence, more than any other factor, pushed both Indian and Metis into a dependent relationship with the dominant culture. When the buffalo disappeared in the 1870s, Friesen concludes, "Indians were on reserves, the Metis in disarray, and the whites in control." Even when reduced to the status of wage laborers, however, Indian people were still beyond the "pale of acceptable class associates for most of the British." Both class and race were powerful determinants in shaping the British Empire, and nineteenth-century western Canada was not immune from those forces.[50]

Much of the skepticism and suspicion directed at Whiggish interpretations of the Canadian past is a reaction to the National Policy. Emerging in the 1870s in response to the American threat to western Canada, the policy was designed to promote national development and to tie the provinces more closely to the central government. It also quickly became suspect as a means for eastern Canadian interests to exploit the West. As a consequence, no grand mythologies about the Canadian nation-state emerged to limit historical discourse.[51] In contrast, the Turnerian tradition in the United States, with its insular regional focus and its emphasis on national exceptionalism, tended for some time to restrict the scope and conditions of historiographical debate.

While frontier themes permeated discussions about the West in the United States, Canadian scholars were effecting strikingly modern theoretical constructs to explain the evolution of the Canadian nation-state. The most significant among those interpretations was the staples theory, first developed by Harold Innis during the 1930s. In a refrain that paralleled the later elaboration of the core-periphery/dependency debate, Innis argued that an excessive dependence on the export of staples characterized Canadian development. The key feature to Canada's economic history was the "discrepancy between the centre and the margin of western civilization," with the nation's entire infrastructure "directed toward the exploitation of staples products." It followed, then, that a staples-producing economy neither manufactured its own consumer goods nor most of its subsistence needs. The consequences were unstable and transient communities, continued dependence on metropolitan economies and external capital, and boom-and-bust cycles.[52]

Staples theory gained a second life during the 1970s when subsequent scholarship focused attention on foreign ownership of Canadian industry, the nation's continued dependence on staple exports, and its inability to finance its own development. For resource-dependent western Canada, with its reliance on exports of grains, timber products, and mineral extraction, the blending of staples theory into dependency modeling was especially pertinent. But as Patricia Marchak has observed, those theoretical constructs ignored fundamental issues: (1) Canada's place in U.S. imperial expansion; (2) the difference between Canada's dependent relation to the United States and that of Third World nations; (3) the lack of attention given to labor and class in Canada's historical development; and (4) the existence, especially in western Canada, of a high-wage and heavily unionized work force.[53] Collectively, however, the discussions about staples and dependency theories have enriched and deepened historical understanding of western Canada.

For Canada's westernmost province, British Columbia, political culture and ideological conventions have fostered an interpretive framework that emphasizes the significance of class, the existence of a multicultural society, and the exploitation of natural resources. Yet through all the reinterpretations, including an early recognition of "division and conflict in the province's life," Allan Smith points to one constant theme: "the idea that British Columbia could not be understood without taking full account of its relationship to the world around it." The best historians in the province, he contends, "never fell victim to the illusion that the community of which they spoke could be understood in terms of anything other than its place in a larger world."[54] That statement may be self-serving, but it is a remarkable testament to Canadian scholarship; it is also a sentiment that mutes the power of grand myths centered on conquest, domination, and progress.

Despite their long tradition of critical analysis of the settlement process and related themes, Canadian historians have not always been so attentive to the native story. That trend began to change with the emergence of ethnohistory in the 1960s and the innovative work of Robin Fisher in the Far West. In his award-winning *Contact and Conflict*, he charges that the original peoples of Canada had been peripheral "rather than a central concern to Canada's past." With the decline of the fur trade, he observes, they disappear from view, since an attribute of conventional scholarship is that it "deals [only] with the successful." For his part, Fisher insists that proper reckoning be given to the significance of the Indian presence because the native response to the intrusion of Europeans is important to Canadian history. He reminds his readers that Indian people actively shaped provincial history and formed the majority of British Columbia's population into the 1880s.[55]

Critics may rightly charge that in this chapter I ignore the more recent scholarship on the American side of the border, a growing body of writing that challenges the conventional accounts of virtue, success, and American exceptionalism.[56] In truth, the number of revisionist studies continues to grow, especially as graduate programs produce scholars who are in the forefront of the assault on the prevailing paradigm. Research agendas that focus on issues of gender, race, class, environmental change, urban/hinterland relations, and studies of postindustrialism

provide some of the more prominent and innovative critiques of the tra-
dition-based, myth-centered story of the West.[57] Even more important,
not all of that scholarly effort casts its investigative limelight on California and the Southwest. The northern tier of states stretching from the
Dakotas west to Puget Sound is the setting for inquiries into market-induced bioregional change; studies of subsistence economies, culture,
and the imposition of new legal forms; and comparative investigations
of transnational, resource-based communities.

To be sure, the collective result of the new research (the New Western History as its proponents call it) will not seriously erode the mythic
power of the American West; myth as fable is too deeply ingrained as
part of the dominant national mood. That is not the issue. But it is important that we understand myth so that it does not control or restrict
scholarly endeavor. Richard White made the point in a faculty profile interview at the University of Washington:

> Myth is just an alternative way of understanding the past. At many
> points it overlaps with history. In fact, there is no place where "real"
> history begins and myth ends. I can't banish myth and I wouldn't
> want to. I just want to understand myth and its role in not just ex-
> plaining people's lives, but in shaping them.[58]

Because Canada's historical roots differ in fundamental respects
from those of the United States, the study of Canadian history provides
fascinating comparative insights for American scholars. The point may
seem trite, but the international border between Canada and the United
States is more than a physical boundary dividing common bioregions on
the North American continent. Donald Meinig, who invariably casts his
ideas in global terms, cites the fact that the American Revolution "created not one country, but two, [and] that these two are coeval and contiguous across a continent." Although they are "interlocked and interde-
pendent in myriad ways," he contends, in other respects they are
"independent, competitive, and distinct."[59]

But the Canadian-U.S. border also serves as a barrier to inhibit intellectual dialogue; it places severe strictures on discussions about historical processes that in fact have much in common (Seymour Martin Lipset
notwithstanding). As a community of scholars, we have much to gain
from one another. In some respects American academics have been as
imperial as their nation-state, and they have been especially insular
when it comes to the work of their cross-border counterparts. Rather
than wasting energy puzzling about our neighbor's unwillingness to buy
into the Turner thesis, American scholars might benefit from more careful study of the material forces that have shaped the Canadian past.[60]

Why, for instance, is there no celebratory counterpart to Lewis and Clark in Canadian history?

In contrast, the power of myth may well be the essential feature of the American experience. The very processes of the phenomenon that has been called exploration and settlement have provided the materials for the creation of a grand mythology, one that is both story and justification for what took place. Among other elements, as the narrative took shape, the power of myth made the original inhabitants virtually invisible. And, in its many forms, the myth is with us still. The symbols of Lewis and Clark, the monuments to Custer, and Indian battle sites everywhere clutter the collective memory in the northern West; as historical artifacts they do little except embellish the myths of the winners: success, development, and state-building for this corner of the United States. Our task is not to celebrate myth but to look beyond it for understanding.

PART TWO

Forces of Transformation

CHAPTER FOUR

In Pursuit of Private Gain: The West as Investment Arena

The nineteenth-century United States was a capitalist economy, in which money—a very great deal of money—was to be made, among other ways, by the development and rationalization of the productive resources of a vast and rapidly growing country in a rapidly growing world economy.

—*E. J. Hobsbawm*[1]

The more nationalistic and patriotic literature about the American West, as many critics have indicated, is filled with irony, ambiguity, and contradiction. On the one hand the region is described as the exemplar of national purpose, a moral success story, a body of literature that Eric Wolf has characterized as "a tale about the furtherance of virtue." The story possessed epic and triumphant qualities; it is at once a tale of high drama, of great determination, of hard work, and of courageous effort. First the fur traders, then the missionaries, the gold seekers, and eventually the farmer-settlers who superseded them all, blazed the way to civilization in the West. But that exceptionalist theme, as Richard Oestreicher has argued, has "rarely been grounded in empirical international comparisons."[2] Still, that sense of an unfolding national purpose in what passed for the westward movement has permeated most works of synthesis on the American West until recently.[3]

Collectively those uncritical, triumphal accounts implied a larger national purpose to the westering press of the population, one that suggested high principle and a greater design to the process that unfolded. No scholar put the romantic, celebratory version of the West more eloquently than Arrell Morgan Gibson:

> The magnificent spectacle of the emergent American nation, breaching the Appalachian barrier and like a human floodtide, surging with incredible velocity and irrepressible force westward across the continent into the Pacific Basin, ranks with the grandest epics of human history. This is the essence of *The West in the Life of the Nation*.[4]

But Gibson also recognized that the grand purpose of western settlement embraced a material element: that is, the region's occupation, the organization of its governments, and the exploitation of its resources "produced countless personal economic successes and a concomitant increase in national strength." Moreover, to underscore the importance of the West in the larger scheme of nation-building, he pointed out that the resources of the West were the principle determinants of "national economic strength and hegemony." As a historical synthesis and as a measure of its time, Gibson's West was a place where virtue triumphed over evil as part of a timeless essence, where the plight of the losers was lamented only in passing.[5]

Gibson and others who pursued similar themes created a false model of reality, a paradigm that evaded the larger questions of market and class relations, that ignored the perpetually changing character of capitalism and its influence in shaping and reshaping life in the West, and the consequences of that often turbulent economic world for the region's population. Remove the mythical elements from those accounts and a different story emerges, one that portrays a darker side to western development in which romantic cowboys are wage laborers, Indian people are forcibly confined to restricted areas as a means of social control, and industrial statesmen manipulate investments in western resources in the pursuit of private gain. Robert Athearn put a kind face to that entrepreneurial influence in the region when he likened it to "exploitation and experimentation carried on by remote control."[6]

In truth, Athearn understated the larger influence of eastern capital in shaping life in the West and the concomitant importance of western resources to a rapidly expanding and industrializing global economy. It is essential to recognize that for the last thirty years of the nineteenth century and into the early years of the twentieth, the American West was the great natural-resource reservoir and the investment arena for eastern U.S. and western European capital. In that sense the region was part of the wider subordination of colonial sectors to the requirements of metropolitan-based economies. With a largely monocultural focus based on the exploitation of natural resources for export, those rural, hinterland economies were linked to centers of industry and manufacturing in a decidedly dependent way.[7] Hence, the great advances in production and in the accumulation of wealth in the Atlantic-centered industrial economy depended heavily on resources from the American West.

By all accounts the West loomed large in the post–Civil War industrial program: as an investment arena for surplus capital, as a source of raw materials, and as a vast vacant lot to enter and occupy. Railroads, cattle, mineral extraction, timber, bonanza agricultural enterprises, speculation in townsites, and myriad other activities attracted both the shrewd and the gullible among would-be settlers and finance capitalists alike. But it was the world of eastern (and European) capital—not the sturdy work of the solitary prospector or the sodbuster—that provided the major impetus to change in the West. Walter Prescott Webb's writings, among others, reveal the shortcomings of historical scholarship in that respect: despite his attention to the colonial exploitation of the West, he failed to see the integrated nature of modern capitalism. For him capitalism was a static system, frozen in time and place. Thus, in light of the historical profession's long preoccupation with the frontier West as the key factor in American development, scholars would have been wise to acknowledge Douglas C. North's suggestion of many years ago: that the worldwide mobility of capital and labor, shifting British and European markets, and a shared international pool of technological information best explained the quality, direction, and rate of economic growth in the western United States. By the last quarter of the nineteenth century, in the words of E. J. Hobsbawm, a tremendous expansion in the world economy had emerged, with several countries already industrialized and with a "genuinely global flow of goods, capital, and men."[8]

The history of the post–Civil War West—and of the nation at large—is the story of dynamic, reciprocal, and interconnected phenomena. That is especially true of the establishment and evolution of modern capitalism and of the integration of the trans-Mississippi West into national- and international-exchange relationships. To attempt to describe change in the West as an isolated, internally homogenous process falsifies the material world; it ignores important and integral relationships involving the modern capitalist world system. It is also important to understand capitalism as a mode of production (or as a particular way of organizing production) that places ultimate significance on the material world and on the manipulation and transformation of that world for the purpose of making a profit.[9]

In the late nineteenth century the French political scientist Emile Boutmy remarked that the most "striking and peculiar characteristic" of American society was its commercial nature: "It is not so much a democracy," he said, "as a huge commercial company for the discovery, cultivation, and capitalization of its enormous territory." When Boutmy made those remarks in 1891, much of the American West fit that description—a vast warehouse of raw materials for the industrial world.[10] As a revolutionary and expanding economic order, unfettered with feudal legacies and with relatively few restrictions on private enterprise, the United States was rapidly emerging as the exemplar of the capitalist state in the modern world. A good beginning point for the study of social change, then, is economic relationships in the larger arena of world affairs and the parallel evolution of more localized economies.

As such, the American West held certain material attractions that fired imaginations. Indeed, it can be said that the great spur to western development was the dynamic, expansive, and internationalizing Atlantic economy, where leading segments of its British and European counterparts had accumulated significant amounts of surplus capital. In that sense, the western United States was but one, albeit unique, component in the extraordinary global economic transformation and in the international movement of capital from points where surpluses had accumulated to distant places where the promise of return was rumored to be high. That movement of investment finance and its accompanying global influence marked the period "when the world became capitalist and a significant minority of 'developed' countries became industrial economies." In the years following the American Civil War, British and European capitalists—in part responding to a crisis in capital accumulation at home—were seeking new overseas investment arenas; earlier preferred offerings for British, European, and Indian railroad and industrial securities were no longer as promising or as lucrative. Although transatlantic financing was only one source of capital involved in the economic development of the American West, it was often invested in railroad construction or other improvements in transportation, and as such it provided the critical opening wedge for further economic expansion.[11]

It can be said with some truth that those who controlled the primary sources of capital also provided the cutting edge for the transformation of the western interior of North America. Whether they worked individually or in concert, theirs was a world that linked areas of primary capital accumulation to peripheral regions rich with the raw materials valuable to the industrial sectors. But most important it was capital invested in internal improvements to provide the necessary infrastructure that made possible the subsequent expansiveness of the western economy. And changing modes of production accompanied the introduction of the market revolution everywhere; investments in the first rail lines to extend beyond the Mississippi coincided with the effort to control and confine the Native American residents of the plains. The coming of the railroad also paralleled the wholesale slaughter of the bison, the animals that provided the native people's chief means of subsistence. That in turn meant an end to their pastoral and communitarian mode of existence and opened millions of acres of grazing land to the range-cattle industry that began spreading northward across the plains after the Civil War.

It is also fair to indicate that establishing a safe and stable environment for investment capital was expensive, a fact generally ignored in the more conventional stories of the American West. In the post–Civil War era costly military garrisons were located at strategic points to ensure that the recently pacified tribes remained confined to reservations. The removal of the native people through a series of forced treaties freed the western land base to market forces. The federal government further served as the interlocutor in ascribing legal attachments to the land and in overseeing its commodification and distribution as private property in the form of grants to railroads and settlers and through low-cost leases to mining companies. Heralded in the settlement literature of the period as a boon to the yeoman farmer, the process in fact freed the land from aboriginal title and opened it to market appropriation. Moreover, it is also clear that by the end of the Civil War the federal policy that directed taking possession of the native land base was not a negotiation between equals but the act of a victorious aggressor dictating settlements to subjugated people.[12] With the final defeat of the Indians on the northern plains in the late 1870s market capitalism had extended its reach to the remote interior of the continent.

The federal distribution of land was an additional expense, borne by the national treasury but with the principal end in mind of placing land at market and transferring legal title to the private sector. In retrospect, there should be little doubt about the ultimate objective and purpose of the disposal of the public domain (at least until the late nineteenth century); the Land Ordinance of 1785 stated clearly that lands ceded by the original states to the federal government and those purchased from Indian tribes "shall be disposed of." John Opie observes that the great land ordinances of the 1780s "put sovereign territory on the market," a principle that was later confirmed under the Constitution through the recognition of private property. Although the desire to acquire land at any one time may have involved all social classes, the larger capital enterprises were better equipped in the long run to buy out or to push aside small holders if such actions were critical to their investment interests. Those enterprises were the primary force in directing the course of capitalist development in the West. Thus, the realities of the story of the opening of the West to the yeoman ideal took an ironic turn; in Alan Trachtenberg's words, "Incorporation took swift possession of the garden, mocking those who lived by the hopes of cultural myth."[13]

The territorial and later the state land office business—whatever the charges of ethical misconduct—was a significant federal service provided largely free of charge to the expanding network of capitalist legal relations. As the officials in charge of overseeing that system, federal and state administrators were important links in carrying out land policy. Beyond the world of the government agencies, those people with surplus capital to invest fueled a series of land-speculation frenzies and the organization of a great variety of land-stock companies. The federal government, as Malcolm Rohrbough has shown, substantially aided the transfer, both legal and illegal, of public lands to the private sector. "The management of the public domain," he points out, "lay at the center of life on the frontier."[14] And federal land policy would remain as one of the central features of economic life, especially in the great public land states west of the ninety-eighth meridian.

Perhaps the greatest of the early federal services—hence subsidies—to would-be financiers and potential investors in western enterprise were the U.S. Army reconnaissance and exploring expeditions of the Corps of Topographical Engineers, including the great railroad surveys conducted in the 1850s. The engineers engaged in several fact-finding expeditions, the best known being those led by the corps' most famous figure, John C. Frémont. His travels through the Rocky Mountains and the Far West between 1841 and 1845, according to William Goetzmann, "helped point out the value of Oregon and California to Congress." The subsequent reconnaissance and boundary surveys during and after the Mexican war in the northern and southern West provided an "incalculable service to the nation as it acted as a vanguard of settlement in the Southwest, clearing away the Indian barrier and laying out the lines of communication." Those federally funded undertakings, and other cartographical and geological information gathered before the Civil War, underscore the substantial role of the government in advertising the West. Collectively those published reports formed a corpus of general knowledge that illustrates the early ties between science and the world of public policy and finance in a burgeoning capitalist state. The surveys provided the first general but reputable scientific knowledge about the geography of the West: its complex systems of rivers, valleys, and mountains and its expansive and awe-inspiring basins and plateaus.[15] Those explorations, it should be emphasized, were less significant as disinterested exercises in scientific curiosity than as the means for providing real and practical information for an expanding American empire, for potential investors in western enterprise, and for those interested in the prospects for settlement.

In a very real sense the pre–Civil War explorations marked the culmination of efforts that date from the earliest pronouncements of men such as Thomas Hart Benton and other visionaries of western development. There was much more, however, than mere mythmaking to the Missouri senator's thinking: from an early period his thoughts about western North America possessed a distinctly commercial tint that envisioned the benefits to be reaped with the construction of a convenient route of travel across the continent:

An American road to India through the heart of our country will revive upon its line all the wonders of which we have read—and eclipse them. The western wilderness, from the Pacific to the Mississippi, will start into life under its touch.

The completion of the great Pacific Railroad in 1869, helped along with an infusion of federally guaranteed bonds, was not quite the poetic undertaking that Benton had imagined. Nevertheless, that first engineering wonder and the other interior western lines constructed before the turn of the century, once figments of the transcontinental imagination, in actual practice closed time and distance across the western interior of North America.[16] The marvelous technical application of steam power to land travel therefore vastly advanced the geographic reach of capital; as a consequence the rail links everywhere boosted speculation in western land and resources.

The new means of travel and transport in fact opened the vast expanses of the West to production. According to John Agnew, new forms of transportation technology were fundamental to the success of capitalism in its ability to organize and expand on a global scale in the late nineteenth century. In the expansion of that system, land and resources were not undifferentiated productive factors but were qualitatively important relative to their proximity to market.[17] The application of steam power to oceanic travel and to rail transportation enabled distant areas to connect to markets. That process also put in motion both capital and a great population shift to newly opened lands in Australia, New Zealand, Argentina, and western North America. The vast movement of continental populations in the late nineteenth century, Walter Nugent contends, was related to several factors: advances in the technology of land and ocean travel, the relative absence of restrictions on migration, and "great agricultural development on several New World frontiers."[18]

Although the propagandists who extolled the virtues of western development date from the early years of the republic, the ties between political and industrial supporters for specific projects did not crystallize until the Civil War decade. The Credit Mobilier scandal may have expressed the baser elements of the politics of that profit-seeking world, but other federally subsidized enterprises carry to this day the reputation for pursuing more noble ends. There is little question that the need for more precise information about the West clearly spurred the federal government to underwrite the four great postwar surveys, led by Clarence King, Ferdinand V. Hayden, George M. Wheeler, and John Wesley Powell. Those last reconnaissance missions reflected the new requirements of the modern industrial state: the need for detailed information about the western landscape, its topography, and its mineral, timber, and water resources.[19]

The California gold rush and the solitary prospector excited the imaginations of enterprising capitalists, but the more far-sighted among them wanted more than random suggestion and rumor before putting capital into western mining enterprises. In that sense the surveys moved well beyond discovery and by the late 1870s had filled in the last of what is now familiar geography. Although the work of the artists and photographers and the specimens they sent to the Smithsonian have captured the imaginations of twentieth-century Americans, the immediate contributions of those scientific undertakings, like the prewar railroad surveys, were more tangible. With some accuracy the surveys mapped large sections of the West in terms that would be useful to railroad builders, to capitalists interested in mineral and timberland investment, and to potential agriculturalists.[20] The components of the landscape, the vital elements so important to capitalist expansion, were much better known when the work of the surveys was completed in the late 1870s.

The establishment of the U.S. Geological Survey (USGS) marked the formal institutionalization of governmental scientific inquiry in the West. Its first director, Clarence King, enjoyed a close relationship with investors in mining enterprises and in the new field of economic geology. The association and increased cooperation among the scientific community, the USGS, and a related and major capital enterprise in the West established precedents and advanced a set of relationships that would become evermore complex (and intimate) in the twentieth century. Scientific inquiry in that sense served as the cutting edge for competitive innovation. If the genius of capitalist enterprise is to anticipate the future, then harnessing science to advance industrial activity should lead to competitive advantage; the USGS served that function well.[21]

The scenario that unfolded in the trans-Mississippi West was linked closely with the dynamics of the eastern industrial system and the Atlantic world beyond. In the years following the Civil War, the rest of the world but especially Europe, Hobsbawm argues, "was keenly aware of the United States" because of its vast expanse and its extraordinary material advances. As an expression of that rapidly expanding system, the actions of the federal government manifested the close ties between the economic and the political realms: through its unrestricted, indeed sympathetic, support for the activities of most business enterprises, through its subsidies to scientific and transportation infrastructures necessary to industrial expansion, through a politics that gave primacy to economic matters (especially in the handling of natural resources), and through an outright hostility toward labor. In that respect, the nineteenth century may be unique, Douglas North has argued, in the lack of governmental restriction on the movement of material, people, and capital; his reference included Great Britain and Europe as well as America.[22]

With an extensive land and raw-materials base in the vast interic continent, the United States had at hand the physical requirements iu. unprecedented growth in productive power. As it moved toward core status among the nation-states of the world, the United States stood at a propitious moment in history, the onset of an era that Henry Luce would later call "the American Century." Its massive resource base made the nation virtually an empire in itself. That natural wealth, John Agnew contends, could be described only as gargantuan:

> huge quantities of all the major minerals needed for industrializa-tion—coal, iron ore, copper, minor metals like zinc, gold and silver, and huge quantities of oil; rich agricultural soils extending across thousands of square miles; a climate of sufficient diversity to permit long growing seasons for fiber crops like hemp and cotton and food crops like sugar; and rich forests providing vast amounts of lumber for housing and a wide range of wood products.[23]

To be sure, competing forces of capital fought for the choicest slices of the federal largesse. Still, a consensus of sorts existed among the eco-nomic and political elites about general polity: there should be a close re-lationship between the requirements of the private sector and the articu-lation of those needs in public policy. That general consensus among the largely metropolitan leadership created an atmosphere favorable to the emergence of an expansive, relatively unrestrained, and innovative capi-talist economy. Those conditions accelerated the pace of change every-where in the world economy: expanding systems of production in one area retarded similar production elsewhere and resulted in a great trans-atlantic and transcontinental movement of people. The increasing inte-gration of the global economy made the fortunes of producers, especially those in agriculture, dependent on world market prices. Hence, the post–Civil War era was truly a revolutionary moment in modern history, and the Atlantic world was the vibrant center of that age of dramatic transformation.[24] Shifting capital, disrupted traditions, and the phenom-enon that characterized capitalism above all else, repeated technological innovation, were the hallmarks of the era. Those changes were also ap-parent in the American West, the great warehouse of raw materials for the eastern United States and the Atlantic-based industrial system.

If in the world of conventional capitalist political economy dominant groups are able to express their power and influence through the control of allocative resources, then the American West provides ample evidence to support that thesis. Even before regulations came to the western ranges, cattlemen and sheepherders had grazed their animals at will on public, territorial, and Indian lands, a form of public subsidy, some would say, because there were no charges for the grazing privileges. Rumors of the great profits to be had in that capital-scarce enterprise attracted both eastern and British investors in the post–Civil War era. High beef prices in Great Britain had prompted a royal commission to inquire into and to report favorably on the feasibility of investing in the American cattle business.[25] At the zenith of its economic power and with its venture capital literally probing the far corners of the globe, the British government both advanced the prospects for such financial activities and then stood ready to protect those securities once they were in place. The government of the United States would prove itself no less decisive in promoting the interests of capital in the American West and guarding against the forays of labor and an occasional state government.

Soaring slaughterhouse prices continued to brighten prospects, and the number of investors interested in placing cattle on the great western commons multiplied as did the problems in policing those increasingly crowded activities. While some cattlemen attempted to establish vaguely acknowledged local range rights to sanctify and to bring order to their use of the public domain, others (especially those backed by foreign capital) tried to purchase or lease huge grazing acreages. Yet with the virtual absence of any federal restraints or an infrastructure to oversee the orderly occupation of the plains, the number of individual operators and grazing animals increased rapidly. Out of the anarchy and chaos that ensued, the owners formed politically influential cattlemen's associations to protect their herds and to gain agreements to regulate grazing, but to no avail.[26] Too many cattle continued to overgraze too many ranges until disaster struck in the infamous winter storms of 1886–1887.

Across the grazing lands of the trans-Mississippi West the day of the range-cattle industry had begun to ebb by the time of the "big die-up," as the cattlemen termed the great blizzard that devastated the western herds. While some observers saw the hand of Providence amid the dead and starving cattle during that long, harsh winter, many of the eastern and European investors (who knew better) had already begun to seek other, more lucrative markets for their capital. In effect, the cattle industry in the West was experiencing a restructuring of sorts because competitive conditions had changed: the market was sluggish; open-range grazing was no longer bringing satisfactory returns for investors, and legal challenges to the unlimited and free use of the public domain had arisen. Those challenges reflected a more aggressive assertion of the principles of republican landownership and changes in capitalist property relations. "When the investor in cattle deduced that his cattle company was not going to shower him with manna," Gene Gressley has pointed out, "he sought other avenues of profit."[27] Thus, in its grand pastoral style of extended trail drives over vast distances, the classic range-cattle industry was a relatively short-lived phenomenon.

Some of the great outfits did survive the climatic and economic shakeout that occurred between 1885 and 1895, but they were usually the well-established firms that had already adjusted to the new conditions for conducting business. The Swan Land and Cattle Company and the Matador Land and Cattle Company, both Scottish-owned, reduced stocking on their home ranges, moved their cattle to predetermined locations during certain periods of the animals' lives, introduced the use of purebred bulls, installed wells and reservoirs, and in other ways took advantage of new forms of technology to improve their herds.[28] But that new age in the ranch-cattle business, no matter what its scale, was tied firmly to eastern and overseas markets, to innovations in technology, and, as we have witnessed in the late twentieth century, to the changing dietary tastes of consumers.

The displacement of buffalo with range cattle on the arid reaches of the high plains was but the opening wedge in a series of market-induced disruptions that have persisted in the region. The burgeoning industrial population in the late nineteenth century provided commercial agriculture worldwide with an ever-increasing demand for a growing variety of products: meat, dairy products, wheat, corn, and fruit. For the Great Plains, then, we should not wonder that the day of the cattleman was short-lived, bankrupted by weather, overexpansion, and the changing nutritional requirements of an industrial economy.[29] But that shift was only the first in a succession of disruptive forms of production, of human efforts to adapt and to carry on agricultural enterprise in a land of marginal precipitation. From the Texas panhandle northward onto the Canadian prairies other interests were at work, some of them originating in places far removed from the region, that served to fire the imaginations of would-be settlers and that led to a mad scramble to take up land in much of the old cattle kingdom. The point is important because the agricultural advance onto the high plains was not inevitable; an active capitalist class, sometimes working at cross-purposes, strove mightily to bring it about.[30]

Ultimately there was little that was natural about the emigrant movement onto the Great Plains in the last thirty years of the nineteenth century. Settler-farmers were not responding to an inherent wanderlust or to suprahuman economic laws in taking up land on the former buffalo commons. To suppose that such motives prompted similar global demographic shifts during this period is to deny the active, conscious efforts of an aggressive emergent capitalist class working to shape potential investment environments to their liking. Human agency, therefore, in the form of a concerted corporate and governmental effort endeavored to bring about the agricultural occupation of the Great Plains. In short, to make the rail systems that penetrated the plains a paying proposition, corporate capitalists elaborated an attractive advertisement campaign— couched in language extolling the virtues and potential of a garden in the western grasslands—that appealed to the acquisitive values of subject populations. The advertising effort was a willful historical event, as significant as the great demographic movement that followed in its wake.[31]

Whereas a single transcontinental line spanned the United States in 1870, by the turn of the century there were five. And therein rests much of the explanation for the surge in agricultural expansion and the repeopling of large sections of the high plains with settler-farmers by the first decade of the twentieth century. Within two generations rising demands in eastern U.S. and European markets had transformed the subsistence and pastoral economy of the West into integral and dependent components of an Atlantic-dominated agricultural marketing system. "The ever-growing demand for food for urban and industrial parts of the world," Hobsbawm concludes, was the critical element in agricultural development worldwide.[32] In the United States eastern financiers, acting both in their own right and as agents of European capital, were intimately involved in promoting that great westward agricultural push in the late nineteenth century. James J. Hill and the Great Northern Railway and its financial associates in London and western Europe provide an interesting case study of that phenomenon.[33] Although railroad companies were not behind all the settlement schemes, their land-office promotions dwarfed all other interests in terms of influence.

Begin with George Armstrong Custer's famous reconnaissance to the Black Hills in 1872, a federally sponsored venture that led directly to the pacification of the Sioux, to the opening of Dakota Territory to large-scale mining enterprises, and to the introduction of extensive wheat production. During the Great Dakota boom of the late 1870s and into the 1880s (years of unusually good precipitation), James J. Hill's Manitoba Road promoted settlement in the Red River Valley and the Northern Pacific Railroad pushed west across the Dakotas. Agricultural expansion during those years—much of it involving the huge bonanza farming enterprises that subsequently dwindled away in the late 1880s, victim to both climatic and financial failure—occurred close to the major rail lines, the Northern Pacific and the Great Northern.[34] The events of those years also demonstrate the central importance of the railroad to western economic development, the vital transportation arterial that linked points of agricultural production to the great population centers and the equally strategic Atlantic ports.

The westerly push of Hill's expanding rail network illustrates the point: the Great Northern crossed the Red River at East Grand Forks in 1880, reaching Minot in 1886 and the Montana territorial line in 1887. Unlike the more ambitious but less astute Northern Pacific officials who focused on extending their line to the Pacific Coast during those years, the Hill interests built several feeder lines and furnished loans, animals, and seed to prospective settlers. The population increases for North Dakota and Montana after 1890 indicate the successes of the transcontinental railroads' advertising effort—especially that of the Great Northern—in attracting farmers to settle marginal and submarginal lands in the two states. Montana's population increased from 39,000 in 1880 to 143,000 by 1890; its eastern neighbor, North Dakota, grew from 37,000 to 191,000 in the same period.[35] What the statistics do not reveal, as the great Montana journalist Joseph Kinsey Howard observed, were the failures when prices dropped, when grasshoppers and locust plagues swept the countryside, or when the cycles of drought returned to the northern plains. That reality was affirmed by the empty trains rattling through dying towns and by the "neat little green fields" transformed into "fenced deserts."[36]

For a time the big attractions for venture capital were the large-scale wheat operations in the great Red River Valley of the north, an innovative effort that involved strict business principles of management, absentee ownership, mechanization, and specialized forms of production. The bonanza enterprises ironically had their beginnings in industrial failure: the bankruptcy of the Northern Pacific Railroad Company. Following the panic of 1873 the Northern Pacific began the practice of exchanging grant lands for its depreciated securities; one of the largest of those bond sales involved 28,352 acres to the Amenia and Sharon Land Company, a group of New York and Connecticut investors. To "block-up" those immense holdings (to take up contiguous acreages), companies acquired intervening public lands under one or more of the federal laws. The executives in charge of the Northern Pacific had disposed of nearly 3 million acres of its grant lands in this fashion by the end of 1880.[37]

The bonanza farms were huge, spectacular, and for a time immensely profitable. They served as large laboratories for testing the most recent developments in agricultural technology, especially the latest advancements in mechanized equipment. Those corporate agriculturalists operated factory-type systems, with large groups of laborers; and the monopolylike business entities dramatized a modus operandi that William Appleman Williams termed "absentee control by metropolitan interests." The farms attracted attention in other ways: two members of the British Parliament visited the Red River Valley in 1879; letters describing the operations appeared in the London *Times*; and *Harper's*, the *Atlantic*, and *Scribner's* printed articles on the farms. The big wheat enterprises required large, seasonal work forces and thus were inimical to community development.[38] Clearly they were the antithesis of Jeffersonian mythology and the yeoman ideal.

As large-scale capital operations, the long-term success of the bonanza enterprises rested on the twin requisites of capitalism: predictability and a semblance of stability. But as time was to prove, the huge Red River Valley farms offered no such assurances. The climatic patterns, which fluctuated wildly, were never predictable enough to provide sufficient precipitation year after year to guarantee a margin of profit. As wheat prices declined in the 1880s, resident managers complained of the difficulty of making ends meet. The bonanza farmer's main problem, according to Gilbert Fite, was that he "could not regulate his production nor determine the prices of things he bought or sold." The big profits of the early 1880s evaporated as the decade advanced and wheat prices plummeted. "When cash returns dried up because of poor yields or low wheat prices as was true in 1889 and 1890," Fite points out, "it made good sense for these operators to sell or rent part or all of their land and invest their money in something that would produce better dividends."[39] The advent of more lasting enterprises of this kind would await the federal price supports and disaster-relief subsidies of the last half of the twentieth century.

What followed was the gradual parceling off—by sale or leasehold—of the largest estates. Although in their classic form the farms lasted for only one decade, they did contribute to a revolution in agricultural production: they advertised the agricultural potential of the West; they helped stimulate a large population movement to the northern plains; they speeded up the mechanization of wheat production; and they made the two great rail systems through the country—the Northern Pacific and the Great Northern—paying propositions.

The same set of circumstances that beset the bonanza enterprises—unpredictable climate and price instability—plagued the small farmers who followed in their wake, especially those who ventured farther west in the Dakotas. In a moving and personal story about his maternal grandfather, Benjamin Franklin McCardle, Gilbert Fite has described the efforts of one generation of settlers to homestead on the Dakota frontier. A native of Virginia, Frank McCardle "struck out West" in 1888 without sufficient capital to establish a farm "even on free land." After working as a farm laborer for two years, he married Mary Alquire, a neighboring farmer's hired girl; together the two began homesteading in Jerauld

County, South Dakota, on land located astride the ninety-ninth meridian, the infamous and historic area of marginal crop production.

Through diligence and toil McCardle appeared to be a successful farmer by the advent of World War I. Because he had amassed a sizable acreage through purchase, however, McCardle was in deep trouble (and land poor) when prices slumped during the early 1920s. His farm was foreclosed in 1927, and he gave up farming in the midst of the Great Depression. Although he was able to provide a modest living for his family, by most measures of success, "Frank McCardle was an economic failure."[40] McCardle struggled under conditions familiar to farmers elsewhere, especially those who were attempting to eke out an existence in places where precipitation was at best unpredictable and who were without recourse to irrigation. The region, Kathleen Norris reminds us, is a land of hopes:

> hoping that droughts will end; hoping that our crops won't be hailed out in the few rainstorms that come; hoping that it won't be too windy on the day we harvest, blowing away five bushels an acre; hoping (usually against hope) that if we get a fair crop, we'll be able to get a fair price for it.[41]

Conditions similar to those that occurred in the Dakotas and Montana also prevailed in the territories and states to the south. Sod-house farmers began to enter the heart of the Great Plains in the 1870s, a movement that became a land rush in the 1880s. That demographic shift took settlers west of the ninety-eighth meridian, to western Nebraska and Kansas and to eastern Colorado. The writer Wright Morris, who was born "just west of the 98th meridian" in the Platte Valley of Nebraska, understood the geographic significance of his natal environment: ["It was] just to the north, or south, or a bit to the east of where it sometimes rained, but more than likely it didn't."[42] Conditions such as those described by Morris and others who attempted to farm the high plains country were conducive only to the naive and to the most wildly imaginative of the risk takers.

And many people were offering inducements—land promoters, newspaper boosters, railroad officials—and with a few years of above-average precipitation, the promise of success seemed bright and assured. Railroads were of course critical to agricultural expansion on the central and southern plains, especially the more strategically located lines such as the Atchison, Topeka, and Santa Fe. With the assistance of a sizable federal land subsidy, the Santa Fe had constructed a road during the 1870s from Topeka to Pueblo, Colorado, and then southwest to Albuquerque in New Mexico Territory. Through an agreement with the

Southern Pacific, the Santa Fe began running trains to the Pacific Coast at the onset of the 1880s.[43] The railroad's most immediate influence was in Kansas, a state that experienced a phenomenal rate of growth in the 1870s and into the 1880s.

The Santa Fe subsequently proved itself to be a striking financial success: in Kansas it was able to dispose of nearly 3 million acres of its federal land grant. The state's population grew from 364,000 in 1870 to 996,000 in 1880 and to 1.4 million by 1890. The accounts of success in the new agricultural mecca were impressive, especially in those counties traversed by the railroad where the rate of growth was higher than in other parts of the state. Along with the Missouri, Kansas, and Texas Railroad (the Katy) and the Kansas Pacific (part of the Union Pacific network), the Santa Fe gave the state of Kansas the highest per capital rail mileage in the United States.[44] Cattle, wheat, and corn production burgeoned during those years when the southern plains enjoyed above average precipitation.

But as James C. Malin pointed out over fifty years ago, those people who settled in western Kansas and in neighboring states were a notoriously mobile group. Whether forced out by an unpredictable and wildly fluctuating climate or by equally unreliable market conditions, settlers simply did not stay in one place for very long. Many newcomers to Kansas took up claims, Malin argued, not as a permanent enterprise but as a speculative activity that would reward them with sizable profits at some point in the future. Whatever their acquisitive drive or motive, and no firm evidence supports Malin's argument, those new settlements beyond the ninety-eighth meridian were in jeopardy. Falling international prices for agricultural crops of wheat and corn and recurring cycles of drought beginning in the mid-1880s brought failure to farmers all along that line of marginal precipitation.[45] To impute motive to the obvious transiency among the early Kansas farm population is beside the point; for those settlers who were forced to move on, simple survival instincts were at work as well.

Whether those farmers who tested the limits of agriculture on the high plains in the late nineteenth century were aspirant speculators or sturdy yeomen agriculturalists and builders of community in the Jeffersonian tradition seems a moot point. Indeed the most significant historical feature of the effort to farm the arid plains—or the equally marginal areas on the Canadian prairies such as the Paliser Triangle—is its boom-and-bust character, its transiency. Donald Worster's assessment of the soddy entrepreneur may well be correct: that the settlers merely wanted to establish a more democratic system of tenure on the old range-cattle grazing lands; that capitalism defined the sodbusters' attitude toward the land; and that as a group they viewed farming increasingly as a business, the object being "not simply to make a living, but to make money."[46]

Yet that argument, like Malin's reference to the aspirant speculator, obscures larger explanations of transiency and excuses more than it clarifies. In a sense it blames the victims in situ for the environmental and economic tragedies that occurred. Larger forces were at work (the sodbuster might be described as their gullible and willing foot soldier) that better explain the ephemeral character of all agricultural practice on the high plains. The settler population, it must be remembered, lacked capital and accurate and easily available knowledge about the region's climate; nor did they have at hand helpful advice or guidance from government agencies. The high-plains sodbusters of those early years, beguiled by advertisements extolling the agricultural potential of the region, became victims of human and cultural forces beyond their control. As a group, their experiences fell a bit short of the settler population William Kittredge refers to as "white people in paradise."[47]

In the general expansion of capitalism in late-nineteenth-century America, land and natural resources were the critical ingredients to sustained economic growth, providing incentive and opportunity to the great entrepreneurs who were relentlessly seeking to expand their financial empires and to the aspiring middle class who were also striving for a piece of the action.[48] Collectively their activities revolutionized productive relations and altered the legal status of land and natural resources, their social and economic worth, and the particular moral value that landownership held for common citizens. Hence, given the thrust of American development in the nineteenth century, it is not surprising that undercapitalized farmers, persuaded by an all-pervasive collectivity of propaganda, would sometimes push subhumid agricultural practices beyond environmental limits.[49] Indeed, every cultural value and social virtue in the larger society urged them to do so. Moreover, the foremost private institutions of the day—the great transportation systems, with an advertising reach that spanned the Atlantic Ocean—were aggressively promoting western settlement at every opportunity. The ad campaigns of the transcontinentals, according to Walter Nugent, brought "Volga Germans to Kansas in the 1870s and Ukrainians to Alberta in the 1920s."[50]

Railroads were the great agencies of change in the interior West, everywhere bringing alterations to agricultural production. The great roads that traversed the plains meant higher land values, the transition from subsistence to commercial farming, the end of open-range grazing in many areas, and in various instances the introduction of some form of agriculture where none had been practiced before. Representing a gigantic leap in the technical ability to transport people and goods, the railroads intensified the need for still more capital and triggered additional technological advances through the introduction of a cornucopia of mass-produced farm equipment: disc gang plows, five-section disc harrows, grain drills, checkrowers, and increasingly improved harvesting and threshing machines.[51] The impetus of capital in advancing the technology to produce more goods was the real force behind the great boom in world agricultural output in the last quarter of the nineteenth century.

Progress came at a cost, of course. Because most farmers lacked the financial resources to purchase the new technological marvels, the field was open to bankers and mortgage companies, human adversaries as it turned out who were often more threatening than the natural ones. Although the proliferation of mortgage houses and credit agencies fueled the agricultural boom of the 1870s and 1880s, the financiers did little to urge caution upon farmers. That this tenuous structure of financing would prove fragile is not surprising. When a fractious climate and an equally unruly economy subsequently combined to end the narrow margin of profitability for farmers on the high plains, many of the mortgage brokers who had financed the operations west of the ninety-eighth meridian fell victim to those same forces.[52]

There was a period of several years when all seemed well and good, however. The westward tide of settlement, aided by a cycle of above-average precipitation for the high plains, pressed relentlessly into eastern Colorado, into Texas north of the huge cattle baronies, and in a great frenzy in the late 1880s into Oklahoma. A Burlington Railroad pamphlet published in 1887 observed that the belt of adequate rainfall had moved westward toward Denver and that the eastern Colorado plains were "not to be excelled in productiveness by any country upon earth." As numerous scholars have indicated, the collective public-relations work of the railroad boosters, the townsite promoters, and others who stood to profit from agricultural expansion acted in the face of growing scientific evidence to the contrary. Considering those settlers who staked out claims in eastern Colorado's sagebrush and buffalo-grass country during those years, Marshall Sprague puts an ironic spin on the corporate manipulation of the realities of climate: "Railroad agents were careful not to prepare them for the reality of their Colorado Eden." The boosters ignored, resented, and shunted aside the careful investigations of John Wesley Powell and others whose scientific findings simply did not fit the prevailing ethos. Yet many of Powell's observations about agricultural problems west of the 100th meridian were essentially valid and particularly so for the area that subsequently suffered the great dust storms of the 1930s.[53]

That region of sporadic and fluctuating precipitation, high winds, and periodic grasshopper and locust plagues did not prove to be the lotusland the boosters had promised. As would happen again in the twentieth century, environmental and economic conditions combined in the late 1880s to limit expansion and to place restrictions on the new mode of capitalist agriculture that had pushed beyond the ninety-eighth meridian. But for a culture possessed of a spare memory, the incidences of failure were remembered momentarily and associated with areas where cycles of drought were of longest duration. In the long run those abortive efforts to farm the arid plains made little impression upon succeeding generations.

For the unfortunate who were caught in a spiral of crop failures, falling agricultural prices, and high mortgage rates, however, the crisis was immediate and real. For the Great Plains as a whole the cycle of dry years began in 1886 and persisted for at least a decade in most places, with the lack of precipitation especially severe on the central plains in 1889. The drought eventually affected every state from Montana and the Dakotas south through Oklahoma and Texas. In the wake of those failures, many western counties in the Dakotas, Nebraska, and Kansas and counties in eastern Colorado experienced a net decline in population between 1890 and 1900. The number of settlers displaced during the period may have been as high as 200,000, a figure that ranks second only to the approximately 500,000 who relocated during the Great Depression. Following that human exodus, the average size of farming operations increased as many of the acreages reverted to cattle raising.[54]

Like advancing and receding waves moving with the rhythms of climatic and economic conditions, settler farmers repeatedly attempted to practice agriculture beyond the ninety-eighth meridian. Those recurring cycles of failure were always linked to larger arenas of action, in which American agriculturists functioned as part of a wider and increasingly integrated world economic system. Some scholars have cited the existence of a crisis in capital accumulation in the advanced industrial world, beginning in the mid-1870s and gaining momentum in the succeeding years, especially in Great Britain, the country that pioneered the way to the industrial revolution. Railroad and related securities, hitherto the centerpieces of accumulation, entered a long period of declining profits. At the same time, there was as yet no new form of investment, such as chemicals, internal-combustion engines, and the like, to replace the railroad as a motive force for rapid economic expansion. The onset of the worldwide depression in the 1890s marked the beginning of a new phase in world capitalism that encroached heavily on subsistence modes of production everywhere.[55] Aside from shifting power relations among the industrial nations, the rapid expansion of the capitalist mode of agriculture and the huge increase in production may have been the most significant and far-reaching of the changes that occurred in the last quarter of the nineteenth century.

The great successes of the railroad and the improved and more rapid means of ocean transport contributed both to the advance of capitalist agriculture around the globe and to the increased intercontinental movement of people. Those developments had reciprocal implications for social systems everywhere. In the last quarter of the nineteenth century, and with seemingly alarming rapidity, market agriculture spread to New Zealand, Australia, Argentina, India, and to the southeastern steppes in Russia. The advances in technology now made it possible to ship beef, cotton, corn, sugar, wheat, and other grains to Europe in a matter of days. Those developments took place in the midst of a deflationary period that witnessed a dramatic decline in prices for all commodities, including those for grain crops like wheat and corn. The consequences for European agriculture, especially for marginal peasant farmers, were disastrous, forcing a large-scale emigration to urban centers on the Continent or, as happened in many cases, a move to the United States or to Canada. The reverberations, according to Eric Wolf, were far-reaching:

> American wheat, sold in Europe at lower prices than the domestic product, brought on a crisis in European peasant agriculture, sending a migrant stream of ruined peasants to seek new sources of livelihood in the burgeoning Americas. Ironically, many of them made the journey westward on the same ships that carried to Europe the wheat that proved their undoing.[56]

Those interrelationships in a world economy that was becoming increasingly integrated, although not the first of their kind, would gain momentum as the twentieth century advanced.

The millions of new acres brought into agricultural production beyond the continental United States after 1870 compounded the marketing difficulties for the 6 million people living on the Great Plains by 1890. Indeed, climatic problems combined with the great agricultural depression in the latter part of the nineteenth century to sharply limit migration to the Great Plains region.[57] But farmers on the plains were not alone in suffering hardship. Agriculturists elsewhere in the country, including those who operated marginally productive units in the South or in New England, faced similar problems. Even in the expanding agricultural mecca of California, farmers felt the impact from international commodity price swings. While it always lacked the agrarian, small-freeholder tradition of the Midwest and Great Plains states, capitalist agriculture in California confronted marketing problems similar to those east of the Rocky Mountains.[58] Although it was not apparent for a time, operators in the Sunshine State ultimately would take advantage of the increasing diversity of their grain crops and vegetable, fruit, and fiber production—along with public subsidies for great water-diversion schemes—to forge a powerful agricultural economy.

After visiting California in 1835, the peripatetic Richard Henry Dana remarked, "In the hands of an enterprising people, what a country this might be!" Although Dana did not say, given his New England background, we might hedge a safe bet on whom he had in mind. But the situation that eventually emerged in California was quite different from anything that Dana (and many others) had envisioned. Indeed, if an argument is to be made for a feudal tradition in the United States, it rests in the great Mexican land-grant system that remained largely intact (albeit under different owners) after the conquest. Moreover, the emerging social and economic base of California's power structure was apparent from an early period: Josiah Royce observed that the inherited system of Mexican land grants, well suited to a pastoral people, was bound to cause problems when the population increased and the land appreciated in value. The bookdealer and publisher Hubert Howe Bancroft pointed to land monopoly as the state's special evil, particularly when a clamor arose during the 1870s for redistribution of the old Mexican grants on a more equitable basis. Although railroad monopoly existed in California, "more formidable," Bancroft insisted, "is land monopoly."[59]

In the rapid westward press of the American population after the Civil War, federal land policy loomed large in shaping the social matrix of new agricultural communities. "To a greater or lesser extent," Carey McWilliams has argued, every western state "experienced the leavening effect" of the government's "free or 'cheap' land policy, . . . that is, every state except California." The state's best farming land, including that deeded by the Mexican government to a few hundred owners before the conquest, was subjected to a period of frenzied speculation and eventually wound up in the hands of San Francisco and Sacramento capitalists who manipulated state and federal land laws to amass huge holdings. Hence, in the case of the landownership pattern in California, the present is at one with the past: the large agribusiness holdings of today are largely a consequence of those early estates accumulated well before the end of the nineteenth century.[60]

The capitalist mode of agriculture was introduced to California in a series of waves—the hide and tallow trade of the Spanish and Mexican period; the livestock boom from the conquest to 1870; the emergence and domination of bonanza wheat farming into the 1890s; and finally the growing speculation in land for irrigation purposes and the diversification of crop production. But through that series of transitions, one great constant remained: monopolization in landownership. Henry George wrote as early as 1871 that California was "a country of plantations and estates." According to Carey McWilliams, the state skipped the frontier stage of agricultural development because it never experienced the small family-farm tradition; in that sense Donald Pisani agrees: California was "the great exception." By the early twentieth century "wealthy, nonresident land barons and migratory farm laborers or tenants" characterized agriculture in the state.[61]

While agriculture in the West, including that in California, was being increasingly integrated into worldwide patterns of trade relations and capital movement during the last quarter of the nineteenth century, other forms of regional economic activity were even more closely linked to the expanding capitalist world economy. The rapidly growing industrial sector, primarily in mineral resources, was foremost. Mining was a boon to early commercial agriculture in the West, beginning with the great California gold rush and continuing through a series of more lasting mineral finds elsewhere in the region. It was also mining activity that triggered the interests of eastern U.S. and European investors in the West and brought the industrial world directly to the region.

CHAPTER FIVE

The Industrial West: The Paradox of the Machine in the Garden

Cosmopolitan, aggressive and diverse, Butte was a city—some say Montana's only city. More to the point, the metropolis that copper built was an industrial city that operated by a different clock than the state's agricultural settlements. It stood alone as a smoking island of intense activity.

—*William L. Lang*[1]

Gus Masciotra, an early twentieth-century immigrant from the small town of Agnone Cilento, near Naples, does not fit the conventional image of the preindustrial westerner. His ethnic background, occupation, and place of residence fall beyond the bounds of the mythical agrarian and subsistence stereotypes that characterize the region. Shortly after his arrival in the United States, the teenaged Masciotra made the seemingly unorthodox move west and hired on with the Colorado Fuel and Iron Company in Pueblo. Between the turn of the century and the outbreak of World War II the sprawling complex of mines, mills, and smelters was the preeminent industrial enterprise in the state, employing one out of every ten wage earners in Colorado. With savings accrued from his earnings at the Rockefeller-controlled firm, Masciotra purchased a home near the Pueblo operation, added a grocery at the same location in 1926, and then with the end of prohibition, opened a tavern in front of the grocery.[2]

Gus' Place, Colorado's most historic and celebrated blue-collar bar, still serves up the chilled brew and the lunch platters that made it the foremost working-class neighborhood saloon in Pueblo. As such, Gus' Place reminds us of the hundreds of social gathering places in those once bustling industrial communities scattered throughout the West. Like the Jameson Saloon in Wallace, Idaho, and others of its kind, Gus' Place defies the pastoral and agrarian images associated with the premodern West of subsistence farmers, cattlemen, and solitary mining enterprises. The classic West, as one writer put it, "was simply no place for wageworkers." The history of Gus' Place points to a different story about the West, one set very much in an industrial environment in a place linked to the far corners of the globe and peopled with a great diversity of ethnic types.[3]

Despite the abundance of published work on the western mining industry and other parallel forms of mineral extraction where large numbers of people worked in labor-intensive and partially mechanized undertakings, most writers fail to link those activities to industrial/manufacturing occupations. The consequence is a story that describes a capital-poor but resource-rich region largely subject to the fluctuations of distant financial houses until the liberating influence of World War II. That interpretative lineage includes the western colonialist arguments of Bernard DeVoto and Walter Prescott Webb before World War II.[4] More recent assessments can be found in Earl Pomeroy, Gerald Nash, Michael Malone, Richard Etulain, and a host of others.[5]

Those conflicting images of a preindustrial and largely pastoral West (i.e., prior to World War II) and the emergence of the region as an important industrial partner after 1945 may seem reductive and simplistic; however, they do reflect a sense that the region was generally lacking in those qualities that we attribute to industrialism. "The Second World War," according to Earl Pomeroy, "brought the most drastic changes in the Far West *since 1849*"; the region's wartime industrial growth was the principal factor in that transformation.[6] According to Gerald Nash, the war stimulated manufacturing and industry "as no other single event in the history of the West." A region heavily dependent on agriculture and raw-materials production was diversified and made increasingly self-sufficient: "Sleepy western towns had been transformed into teeming cities; ethnic diversity had become a new reality."[7]

Although World War II unquestionably brought change to all of western North America, scholars have exaggerated the influence of the war on the industrial attributes of the West.[8] If, as Patricia Limerick contends, "mining set the pace and direction of western development," then we have much to learn by examining more closely the region's oldest industry and its quick evolution from individual treasure hunt to large-scale corporate enterprise. Mining had a greater influence on western history (and over a more protracted time) than any other industry. And from an early period it reflected the basic elements of industrial activity elsewhere in North America: the development of urban living patterns, the striking pervasiveness of wageworkers in those growing communities, and a reliance on global markets for capital, prices, and labor.[9] Mining and its vast support network, including its supply and delivery arterials, made the West an integral element of the industrializing Atlantic economy.

Mining enterprises of any consequence required the accoutrements of industrialism: railroads, mills, smelters, and the investment capital to make that infrastructure possible. Ultimately, as one writer pointed out, "the entrepreneurs began to mine the miners." Towns and mills replaced camps and claims, and the capitalists "took from the prospector . . . a nascent vision of laissez-faire and elevated it to an iron art."[10] As an investment arena for continental and global capital and as the workplace for foreign-born wage earners, the West began developing the symbols of industrialism at least as early as the 1860s with the opening of the Comstock Lode. Those deep mines, some of them achieving depths of more than 3,000 feet, required a degree of capitalization and heavy industrial equipment hitherto unknown in the West. The mining camps of Virginia City and nearby Gold Hill quickly grew into urban, industrial settlements with a combined population of approximately 6,000 people as early as the 1860s. Virginia City's population may have reached as high as 25,000 just before the mines began to run out in the mid-1870s. In the foothills on the western side of the Sierra Nevada, according to Ralph Mann, Grass Valley and Nevada City developed "large-scale industrial mining economies by the late 1860s"; mining became increasingly specialized and the proportion of miners declined; but the number of people employed in the industry as a whole increased.[11]

The first stirrings of the western labor movement also occurred on the Comstock, another indication of the industrial influences in the region. The formidable Comstock miners' union, according to one authority, achieved for its membership "a level of wages and benefits unsurpassed in the western mines," and it sustained the movement elsewhere in the West long after the Comstock had ceased to be productive. When the intense activity on the Comstock began to play out in the late 1870s, the veterans of that experience took their skills (and their ideas about worker cooperation and labor unions) to already developing enterprises in new districts scattered from Idaho and Montana south to Utah, Arizona, and New Mexico.[12]

The building of transcontinental railroads through the region, beginning with the Central Pacific/Union Pacific line in 1869, aided and abetted the development of the region's industrial infrastructure and provided a further stimulus to foreign capital, especially in the mineral-rich Rocky Mountain cordillera. Those developments reveal a certain logic, a portrait that is less agrarian than it is a picture infused with the symbols of industrial capitalism.[13] To be sure, western industrial communities in the nineteenth century were often dependent on a single unstable extractive activity; still, the conventional attributes associated with industrialism appear everywhere in the years following the Civil War: (1) diverse and ever-expanding forms of technology in transportation, communication, agriculture, mining, and lumbering; (2) the emergence of the labor question in the more industrialized sectors; (3) the appearance of sizable ethnic enclaves in virtually every industrial enterprise; and (4) the progressive incorporation and consolidation of the western business world.

Largely because its strategic location provided access to oceanic routes of travel, San Francisco quickly established itself as the preeminent manufacturing center of the nineteenth-century West. And since it was relatively isolated from the great industrial centers of the East Coast, San Francisco developed a broad-based and regionally significant manufacturing sector by the 1880s. The city promptly gained a regional monopoly on the manufacture of custom-made and locally designed mining equipment, and its production facilities quickly expanded from cottage-industry capacity to primary supplier for a sizable hinterland area.[14]

As western European, eastern U.S., and San Francisco capital investments in mining activity expanded through the western American backcountry, the symbols of industrialism appeared nearly everywhere throughout the region. The point may be trite, but it should be emphasized that nineteenth-century mining settlements were centers of industrial activity with certain common characteristics: the communities usually included large concentrations of male, blue-collar workers, diverse in their ethnic makeup, who were employed as wage laborers. Indeed, the region had a higher percentage of the foreign-born people than the East. In Grass Valley, the number of Cornish workers increased as American-born laborers gravitated toward other occupations. That "real West," historian David Emmons suggests, was the polar opposite of Frederick Remington's "primeval and frontier" region and the cultural antithesis of the Anglo-Saxon virtues of Owen Wister's *Virginian*. "For every cowboy town like Medicine Bow," Emmons argues, "there were three or four coal-mining and railroad towns like Rock Springs."[15]

The industrialization of the United States during the last half of the nineteenth century reflected the increasing global reach of capital to potentially lucrative sectors of investment, including sizable commitments to western railroad construction and to speculation in the region's mineral development.[16] Because of a profitability crisis in Europe by the 1870s where investments in traditional industrializing sectors such as railroads were no longer returning acceptable profit margins, American financial ventures proved especially attractive. Among those interested were British capitalists who had become disenchanted with the declining profits in railway and industrial securities in Great Britain, Europe, and India.[17]

In the context of global capital flows in the nineteenth century, it is important to recall that in conventional economic terms the United States was among the rapidly developing nations of the world. The data for British overseas investment between 1865 and the outbreak of World

War I (Britain was the leading creditor nation prior to 1914) indicate that 34 percent of its overseas investment portfolio went to North America, with the United States "the most important foreign source of new security issues in the British capital market." Moreover, in relation to that sizable commitment of capital, the most important factor, according to one scholar, "was the huge demands for building and maintaining the 216,000 miles of the American rail network." The objective of British investment was the development of infrastructures that in turn would increase the capacity of nations such as the United States to export its surpluses to Europe. And yet, even though European migration has been the subject of numerous monographic studies, scholars have found the transoceanic movement of capital less interesting. How important, then, was British capital to American development, especially in railroad construction? During one critical period following the American Civil War, foreign capital (most of it British) was almost wholly responsible for the doubling of railway mileage in the United States.[18]

British financiers, some of whom were gulled into backing bogus claims, also provided capital for the development of a significant segment of the western mining industry between 1860 and the close of the century. Clark Spence, author of an early study of British investment in American mining enterprises, argues that during the great mining boom after 1870, British firms stand out among all others. While continental capital was also important, it paled before the efforts of the British, who registered 518 companies between 1860 and 1900.[19] It would seem fair to say, then, that foreign investment contributed mightily to the capitalist transformation and industrialization of the American West.

It also should be emphasized that entrepreneurs in the region were not the passive victims of capital-rich aggressors from without who came to fleece them. San Francisco capitalists provided the bulk of the initial financing for western mining ventures, but those sources soon proved inadequate; hence the business community quickly turned to more distant places of greater capital accumulation in the eastern United States and in Europe. Former California governor Milton S. Latham told the members of the American Mining Stock Exchange in 1880 that San Francisco was no longer the major player in mining finance: "The center of speculative mining is now transferred . . . to Boston and New York." And the invitees, according to Clark Spence, were not reluctant to take up the requests. Between 1860 and the turn of the century natural resources in the United States were thrown open "to rapid and often ruthless exploitation. . . . From all sides in flocked hungry capitalists, all eager to drink deeply and to feast greedily." In the end, Spence concludes, British investments in the West accelerated the development of the region's industrial structure and ended the need for external capital.[20]

The closing of time and space through technological advances—improved rail and steamship transport and the completion of the transatlantic cable in 1867—boosted the attractiveness of the West to outside capital and vastly accelerated the process of the capitalist transformation of the region. For the northern West, the railroad was the key instrument in transforming the area from preindustrial forms of economic activity to modern industrial technology. The correspondence of Samuel T. Hauser, Montana's leading banker and mining and railroad entrepreneur of the 1870s and 1880s, indicates a sharp expansion of business activity beginning in 1880, especially in exchanges with distant investment houses in the East and in Europe.[21]

The great boom in silver production in Montana, according to one authority, "required the piecing together of an industrial infrastructure— mills, smelters, and especially railroads to connect mines with smelters and markets," and, the author might have added, the capital necessary to finance those undertakings. The railroads (to Butte in 1881 and to Helena and elsewhere in 1883) attracted capital, the quintessential ingredient for the building of an industrial base. The rails, the critical and necessary "lifeline of the industry," also made possible the importation of heavy equipment and supplies: stamping mills, machinery for the mines, tools, cables, food stocks, and the other requirements for milling and smelting.[22] The ribbons of steel that everywhere penetrated the Intermountain West both speeded up transportation and drastically reduced its costs.[23] Thus the dramatic changes in the region after 1870 were directly related to the links between technology and finance that tied the emerging industrial West to continental and global influences.

In a sense, the last thirty years of the nineteenth century saw the rapid expansion of an integrated, metropolitan-industrial system surrounded by peripheral population centers in resource-rich regions that paid tribute to the manufacturing core. New Orleans, San Francisco, and Minneapolis, according to historical geographer John Agnew, were gateway cities, providing ready access to a variety of hinterland areas: the Mississippi basin, California's Central Valley, and the northern plains. As the century drew to a close, other gateway cities such as Denver emerged to serve the increasing number of primary industrial communities in the countryside and the distant markets and centers of capital to which they paid homage. Metropolitan centers established the conditions for economic growth in the outback and dictated the respective roles that peripheral areas would play in the national economy. The movement of raw materials toward the center and the shipment of finished products outward articulated that reciprocal command and reactive relationship.[24]

To a significant degree, then, the emerging western industrial program was an extension of capitalist relations in eastern North America and in Europe where surpluses had accumulated. Moreover, that push into the mineral-rich Rocky Mountain cordillera did not come about as a natural consequence of evolutionary processes; rather, human agency effected the historical transformation of the West through conscious and deliberate decisions made in the capitalist marketplace.[25] Clearly the agents of eastern U.S. and European capital—and the technical experts they hired—provided the vital ingredients driving the industrial infrastructure necessary to mineral exploitation in the region.

Nowhere is this phenomenon more evident than in the hinterland Southwest where the link between the arrival of the railroad and industrial activity is most apparent. The revolutionary world of industrial capitalism was extended to the desert borderland country with the construction of railroads across New Mexico and Arizona between 1878 and 1883. The Southern Pacific Railroad and the Atchison, Topeka, and the Santa Fe Railway lines brought potential copper-mining enterprises within reach of a vast transcontinental rail system. Where single prospectors and miners had formerly rushed from one digging to the next, mining districts were quickly transformed into communities of wage earners. At the same time the districts came under the control of outside capitalists who introduced branch lines, tramways, and heavy smelting machinery. The firms themselves hired trained mining engineers, metallurgical scientists, and bookkeepers and accountants to direct their industrial activities.[26] The onset of the copper boom in Arizona indicated that the region had become an integral part of the larger continental and transatlantic world of industrial capitalism.

The influence of the transcontinentals caused Arizona's population to boom; it grew from fewer than 10,000 people in 1870 to nearly 123,000 by the turn of the century. In the case of the Phelps-Dodge Corporation, the effect of the railroad was immediate. In the early 1880s, with its interest in Arizona's mineral potential quickening, the firm dispatched James Douglas, an expert on copper ores, to the region. As a result of his investigations, the company purchased claims at Bisbee and Morenci that were to make Phelps-Dodge the leading and most notorious copper producer in the Southwest. After acquiring adjacent ore bodies in the vicinity of Bisbee, Phelps-Dodge began large-scale production under the Copper Queen Consolidated Copper Company in 1885. With an immensely profitable operation and with rail lines linked to the transcontinentals, Phelps-Dodge directors authorized the construction of a new company town, Douglas, and a new state-of-the art smelter adjacent to the Copper Queen in 1904. As the company's representative in Arizona, Douglas directed a paternal operation that excluded Chinese laborers from the Phelps-Dodge communities after nightfall and that shunted Mexican workers to employment in the smelters and on railroad construction projects. The company firmly opposed all forms of union activity. By the turn of the century Phelps-Dodge dominated the copper business in Arizona from the pit to the refinery, and within the decade it extended a railroad from its Morenci plant to the rich ore bodies in northern Mexico. Phelps-Dodge continued to integrate its entire production network in the Southwest, and in 1908 the firm formally incorporated as Phelps-Dodge and Company.[27]

The Company, as it was referred to in Arizona, loomed as large in the territorial polity and economy as Anaconda did in Montana. Although the Phelps-Dodge operations were isolated and in many instances distant from one another, the wealthy and paternalistic company wielded great power in an otherwise sparsely populated area. Its company-controlled settlements were discrete industrial communities with a substantial mix of ethnic groups: Hispanics, Cornish, Welsh, Irish, Finns, Italians, and an assortment of eastern Europeans.[28] It should be added that the population of those company towns, like similar communities elsewhere in the region, was extremely vulnerable to fluctuations in market conditions and to the paternal nature of the capitalist enterprise in question.

Though prospecting and occasional mining rushes are part of the immediate postconquest history of the territories of New Mexico and Arizona, the influence of those activities was negligible until the industrial boom that occurred during the 1880s. The transition from a predominantly pastoral (i.e., agriculture and livestock) to a mining-industrial economy took place in less than two decades. By the turn of the century—and largely as a consequence of rapidly expanding copper production—mining was the most important single industry in the Southwest in terms of the number of people employed and the value of mineral production. Only copper mining could explain the existence of communities such as Bisbee. "Copper," Carlos Schwantes observes, "equaled prosperity or adversity: a rise in the price in Paris or the opening of a new mine in Chile would impact life in Bisbee." Like other single-industry towns in the mining region, Bisbee's economic health resembled an economic roller coaster for most of its existence. Eastern investors supplied the capital and paid for the infrastructure to exploit the region's minerals and in turn reaped the bulk of the great profits that were made.[29] And until the development of publicly subsidized irrigation systems and the coming of war-related economic growth, industrial mining remained Arizona's principal economic activity.

One of his advisers warned Pres. Grover Cleveland early in 1894, "We are on the eve of a very dark night." That comment both explains and obscures the realities of the nationwide depression that settled on the

United States between 1893 and 1897. Conventional reasoning for the national economic collapse usually addresses such themes as overproduction, bank insolvencies, the bankruptcy of the Philadelphia and Reading Railroad, and the failure of the National Cordage Company. Widespread unemployment, homelessness, and social unrest, especially in the great manufacturing centers of the East, accompanied that first industrial depression in the United States. "Men died like flies under the strain," wrote Henry Adams about Boston; the city "grew suddenly old, haggard, and thin."[30] But that sudden reversal in the nation's economic development and well-being was felt far beyond the industrial cities in the East.

Although the American West figures in the larger story of the economic collapse of the 1890s, conventional accounts usually treat the region as a colorful sideshow for silver zealots, agricultural protest, and the Coxey movement. And yet more than any other single factor the economic collapse of the 1890s indicates the importance of industrial activity to the West and the remarkable degree to which the region already was linked to the fortunes of global economic conditions. The mining of silver was labor-intensive, and it required repeated infusions of capital to pay the charges of installing underground timbers, water pumps, and lifting machinery.[31] As the events of 1893 would show, decisions made in the distant transatlantic world of investment capital had a direct and immediate effect on the tiniest of industrial outposts in western North America. Malcolm Rohrbough has summarized that threat in his study of Aspen, Colorado: "The dangers to the city and its people lay not within but without, in the vast arena of national and international finance."[32]

Silver prices, which had been declining since the end of the Civil War, took an ominous plunge downward in the spring of 1893. Then on June 26 came the thunderbolt: a British House of Commons committee published a report recommending that the government's mint in India cease the practice of coining silver rupees. That information brought immediate chaos to world metal exchanges and to mining and smeltering centers of the American West; literally within hours silver prices dropped 20 percent.[33] Given our instant global communications systems, the frenzy of activity following the cabled dispatches of late June 1893 is impressive.

News about the British report reached the silver-mining and smeltering centers of the Intermountain West simultaneously with corporate orders to close mines and smelters or to reduce wages. In Aspen the *Rocky Mountain Sun* reported on July 1 that mines were being closed everywhere in Colorado, the nation's number-one silver-producing state, and that 200,000 people were destitute. Employment in Aspen's mines had dropped from 2,500 to 150 within a week, and on July 22 the community's prestigious Wheeler Bank, closely linked to the high-country's silver economy, ceased operations. Mines and mills were shut down elsewhere in the region—in the Colorado high country of Leadville and San Juan, in the Salt Lake Valley, and in northern Idaho's Coeur d'Alene district. The collapse of silver and the ravages of the panic of 1893, according to James Fell, "brought the entire silver-lead industry to a virtual standstill."[34]

Montana's oldest financial institution, Samuel Hauser's First National Bank of Helena, with sizable investments in silver enterprises, also suspended operations in summer 1893. Similar conditions prevailed elsewhere in Montana's rich silver-lode country, where the mining towns of Granite, Castle, and Elkhorn began to slide into oblivion.[35] When the order arrived on July 1 to close the fabled Granite Mine for good, 3,000 people left the mountain town and headed downslope for Phillipsburg. A. L. Stone, a child participant in the leave-taking, remembered the exodus:

> Everyone was in a hurry and pushed and jostled to reach the bottom first. . . . [Some walked] carrying their hand luggage, frying pans or teakettles. Wagons that hadn't been used for ten years, creaked and screeched down the incline. Bandboxes, babies and bull dogs, brought up the rear, and so it kept up all day and night—a continual stream of almost panic-striken people, leaving, perhaps forever, their home on the mountain.[36]

As "the year of calamity" drew to a close, unemployment in Montana may have been as high as 20,000, one-third of the thinly populated state's work force. A floating population of idle men filled the streets in industrial towns such as Butte and Helena. "Butte," Marcus Daly observed, "is looking very savage. There are over 3,000 idle men on the streets. They are discontented and dissatisfied." Elsewhere in silver-lode country, smelting and refining companies announced that they would receive no further ore shipments. The Pueblo Smelting and Refining Company telegraphed its suppliers that it would "neither unload . . . nor pay freight charges thereon until market conditions are fully settled."[37] With a few exceptions, the precipitous collapse in the price of silver marked the close of the booming years of the precious-metals industry in the West.

Clearly the silver debacle (combined with the national financial contraction) devastated the Rocky Mountain mining districts. Only those mining centers—Butte is the most notable example—able to exploit alternative ore bodies survived into the twentieth century. Many of the silver mines—the bulwark of the industrial infrastructure of the West since the 1870s—remained closed. The physical impact of the industrial shutdown was apparent everywhere: banks failed, businesses closed, jobs disappeared, and legions of the unemployed took to the rails and wandered the region in search of work. The events of the summer of 1893 had rent asunder the pacesetting industrial sector in the region. Only the revival in gold extraction in a few places and the continued expansion of the copper business carried the industry into the twentieth century. Henceforth, copper emerged preeminent in western mining, and the extraction of precious metals became largely a by-product of that process.[38]

During the wartime production peak in 1917, it is said that Park and Main streets in Butte, Montana, were crowded twenty-four hours a day. Legend has it that cafes, bars, and whorehouses operated around the clock as the "richest hill on earth" poured forth prodigious quantities of copper to meet national requirements. By the time the United States was sending its troops to fight in World War I, Butte had already established itself as the most colorful industrial center in the West. In brief, Butte was brash, exploitive, fundamental. Butte was everything that the mythical West was not: it was heavily industrial; its population was composed of people who worked for daily wages; it was the scene of episodic labor warfare; its citizenry represented myriad ethnic groups; and it was linked by investment and markets to global corporate strategies.[39] The process of industrialization in Butte followed paths familiar to industrialism elsewhere in the West: dependence on ever more sophisticated technology; increasing amounts of capitalization; the development of greater complexity in skill levels; and the progressive diminution of worker autonomy.[40]

Pueblo, Colorado, like Butte, is one of the more enduring and celebrated working-class communities in the American West. But if Butte was red brick and volatile, Pueblo was gray and nondescript in comparison. While industrial activity in Butte centered on mineral extraction, Pueblo enjoyed a more diverse economic base of refining, smelting, and the more conventional industrial forms of manufacturing. Both communities, however, shared common ties to the world of finance capital in the form of domination by the Standard Oil Gang, the relatives and associates of John D. Rockefeller. For Butte the Standard Oil initiative involved the formation of a copper trust, the Amalgamated Copper Company.[41] In Pueblo the Rockefellers intervened more directly with the purchase of the community's foremost enterprise, the Colorado Fuel and Iron Company (CF&I). While the Standard Oil associates—through Amalgamated and subsequently its operating company, Anaconda—sat astride Montana's economy as a corporate colossus, Colorado Fuel and Iron exercised a similar if slightly diminished influence in Colorado.

The Colorado Fuel and Iron Company originated in a series of Pueblo business enterprises, many of them associated with the dramatic surge in silver mining in the 1870s. Situated on the broad flatland where the Arkansas River enters onto the high plains, Pueblo provided natural advantages to railroad builders with easy access routes up the Arkansas valley to the booming town of Leadville and south to the Trinidad coal fields on the Colorado–New Mexico border. Linking Pueblo to Denver and points east and south, new transportation arterials—the Denver and Rio Grande and the Atchison, Topeka, and the Santa Fe railroads—were critical to its emergence as a smelting and refining center.[42] Pueblo's advantages as a transportation hub attracted capital, industry, and an influx of wageworkers and for several decades made it the leading industrial center of the West. By the early twentieth century, CF&I's Pueblo-based industrial operation represented the only fully integrated iron and steel manufactory in the western United States; it controlled mining enterprises in four states and territories and operated sales offices throughout the Rocky Mountains and the Far West. The company remained the only operation of its kind west of Saint Louis until the outbreak of World War II.[43]

Colorado Fuel and Iron traces its lineage to the corporate efforts of the Denver and Rio Grande Railroad and to its principal architect, William Jackson Palmer, who consolidated three smaller firms in 1880 to form the Colorado Coal and Iron Company. The new operation was intended to engage in residential and agricultural real estate, to extract and sell coal, to produce coke, and to manufacture iron and steel at Pueblo. The modern steel operation that opened in 1882 included blooming and rail mills, a foundry, and machine shops. For the next ten years Colorado Coal and Iron sold pig iron, pipes, spikes, and steel rails, and the expanding Rio Grande system was its principal customer for rails. When a new competitor, John Osgood and the Colorado Fuel Company, emerged in the mid-1880s and won contracts to supply coal to the major railroads operating through Colorado, the result was the merger of the two firms in 1892 and the formation of the Colorado Fuel and Iron Company. Until well into the twentieth century, the company's principal sales remained in rails and accessories and in coal production.[44]

As the principal manufacturing and refining center for CF&I, Pueblo served as an industrial way station that linked eastern capital, hinterland resources, industrial processing and manufacturing, and markets in a kind of productive symbiosis. While Denver's economic base was relatively diverse, Pueblo's was more directly tied to the immediate industrial infrastructure of the West: the manufacture of steel rails for the expanding railroad system in the Rocky Mountains and beyond and the mining of coal to fuel steam-powered transportation throughout the region. The residents of Pueblo saw clearly that outside forces—aided and abetted by the occasional local booster—drove economic expansion. Such a system of capitalist power relations had little to do with the larger Pueblo community, its backcountry satellites, or the development of a self-sustaining economic base, except as a constellation of profit-producing phenomena. Indeed, the economic command structures that controlled such resource-rich industrial areas were predicated on destroying that which brought the communities into existence in the first place.[45] Pueblo and its tributary company towns prospered and decayed according to the availability of the appropriate ores, the demand for coal, and the marketability of its manufactures.

The most important of the CF&I/Pueblo tributary communities was Crested Butte, a small town on the western slope of the Continental Divide. The former hard-rock camp turned to the successful mining of coal and then became part of CF&I's expanding Colorado empire in 1892. At the outset, American-born, British, and northern European miners dominated the Crested Butte work force; however, the 1900 census shows a complete turnabout in the ethnic makeup of the settlement: 62 percent Austrian, 8 percent Scots, 8 percent Italian, and 8 percent American. The small community had a three-room schoolhouse in 1902 and the local coal-mining operation employed 370 workers. Although it avoided the violent clashes that erupted at Ludlow, Crested Butte remained until its last coal mine closed in 1952 a settlement of ill-paid blue-collar workers who labored in a dangerous environment under physically demanding conditions.[46]

But Crested Butte was not a fortuitous historical accident for its investors; rather, the community's raison d'être signified capital's pursuit of its logical end: procuring its requisite resource base. Crested Butte's world was always linked to CF&I, the company that had dominated Colorado's industrial economy from its inception in 1892. By the turn of the century CF&I provided 75 percent of the state's coal output (a significant figure given the fact that Colorado was the leading coal producer among the western states), manufactured 7 percent of the steel-rail production in the United States, and employed 15,000 workers in Colorado, Wyoming, and New Mexico. Crested Butte provided an explicitly industrial-oriented labor force of mill hands, smelter and coking operatives, coal, iron, and limestone miners, and the other occupational categories necessary to such a vast undertaking.[47]

The industrialization of the world beyond Pueblo was a wrenching experience, especially for the scattered Hispanic villages in southern Colorado. When CF&I moved to exploit the rich deposits of coal in the region, it established a series of satellite company towns in the midst of existing Hispanic villages. The new industrial communities attracted wage laborers from settlements in northern New Mexico where the imposition of federal control and pressure from Anglo commercial interests were already placing strains on traditional Hispanic villages.[48] Similar conditions prevailed in southern Colorado; in Tercio, a CF&I town built in 1901, the firm declared the original Hispanic settlers squatters, thereby denying the existence of legitimate settlement in the area. CF&I officials further argued in the company's newspaper, *Camp and Plant*, that Tercio had come into being through the aegis of "modern energy and science," which combined to turn "a non-producing isolated mountain village" with only scattered herds of grazing sheep into "a scene of bustling activity."[49] The company's industrial domination of the regional economy eventually destroyed the fabric of Hispanic village life in southern Colorado.

John C. Osgood, who represented a group of capitalists known as the Iowa Crowd, held controlling interest in CF&I through the 1890s. As the company's chief executive officer, Osgood was a proponent of industrial paternalism, the belief that maximum production would be realized through the parental solicitude of the firm's managers. To achieve that end, CF&I published *Camp and Plant* and formed a sociological department to promote worker morale through a variety of self-improvement schemes. Despite its seeming success in resolving the labor problem, CF&I confronted serious fiscal problems shortly after the turn of the century: a limited market, access to capital, and severe competition from eastern steelmakers.[50] Those circumstances, most of them external to the company's home base in Colorado, eventually forced a change in the fiscal control of CF&I.

The restructuring of the Pueblo-based firm exemplified the reshaping of the larger corporate world early in the twentieth century when the CF&I leadership surrendered control in late 1902 to the interests of George Jay Gould and John D. Rockefeller, a joint partnership that assumed responsibility for the company's heavy burden of indebtedness. Monopoly capital had now come to Colorado's front range. In *The Great Coalfield War*, George McGovern and Leonard Guttridge point to the more obvious changes in the directorship of CF&I, a shift from Denver and Chicago capitalists to the "men of Wall Street." Although Rockefeller money was firmly in control, the family name was kept out of the news until spring 1903. When that information was made public, Colorado newspapers charged that the state had been annexed by eastern capitalists.[51]

For better or for worse the 1903 takeover linked the world of Colorado Fuel and Iron and its more than 15,000 employees firmly to the Rockefeller financial empire. Because the founding father of Standard Oil was passing into semiretirement, John D. Rockefeller, Jr., assumed the more active role in Colorado affairs. Elected to the board of directors of CF&I in 1904 along with Standard Oil/Rockefeller associates Frederick T. Gates and Starr J. Murphy, the younger Rockefeller exercised a powerful and influential role in company affairs. His staunchly antiunion beliefs undoubtedly exacerbated the industrial violence that was linked to the CF&I effort to prevent labor organizers from gaining a foothold in Pueblo and in the company's tributary coalfields.[52]

Colorado Fuel and Iron may well be the turn-of-the-century archetype for absentee financial control in the industrial West, where the one requirement for resident managers was the need to show major investors that the enterprise had at least the potential and promise for profit. To the degree that CF&I managers achieved that objective, they enjoyed the full support of the Rockefeller interests between the initial purchase of stocks in 1903 and the family's final sale of its CF&I holdings in January 1945. As subsequent events proved, the Rockefeller blessing on local management's decisionmaking, especially that concerning labor policy, had reverberations throughout the CF&I industrial empire.[53]

Under the control of its new investors, Colorado Fuel and Iron enjoyed at best a limited autonomy. Because the company continued to languish as a profit-making enterprise, the Rockefeller interests appointed a trusted family friend, LaMont Montgomery Bowers, as executive vice-president of its CF&I operations in Pueblo. Frederick T. Gates, financial mentor to John D. Rockefeller, Jr., thought it necessary to learn "the inside facts" about the company because it was "not realizing the promises" of the initial investment. It was "very important that we have a man on the inside," Gates told Bowers, "who can keep his finger on the pulse all the time and keep us informed as to exact conditions." He warned the new appointee that he would "be looked upon more or less as an interloper," that his appointment would create jealousy, and that "the greatest possible tact" would be required.[54]

The exchanges of correspondence between the Rockefeller interests and the CF&I operations in Colorado indicate the obvious; the financial overlords at 26 North Broadway in New York City were something more than disinterested absentee owners. In the years preceding the great strike of 1913–1914, the inflexibly conservative—even reactionary—Montgomery Bowers was the Rockefeller point man in Colorado. Jesse F. Welborn was president of the financially troubled firm, but Bowers clearly exercised the commanding influence in larger policy decisions involving investment, the expansion and upgrading of facilities, and the purchase of competing businesses.

A perusal of the exchanges between Bowers and the New York office gives the impression that the new vice-president's chief responsibility was to whip the Colorado company into competitive shape. For "both

J.D.R., Sr. and Jr.," Gates informed Bowers in 1907, "the interests in Colorado are now paramount." The "financial condition of the country and of the company" dictated that Bowers should give his "entire and exclusive attention" to CF&I affairs. Bowers was to familiarize himself with general company business, with the details of the different departments, and was to devote his "experience, insight, energy, knowledge of men and [the] capacity to master situations" in his new appointment.[55] To the degree that Bowers succeeded in streamlining company operations, his policies led to the dismantling of the paternalism of the John Osgood years, resulting in further alienation and hardship for the industrial work force and ultimately in violence.

From his own account and according to his critics, Bowers was an immediate success; he sharply reduced the number of salaried employees, cut operating costs, and otherwise improved the firm's competitiveness in coal production. But elsewhere in the Pueblo hierarchy, Bowers was looked upon as a corporate hit man. The Reverend Eugene Gaddis, whose sociological department was decimated by the new-economy program, likened Bowers to "a man of Louis the Fourteenth airs," whose repeated posturing would "make a burro laugh." Although Bowers enjoyed the full support of John D. Rockefeller, Jr., the latter was still dissatisfied with the company's operations; CF&I had cut expenses, but coal production still lagged behind the expectations at 26 North Broadway.[56]

A coldly rational economic and political calculus moved the Rockefeller management of CF&I affairs. When the New York office wanted the company's working capital deposited in New York banks where interest rates were higher, Bowers objected. Although Colorado banks could not offer the highest interest on balances, placing the firm's surplus cash in Denver financial institutions would "secure the cordial cooperation of the wealthy officers and stockholders . . . so that we may have their influence to protect ourselves from hostile legislation." Colorado's sizable foreign-born population, Bowers pointed out, was "largely under the heel of labor union agitators and shyster politicians," and if uncontested, they would enact legislation damaging to the company. To effectively combat those potentially harmful political conditions, it was necessary "to secure substantial men of importance in the state . . . to defeat these obnoxious measures." Colorado Fuel and Iron money was important to the Denver bankers; hence, "they will go to great lengths to prevent assaults upon us that would be to our detriment."[57]

Rockefeller, Jr., conceded the importance of retaining "the active interest and support of the leading citizens of Denver" but wondered if their support would "be as secure and cordial with a much smaller bank deposit." Moreover, were the "Denver institutions good for such large deposits? Is there not an element of risk in having so much money in any one of them?" Bowers defended the CF&I policy of using the Denver banks for several reasons: (1) the local banks did not charge for collections and other in-state business; (2) the influence of the bankers was essential "in preventing hostile and destructive legislation"; and (3) the money would have an energizing effect in promoting "the great mining operations and development of these states." The idea that Rockefeller wealth could be used as a political tool on the Colorado legislature evidently satisfied 26 North Broadway; there were no further questions about bank deposits.[58]

Bowers prevailed on the place of deposit for CF&I working capital, but he had greater difficulty explaining a series of mine disasters that killed an alarming number of company workers. The evidence suggests that the spate of publicity following the mining tragedies—especially a series of muckraking articles in *Pearson's* and *Survey*—upset the Rockefeller group. The authors of the articles, according to Bowers, received their information from "political shysters," "foreigners," and "disreputable men" associated with the Western Federation of Miners. Because CF&I was nonunion, Bowers complained that the company was "constantly berated by labor union agitators" who were in "the same class as the McNamaras and their clique."[59] Indeed, both the CF&I offices in Pueblo and the company's financial backers in New York went into a denial mode when the spotlight focused on industrial conditions in Colorado.

With its system of labor spies and detectives scattered everywhere among its work force, CF&I had in effect laid siege to its industrial operations by 1912. Even the smallest of the company's coal camps employed mine guards and camp marshals to keep an eye out for union organizers. Bowers's correspondence was filled with references to "enemies of the company," expressions that became ever more vitriolic as the threat of a major strike in the coalfields loomed in 1913. At the same moment, however, as the pacesetter for Colorado's nonunion mining companies, CF&I attempted to mitigate discontent among its employees by issuing a 10 percent wage increase, abolishing the use of script, and introducing the ten-hour day.[60]

Through all the turmoil and labor strife in Colorado, the CF&I officials enjoyed the full support of the New York office. As the United Mine Workers' unionization effort proceeded apace, Rockefeller confided to Bowers that his position opposing the union was correct: "We feel that what you have done is right and fair and that the position you have taken in regard to the unionization of the mines is in the interest of the employees." He assured the Pueblo management that "its strong and just position will not lack backing at this end."[61] That policy of unqualified and rigid support for the resident managers was a major factor contributing to the ensuing conflict. In essence, the CF&I leadership in Colorado and the absentee financiers shared similar dogmatic views. The United States Commission on Industrial Relations later placed responsibility for the strike squarely on CF&I management because of its "ruthless suppression of unionism, accomplished by the use of the power of summary discharge, the black list, armed guards, and spies, and by the active aid of venal state, county and town officials."[62]

When the United Mine Workers demanded union recognition for miners in the southern Colorado coalfields in fall 1913, the operators, including CF&I, refused. Their reaction set the stage for a widespread walkout throughout the region, an increased armed presence on both sides, and the subsequent calling out of the Colorado militia. Matters came to a tragic climax in April 1914 when the militia and company-hired guards fired on a tent colony of mine families near Ludlow and killed eighteen people, the majority of them women and children. During the next few weeks company guards and miners engaged in a series of running battles that resulted in seventy-four additional deaths, federal intervention, and eventually an uneasy truce.[63]

The point here is not to detail the industrial storms of 1913–1914 in the southern Colorado coalfields but to indicate the common ideological bond between company management in Pueblo and the corporate directors in New York City. The conditions and circumstances of labor in the industrial West were always linked to distant markets and the long reach of the absentee investment houses. Although it was only one of many similar corporate industrial arrangements, the Rockefeller/CF&I connection illustrates the arbitrary character of decisionmaking under those conditions. The great strike of 1913–1914 in the Colorado coalfields—and its tragic consequences—was not the last of such CF&I/worker clashes. Despite the company's efforts to create a docile labor force among the great ethnic mix of wageworkers, the widespread participation of all groups in mining strikes indicates that solidarity across ethnic lines was greater than the common bonds of agreement between employer and employee.[64] Violence continued to plague the industrial towns and smaller camps for at least the next two decades, and through it all stood the firm resolve of the Rockefeller group, determined to keep true unionism from the coal communities.

Despite the much-heralded adoption of the Industrial Representation Plan, Rockefeller continued to maintain a substantial influence in the company even after he resigned from the CF&I board of directors in 1920.[65] When the national economy went into a tailspin following World War I, CF&I officials used industrial conditions in coal and steel to implement wage reductions and thereby precipitated another coalfield strike. Company president Jesse Welborn, who served as the firm's chief executive officer from 1915 to 1929, informed Rockefeller that employee representatives in the steel mill and in most of the mining towns had expressed "a willingness to accept a reduction in wages" to enable the firm to cut its costs. From 26 North Broadway Rockefeller applauded CF&I employees for their cooperation with management "in laying plans for retrenchment which will be in the interest of both." For the New York financier this was "a most pleasant situation" because "the more we can trim our sails the less apt we will be to be seriously buffeted by the storm."[66] But that most pleasant situation turned to industrial warfare three more times in the next decade when laborers walked off the job to protest wage cuts and working conditions.

The industrial infrastructure of Colorado Fuel and Iron was uniquely fitted to a rapidly expanding, primary-production economy centered on mining and rail construction, highly volatile sectors that were extremely vulnerable to the warp and woof of national economic trends. The combined circumstances of limited markets, a narrow production line in steel rails and the mining of coal, and eventually the emergence of competing sources of fuel and new modes of transport placed CF&I at financial risk, however. The company's entire operations until World War II, according to one historian, "were on an economic roller-coaster."[67] Those severe fluctuations brought periodic havoc to the working-class towns that constituted the CF&I production system. Yet those circumstances were merely an extension into the twentieth century of industrial conditions whose lineage can be traced to the point in time when mining made the transition from individual treasure hunt to corporate enterprise. Although lone prospectors loom large in the story of western mining, Duane Smith reminds us that they had little influence other than to furnish the materials for legend. In fact, industrialism in the form of outside corporate capital and technical expertise came early to the West. The story of mining as large-scale industrial activity mirrors the increased integration of major western economic enterprises into world market conditions.[68]

The Smuggler Mobile Home Park nestles against the foot of Smuggler Mountain on the northeast side of Aspen, Colorado. Once the location of the Mollie Gibson Mine, the most famous of the 7,000 mining claims in the Roaring Fork District, the base of the mountain is presently dotted with condominiums and the mobile home park, the latter established before Aspen became the home of the rich and famous. The condominiums range from the modest to the exclusive by the standards of upscale, ostentatious Aspen. Except for occasional difficulties with toxic residues in the soil and with water problems that the United States Environmental Protection Agency has attributed to the tailings that surround the town, there is little evidence to indicate that the area once sprouted smokestacks sufficient, according to one resident, to make Aspen look "like New Jersey."[69]

The glamour and glitz associated with affluent, postmodern Aspen are symbols of historical deception. The front-range city of Pueblo still has an industrial appearance, but it requires the expertise of the historical archaeologist to uncover Aspen's working-class roots. The town's historic Clarendon Hotel houses a vintage bar that predates Gus Masciotra's Pueblo saloon by nearly thirty years, but the similarities between the two establishments are few because the Clarendon is worlds removed from Gus' Place in appearance, in the wealth and social cast of its clientele, and in the character of its surroundings. But the historic Aspen bar is at one with other Rocky Mountain mining towns in its efforts to overhaul its industrial trappings to better fit its image as a playing field for affluent Americans. At least on the surface Aspen has succeeded better than most communities in erasing its industrial past.

Although evidence abounds that current investors are turning many of the old industrial towns into tourist resorts, retirement retreats, or information-age settlements for the affluent and occupationally mobile, those manifestations of change are merely historical reminders of the tenuous existence those communities have always experienced. Let Julia Welsh, a self-described "miner's kid" and now "an ancient westerner," have the final word. Welsh cautions those who look for exotic fixes—snow and tourism—as the economic savior for the old industrial mining towns of the West. Tourism, she discovered on a trip to the British Isles, breeds two kinds of people, "the professional tourist lovers who [make] their money off them, and the ones who [make] their living by working at the usual tasks." The former, according to Welsh, were neither honest about themselves nor about their history: "They trotted out all the old superstitions and myths for you." The working people, on the other hand, "snooted" at people like Welsh, "Americans rich enough to travel." Although she carried her own luggage, Welsh observed, "they no doubt regarded me as a capitalist pig." Tourism, she concluded, "made for phony relationships."[70]

The irony in Julia Welsh's remarks reminds us that it requires stark language to describe the forces that have shaped life in the old industrial communities of the West. The extractive economies so common to most of those enterprises have familiar contours: they have been extremely volatile, prone to cycles of boom and bust; they have produced their share of ruined and blighted communities; and not one enterprise has brought sustained prosperity to large numbers of its dependent populations. In both human and environmental terms those were fragile communities in fragile natural settings. And today's generations still bear the century-old legacy of the social and environmental costs and the prospect of the continued instability of those communities through control from afar.

From Capitalist Patriarchy to Corporate Monopoly: The Life and Times of Samuel T. Hauser

The truth is, we are all caught in a great economic system which is heartless.
—*Woodrow Wilson*[1]

From all accounts the evening gathering at fashionable Sherry's Restaurant was a grand and sumptuous affair. Hosted by John D. Ryan, the corporate head of the powerful Anaconda Copper Mining Company, the New York City dinner in December 1913 attracted 200 of the city's principal bankers and financial power brokers. After feasting at a table arranged in the shape of a giant horseshoe, the audience turned its attention to another Ryan extravagance, a motion picture exhibition of the developments of the Montana Power Company, Anaconda's newly created hydroelectric subsidiary. The film extolled the virtues of electrical power as the vital source of energy for the Anaconda colossus now firmly astride Montana's rich copper-lode country. With James J. Hill of the Great Northern Railway and Albert J. Earling of the Milwaukee Road seated beside him, the youthful Ryan appeared the exemplar of the successful corporate executive of the modern age.[2]

Unlike the highly competitive, patriarchal, and combative founders of Anaconda—men like Marcus Daly and others associated with Montana's early mining industry—John D. Ryan personified both the managerial revolution in American business, which had its roots in railroad enterprises, and the emergence of the newly integrated world of monopolylike industrial combinations. That transition marked the historic passage of the U.S. economy from competitive, free-market conditions to industrial oligopoly and the emergence of a new market ideology based on concentrated, heavily bureaucratized corporations producing for large-scale national and global markets. The rise of the corporation, as Spencer Olin has argued, rendered obsolete the "classical equilibrium model of the market."[3] In practice, the new oligopolies were attempting to constrain and control the market in the interests of future predictability.

At the point of American entry into World War I, according to historian Alfred D. Chandler, "the integrated industrial enterprise had become the most powerful institution in American business." In the case of the vertically integrated corporations, the new enterprises made an effort to control production at several levels—from jurisdiction over the raw materials through the manufacture and distribution of the end product. The successfully integrated organizations, therefore, moved to consolidate both the marketing end of operations and the purchase and control of raw materials. Significantly, most of those mergers, consolidations, and takeovers involved "high-volume, large-batch" producers, especially primary-metals groups, industries with "capital-intensive, energy-consuming technologies."[4]

Moreover, as David F. Noble has argued, that new corporate world was a Catch-22 of sorts, tied to world markets that were notoriously unstable:

> With their massive investment in machinery, plants, and manpower, . . . the corporations were economically viable only given maximum utilization of resources—that is, large-scale, continuous production. And such production was economically viable, in turn, only given large-scale consumption.[5]

The spokesmen who articulated that new ideological view understood economic activity as an interrelated system in which conventional free-market forces were destructive and antithetical to the conduct of efficient, predictable, and profitable business enterprise. Moreover, under the new, modern arrangements, individual property holders yielded authority to the emergent corporate bureaucracies. With the incorporation of hydropower into its already well-integrated and extensive operations, the Anaconda Copper Mining Company was at one with the rise of that corporate order.[6]

Anaconda's emergence as Montana's preeminent corporate power was part of the broader reorganization of property relations and investment policies in the United States between 1890 and World War I. Since much of the consolidation and combination in the United States was occurring between 1899 and 1906, it is important to understand that Montana's emerging corporate world reflected changes in the material relations of capital far removed from the northern West. Capitalism, broadly construed as a related set of values and perceptions and their accompanying social, economic, and political relations, was transformed during that period from a "proprietary-competitive stage" to a "corporate-administered stage." With the considerable influence (and intrigues) of British and European banking houses on the financial side of the corporate mergers, that transformation embraced every sphere of American life—political, legal, intellectual, and economic, including the vital trust question and the antitrust debates.[7]

That new world of capital organization was vastly more expansive and integrative than the older style of proprietary capitalism. The novel and innovative corporate organizations recognized neither geographical nor political boundaries; their reach extended from metropolis to hinterland, embracing at once the urban nexus and the most distant outposts of settlement. Moreover, the transformation from the proprietary and competitive stage to the corporate-administrative phase worked its will through different industries at different times. Although the nation's largest and most heavily capitalized enterprise, railroads, led the way, others—including oil, steel, and copper—followed in short order. Much of the centralization and consolidation that transpired at the turn of the century was in part a reaction to the economic crisis of the 1890s, which had prompted investors to coordinate their activities in a concerted effort to gain command over market forces. In seeking appropriate strategies, corporate leaders attempted to control their relevant markets to contain an environment they viewed as destructively competitive.[8]

With its relatively small population, its lack of capital, and its abundance in natural wealth, much of the rural West was positioned at the cutting edge of that transformation; in truth, it was a place where "the ascendancy of corporate capitalism" was most apparent. Understanding the far-reaching implications of that newly emerging corporate order, therefore, casts light on the often disruptive, incessant change that took place in Montana's rich mineral-lode country and elsewhere across the West in the late nineteenth and early twentieth centuries.[9] Because of its relative liabilities in capital and population and because of its wealth in natural resources—especially the ore deposits that lay beneath its mountainous slopes—Montana was particularly vulnerable to the twists and turns of powerful capital institutions beyond its borders. Or, to give the story a different spin, the Montana industrial world that emerged in the late nineteenth century was little more than a creation, an extension of eastern U.S. and transatlantic metal markets. The demand, first for precious metals and subsequently for industrial ores such as copper, enticed prospectors and speculators to Montana and, eventually, investors in industrial development who brought dramatic change to the region.

Beginning with the mining rush to Virginia City and Bannack in the early 1860s, the territory and then the state of Montana was slowly integrated into national and international capitalist networks. As the nineteenth century drew to a close, the contours of Montana's future were already firmly established; the discerning observer clearly understood that decisions made in distant corporate boardrooms were increasingly influencing daily life in the region, periodically disrupting local economies, and contributing to a transient and mobile work force.[10] That turbulent environment produced both winners and losers among local entrepreneurs: the former, men such as John D. Ryan, usually had effectively linked themselves to the rising corporate order; the latter—mostly proprietary capitalists from an earlier day such as Samuel T. Hauser—were often left in the wash as relics of a bygone era.

Samuel T. Hauser—civil engineer, miner, lawyer, banker, investor, politician, gambler in grand schemes—may lack the glamorous appeal of his near contemporary, Charlie Russell, but in many respects he was a far more significant Montanan. Hauser's influence careens across the territorial and early statehood years like a shooting star, ascending brightly in its early trajectory and then losing its glow as it disappears into the night sky. In similar fashion, Montana's volatile extractive economy unleashed a frenzy of expansion and then, responding to decisions in New York and London, fell into the process of creating ghost towns for a latter-day tourist industry. With a rhetorical flourish common to the age, Montana senator Thomas Carter summed up Hauser's public life at a testimonial dinner to honor the aging entrepreneur in 1908:

> His career exemplifies the ups and downs of a new country. . . . He prospered with the state and adversity laid its heaviest hand on him. . . . Trail blazer, Explorer, Vigilante, Banker—flush or broke—coal, coke, smelter and general operator, chief of water power creators.[11]

A tough Gilded Age businessman and risk-taker, Sam Hauser was at the center of much of the action linked to Montana's years of expanding enterprise. He was a boomer who went broke, not once, but twice; he was an uninhibited promoter of frontier business activity—Native Americans, the environment, and nearly anything else that got in his way be damned. Hauser exploited others, exposing him to accusations of rascality; he never achieved epic or mythical stature, and by conventional standards, in the end he turned up a loser.[12]

But his is an instructive, not a tragic, story. Unlike his sometime friend William Andrews Clark, who fleeced the territory and the state of Montana and then fled to New York City, Hauser stayed for the long haul, living fifty-two of his eighty-one years in Montana.[13] Like Mark Twain, Hauser "lit out for the territories" in the midst of the Civil War crisis, in his case to the new mining strike at Bannack in 1862. Two years later, with the assistance of borrowed capital, he joined in a banking partnership in Virginia City, and in 1866 Hauser established the First National Bank of Helena, thus beginning a thirty-year career as Montana's leading banker. When his bank failed in the mid-1890s, the tireless Hauser took up the cause of hydropower development on the Missouri River. That venture turned to environmental and financial disaster when Hauser Dam burst in April 1908. Samuel Hauser died in 1914 amid a changing corporate world that he did not understand and one that had again proved his financial undoing.[14] In that sense, Hauser represents a transitional figure, a man who lived into the era of the new corporate environment but who lacked the mental acuity, the passion, and the patience to survive its requirements.

Granville Stuart—early Montana cattleman, diplomat, and writer—captured the risk-taking, adventurous spirit of Hauser the gambler and entrepreneur in an amusing and well-known story. In Montana's booming gold-rush town of Virginia City in the winter of 1863–1864 some items were in short supply, among them a mealtime favorite, molasses. According to Stuart, Hauser, who shared living quarters with several other men, hit upon a plan whereby he kept the only gallon of molasses to himself. When the crew returned home one evening, they found Hauser sitting at the table holding a mouse by the tail, the animal apparently having drowned in the molasses. Stuart and his friends, reaching that conclusion by inference, immediately lost their appetite for molasses. Hauser meanwhile continued to ladle molasses on his bread at every meal until the canister was empty. One day he asked his partners why they had quit eating it. Stuart's brother, James, remarked that he liked molasses "but not well enough to eat it after a mouse had drowned in it." At that point, a grinning Hauser informed his companions that he had killed the mouse and smeared it with molasses to see how they would react.[15]

There are suggestions that Stuart concocted the molasses story to spite Hauser, to whom he owed large sums of money. But apocryphal or not, it was a popular anecdote since for many people it gave the ring of truth to Hauser's career of purposeful risk-taking. His personal correspondence and the judgments that others have made about his character give the impression that Samuel T. Hauser was perpetually in search of the great mother lode. Like the addicted gambler ever in quest of the one big hit, he sought security through endless speculative ventures—living his life, as it were, as the ultimate financial brinksman.

Hauser expressed that buccaneering spirit in an 1889 circular seeking potential investors to purchase a cluster of contiguous mineral claims, the Pony Mines. The time was ripe, he observed, because the Northern Pacific Railroad was building a line from Three Forks on the Missouri River to Butte, passing within twelve miles of the mines.

I feel it is just and right that you should have the opportunity to sub-scribe under the new bond, if you feel like taking the risk.

I can only say that all mining ventures are risky, that we will all probably make a big killing, or lose all we put in.

If the prospect is worth anything, it is worth twenty times what we put in. I am going to put my money in and take chances, and each and every dollar goes in on the same terms as mine.[16]

Hauser's correspondence is absent of further comment on the Pony Mines until May 1891 when he wrote to Missouri senator J. D. Cameron, one of the investors: "Our mining interests have never looked one half as well, save and except the unfortunate Pony, which I fear will be an entire failure."[17]

Unlike the staid, cautious, and bureaucratic corporate world that emerged during the later years of his life, Hauser neither hedged nor hesitated on his bets. When he joined with other Helena capitalists and the Northern Pacific Railroad to build a short rail line in 1902, Hauser confided to his friends that the "honorable directors" of the railroad would "not try to freeze us out, or in any way hamper the contract. . . . It is not our vanity that makes us feel as we do but our confidence in our fellow men. Now from experience we know we will be treated fairly and squarely, *at least we will take our chances.*"[18] The record shows clearly that Samuel Hauser's business conduct matched the competitive, cutthroat ethos of the latter half of the nineteenth century. He worshiped at the same altars of enterprise, emulated a kindred ruthlessness in tactics, and exhibited a similar individualistic disposition.

William Andrews Clark, whose personal background is strikingly similar to Hauser's, provides a contrasting prototype of western entre-preneurship. Clark, who successfully made the transition from banking and silver to copper and then quietly left the Montana playing field to Anaconda, died an immensely rich man. Described by Montana journal-ist Joseph Kinsey Howard as "a tight, white starched little man" with "no humor and no vices," Clark was also shrewd, intelligent, ruthless, and able to pass smoothly into the reconstructed world of corporate capi-talism in the early twentieth century.[19]

Much of Clark's financial success lay in his ability to anticipate the fu-ture, to shift his investment portfolio accordingly, and to strike an amicable (and profitable) accommodation when the odds were against him. Unlike Hauser's, Clark's entrepreneurial genius was to never underestimate the competition. Ventures that proved financially disastrous for other people Clark turned to gain. When it became apparent by 1911 that Anaconda would inevitably dominate hydropower production on the Missouri River, Clark quickly urged Hauser to compromise with the more powerful forces arrayed against the United Missouri River Power Company. When Clark learned that Hauser had underestimated the ability of an Anaconda subsidiary to deliver power to Butte, he warned Hauser: "[They] will have led you and the rest of us into a hole from which it will be very difficult for us to extricate ourselves." Along with one of the New York-based United Missouri financial backers, Clark pressed for a compromise with Anaconda to avoid "wiping out all our interests."[20]

In contrast to Clark, the less compromising and more willful Hauser kept much of his significant investment portfolio in silver, the most speculative of mineral enterprises. Those were fateful decisions as it turned out, judgments that subsequently destroyed both his banking and mining empires.[21] When he attempted to build a second fortune based on hydropower, unlike the discerning and more cautious Clark, Hauser plunged ahead and chose to joust on the same competitive turf with the rising Anaconda colossus. The consequences for the ever-competitive Hauser once more were financial ruin.

But through the doom and gloom of failing banks and the wreckage of a mining economy gone wrong, Sam Hauser maintained his composure, his optimism, his sense that matters would right themselves: *if* only he could get an extension on that overdue note, *if* only the great money lenders in the East would provide one last infusion of fresh capital, *if* only he could make that last sale of bonds to the financial houses on Wall Street. "Competition," he once told Martin Maginnis, "is the life of trade and will be everything for our territory."[22] The year was 1877. Nearly thirty years later from New York's Fifth Avenue Hotel in Madison Square he wrote his son Tom: "I am still, like many other old vain asses, trying to raise two or three million dollars."[23]

And to the end the old man retained a sense of play, a disposition that suggested speculative investment was part fun and games. On one occasion Hauser chastised William A. Clark when the latter cited the press of business for preventing a visit to Helena:

> Now Senator, it is ridiculous for you to plead want of time. What the devil are you working so hard and making so much money for I cannot guess, if it cramps you so that you cannot enjoy a few hours with your fellow men.

Hauser extended that same capacity for repartee to the august officials of the Northern Pacific Railroad, signing a letter to Pres. Robert Harris on one occasion "Samuel T. Hauser, Prest & Figurehead (?) of the Helena and Jefferson Co. R. R." Yet Hauser, skilled in the art of raising capital, could be deadly serious about public perception if it affected his ability to attract investors. When in his view New York newspapers overstated the downstream damage after Hauser Dam burst in April 1908, he asked a Helena business associate, John S. M. Neil, if he could "get the associated press to give out more favorable news and less exaggeration."[24]

Because Hauser was an unrepentant plunger into mining, railroad, and virtually every other form of speculative enterprise, his business world, albeit extensive, was never secure. Hence, those writers who ascribe great financial success and power to Hauser prior to the silver bust of 1893 overestimate the extent of his *real* wealth.[25] Hauser was much more a conduit than a source of capital. In a classic understatement, the Guide to the Hauser Papers in the Montana Historical Society describes Hauser's influence on the course of events: "His activities drew great sums of eastern capital to Montana and set the pattern for the state's economic future."[26] In truth, throughout his long public career Hauser carefully nurtured a persona that emphasized his contributions to the development of Montana.

As an individual entrepreneur Sam Hauser was a survivor in a period of proprietary capitalism, an era characterized by owner-managers, informal agreements, the absence of structured contractual arrangements, price-taking rather than price-making, and appeals to vanity, secrecy, and subterfuge.[27] He played the game with the skill and artistry of a master gambler, exaggerating his hand when its real substance was marginal and downplaying its weakness when it was to his advantage. Friends and business associates alike were aware of his inclination to procrastinate when the note came due, his tendency to issue disclaimers when the ore body proved lean and spare, and—like the crapshooter always looking for the one big roll—his persistent optimism in the face of impending disaster.

Among the more revealing of Hauser's business relationships is his long association with the Northern Pacific Railroad. As the company's key Montana ally, Hauser was involved in the construction of virtually all of the Northern Pacific branch operations in Montana until 1893 when both the railroad and Hauser suffered financial reverses. Before the collapse of silver and the bankruptcy of the Northern Pacific, however, the railroad company interceded regularly with prime lending institutions in the East to obtain financial support for Hauser in the building of the branch lines.[28] Although the Montana capitalist both benefited and suffered from his ties to the Northern Pacific, the correspondence reveals that neither party was innocent of wrongdoing or careful about prudent business practices.

In nearly every instance Hauser was more aggressive than the railroad company in promoting "the development of the country." With James J. Hill's Manitoba Road moving quickly to build a line westward to

Great Falls, Hauser wrote to Northern Pacific president Robert Harris, urging the company "to take advantage of your opportunity to 'tap' and controll the same" by building branch roads. The Northern Pacific could capture all the local business if it took advantage of the opportunity and acted with dispatch. Though he preferred "the roads . . . to be built by your company," Hauser told Harris that he would assist Hill "all I can" because Hill's success would result in greatly developing the Territory and directly benefit me." Harris responded immediately and invited Hauser to New York City to discuss the matter with the Northern Pacific's executive committee.[29]

As an uninhibited boomer, Hauser saw limitless opportunity everywhere, at least if he had the cooperation of eastern financial houses and the Northern Pacific Railroad.[30] The arrangements between Hauser and the company followed the classic pattern of a Gentlemen's Agreement: Hauser would propose a branch road to link a potential mining district with the Northern Pacific main line; the company would underwrite part of the construction costs through Hauser's syndicate; the Helena capitalist then would direct the building of the branch road; and finally arrangements would be made to lease the completed line to the Northern Pacific.[31] The construction of a railroad extension from the productive silver reduction works at Wickes to Butte in 1884 illustrates the informality of such agreements. Northern Pacific vice-president Thomas F. Oakes directed Hauser to "go on and get up your scheme in full faith that when ready to furnish your part of the money, the balance will be forthcoming from some source, either the company or individuals interested in it." With the same stroke of the pen, Oakes warned that "extreme secrecy is necessary in this matter" because of "our relations with the Union Pacific."[32]

Even though he functioned as the Northern Pacific's most valuable ally in the northern West, company officials occasionally chastised Hauser for failing to meet his financial obligations or for otherwise violating informal protocols of agreement. Oakes, who appears as a business associate and friend in much of the correspondence—and who may have been writing for the benefit of his superiors on occasion—was among the harshest of Hauser's critics. In one notable reprimand, evidently involving the Hauser syndicate's cutting of timber on Northern Pacific lands in 1885, Oakes played hardball with the Helena capitalist:

If we have no rights in this property you will respect, I shall at once withdraw our deposits from your bank, put the Wickes branch on a strictly local basis and in every other respect make things so hot for you, you will think the devil is after you.

The Nor Pac Co. has not spent $70,000,000 to be bulldozed by you or any body else.

The Nor Pac Co. has the right to demand of you the fullest support in every reasonable effort to protect its interest. It has never asked a thing of you thus far but has done a great deal for you and your interests thus far with very little return.[33]

Two years later Oakes again scolded Hauser for breaching confidentiality and overstepping the bounds of an informal business agreement. "You have no right to make such free use of our name," the Northern Pacific executive told Hauser. "Our business relations in this matter were of a private nature, and there was no necessity nor sense in saying any thing . . . about it." Construction of the Hill-controlled Montana Central through the Helena valley was nearing completion, and Oakes warned Hauser of "the importance of preserving the most friendly relations" with the Northern Pacific Company. The Hauser-controlled smelter in Helena, he noted, had given the Montana Central a side track, and its management had "a disposition to obtain rate reductions by [unintelligible word] between the two Co's." Oakes then added the heavy hand: "Your policy should be first, last and all the time in the exclusive interest of the N.P. Co."[34]

Because of the company's persisting financial difficulties, Northern Pacific officials were insistent in their demands that Hauser meet debt agreements in those cases where the company was acting as guarantor for his loan arrangements. In the construction of the Boulder Valley railroad in 1887, the firm's auditor informed Hauser, "It would appear proper that we withhold payment of the amount accrued until these bills are paid." Despite such admonitions, company personnel regularly sought Hauser's assistance and advice for a variety of matters: in quieting the protests of Marcus Daly and William A. Clark over rate increases for ore shipments or in convincing Clark to shift his smelter from Butte to Helena.[35]

Ultimately it was not his relations with the Northern Pacific that brought about the collapse of Hauser's banking and investment portfolio. With a precarious financial empire tied largely to the speculative world of silver, Hauser was simply overextended when the national economy went into a tailspin in mid-1893. A lax personal-management style—inattention to detail, tardy reporting, the neglect of important correspondence, and careless bookkeeping practices—aggravated an already shaky financial situation. The collapse of world silver prices and the depression exposed at once the fragility of Montana's industrial mining economy.[36] Samuel

Hauser's world reflected the economic chaos and financial ruin that settled upon the mountain West in summer 1893.

The combined forces of the national depression and regional problems related to the volatile silver industry contributed directly to the failure of Hauser's First National Bank of Helena on July 27, 1893. The chief culprits, however, were the collapsing local economy, the mismanagement of the bank, and excessive loans to bank officers, including one S. T. Hauser. The obvious had occurred: Hauser's careless, speculative management style had caught up with him in the face of Montana's dramatically collapsing economy. As in other financial institutions in western states, notes rather than hard cash provided much of the support for the Helena bank. That precarious situation and the fact that most bankers, like Hauser, were linked to speculative mining ventures compounded the difficulties brought on by the general depression.[37]

In retrospect, it is obvious that Hauser's financial institution was in a precarious situation long before the collapse of silver prices. The comptroller of the currency warned Hauser early in 1886 that his bank was "too much extended" with "too many large loans and upon a class of property on which it would be difficult to realize within a reasonable time." In response to another bank examiner's report later the same year, Hauser informed the comptroller's office that the bank's problems were "not one tenth as bad as the Examiner's report would indicate. *Though it is fair to say that the details have been shamefully neglected.*"[38]

In the spring of 1892 the comptroller of the currency again found that First National of Helena was carrying eight loans in excess of the legal number and that the bank was accepting "overdraft paper" notes. In defense of the practice, Hauser cited the comptroller's previous acceptance of overdrafts and the difficulties of arresting a habit of twenty years. The following year the comptroller's office again warned Hauser that six First National loans exceeded the limits prescribed in banking law and that four directors of the bank had "large loans and large liabilities as endorsers" (the two largest were to Hauser). The directors of the bank, the comptroller admonished, were required under law to reserve money invested in a national bank exclusively for that purpose and "cannot expect that it shall be devoted still to the support and extension of other business enterprises with which they may be connected."[39]

To the bank's president, who was accustomed to living on the edge of "chronically impaired liquidity," those words of advice and caution made little impression.[40] That paper facade of financial success deteriorated quickly with the collapse of world silver prices, a series of developments that wreaked havoc and spread hardship through Montana's mining towns during the hot summer months of 1893. A British House of Commons recommendation in late June 1893 that the government cease minting silver rupees in India triggered the actions of corporate directors in the United States who ordered the closing of silver mines and smelters throughout the Rocky Mountain cordillera. The fabled Granite Mountain mine was shut down on July 1 and other mines followed suit; by the close of the year unemployment in the state had reached 20,000, most of it around Butte and Helena. The consequence was a run on Montana banks, especially those linked with the world of silver.[41]

The panic had an immediate effect on Sam Hauser's banking empire; hitherto cooperative and friendly business associates bristled at one another in an apparent epidemic of fingerpointing, with Hauser again the focus of attention. Andrew B. Hammond, a prominent Missoula capitalist with sizable shares in the First National Bank of Missoula, was one such associate incensed over what he perceived as the mismanagement of the Hauser-controlled bank. He warned the Helena banker about the precarious financial condition of the enterprise but thought there would be no trouble unless something happened to First National of Helena: "I depend on you giving us some notice *and help* if things should get so they could not be handled." When the Helena bank suspended business on July 27, it caused a run on the Missoula institution and brought an angry response from the outraged Hammond. "Your people in Helena," he told Hauser, "gave us notice of their intention of closing *two hours after they posted their notice.*" His words dripping with sarcasm, Hammond charged, "This is the way they protected us."[42]

In an effort to attract depositors to his suspended operations, Hauser wrote to the Missoula bank a few months later requesting that it defray for the moment an outstanding note held against the Helena institution. "It does not seem possible," he implored, "that my own friends are going to refuse . . . to make a reasonable extension upon what we owe them. It does not seem fair to me, although I acknowledge your good management, that you should press me for so small an amount." His bank still struggling at the edge of financial solvency, Hammond responded in a long letter reviewing the relationship between the two banks and the conduct of the banking business by the Helena institution's officers (all Hauser appointees). At one time, Hammond observed, the Missoula bank "was run in the interest of the President and the Cashier and their personal friends. They managed to build up their own private business at the expense of that of the bank's."[43]

Andrew Hammond, who would survive the silver bust and later shift his investments to timberlands and sawmills in Oregon and the redwood country of the California coast, grasped the essentials of the newly emerging corporate world in which individual whim played a subordinate role to collective decisionmaking.[44] In a remarkable bit of candor, he told the older Hauser that the "lack of confidence in . . .

banks and other corporations has been due largely to the fact that many of them have been dominated over by the will of one man regardless of the wishes of the board of directors or stockholders." While Hammond continued to have the "warmest interest" in Hauser's welfare, he informed Hauser that any business with the Missoula bank must be approved by the board of directors in order to instill "confidence and safety in the future."[45]

The First National Bank of Helena reopened early in 1894, struggled on the margins of survival for a few months, and closed permanently in 1896. During those few months Hauser was at his most persuasive in holding off creditors, pleading for time, and indulging in his habit of mixing private with public business, as he did with the New York financial institution J. & W. Seligman Company. When the firm requested payment on its outstanding notes, Hauser asked for patience and reminded the company's Montana liaison, Henry Seligman, that Seligman had promised not to expect repayment at once "where money was borrowed in my individual name, but in reality in the interest of the bank." In response to a request from a Chicago banker asking for payment of an overdue debt, Hauser responded, "I must admit that I had counted upon a renewal of the note, hence have not made the necessary arrangement to pay it."[46]

Shortly before his bank closed for the final time, Hauser wrote to another New York banking house referring to "a verbal agreement" concerning a loan that he described as "my individual loan (made in the interest of the bank)." Those were busy days for the hard-traveling Helena capitalist, who was spending an inordinate amount of time in New York City attempting to circle his financial bagmen to fend off threatening creditors.[47] But the fiscal string was fast running out on Hauser; in late August 1896 the First National of Helena pulled its shades for the final closing, thereby bringing to an end Hauser's career as Montana's leading banker. It took bank receivers several more years to sort through the institution's tangled financial web.

J. Sam Brown, appointed receiver in early 1898 to oversee the failed First National Bank of Helena, provides the best insight to Hauser's personalized business practices and his world of private entrepreneurship. Brown reported to the comptroller general of the United States that Hauser was "enthusiastic" and confident "of his ability to pay every dollar" to those who had money in the bank, but "in the same breath," the receiver observed, Hauser expected to secure his debts through paper worth "less than its face." Brown then directed the comptroller's attention to the central issue:

[Hauser] is a very careless man so far as looking after the details of his business is concerned, and has a very good memory as to what condi-

tions are where it is to his interest, but where it is against his interest
his memory is a little faulty at times. . . . He is a pretty hard man to
handle because he is not specific in his conversation and thinks if he
comes within a few thousand dollars of a matter, that is quite close
enough, *and* he jumps from one subject to another.

Brown urged the comptroller general to "weight carefully" what Hauser
said because "he is apt to say that he has paid into this bank over $100,000,
when as a matter of fact . . . no money has been received from him direct."[48]

Other contemporaries were equally critical in their judgment of
Hauser's management style and business practices. Norman B. Holter,
who directed his father's Montana interests—many of them financially
linked to Hauser ventures—warned the elder Holter shortly after the bank
failure about being too "good to men like Hauser . . . who has been mis-
leading you for years either by making statements that were not true or by
leaving unsaid that [which] should have been said. I do not believe in carrying the burdens of men of this kind." Concerning a cooperative venture in
mining and smelter investments, the younger Holter charged that Hauser
was "less than truthful" to his longtime Helena friend: "Mr. Hauser has repeatedly made statements to you and to me that he had every reason to believe were wrong when he made them."[49] Holter reminded his father that
Hauser frequently promised payments on his debts but never delivered.

At this point in his career Samuel Hauser might have been wise to
heed the advice of Norman Holter's brother, Edwin. From New York City
where he was practicing law, Holter observed a different business atmosphere from that in the West, one that required a "stricter scale" of operation:

when it comes to the large matters every man is as hard as nails—he
will not endorse a note for anybody . . . he will not lend money to his
best friends unless the collateral is gilt edged—and he prefers small
gains to any speculative risks.

Since such conditions prevailed in older, developed communities, Holter
believed that the time had come "in Montana when accomodation and
friendship is the very worst thing for business security." He wondered how
his father had "kept in front of the procession" during the many years that
he had "been carrying the big end of the stick, with such men as Mr.
Hauser" on the light end. He urged his father to take his turn "at playing
the part of the 'bully' with Mr. Hauser."[50]

Edwin Holter provides an excellent counterpoise to Samuel Hauser in
the transition from proprietary to full-fledged corporate capitalism. As an

upwardly mobile, second-generation member of a business-investment family (his father made his fortune as a merchant), Holter fits the profile of the movement of middle-class males away from the proprietary business world to the corporate and bureaucratic environment of the twentieth century. "From small hometowns, to corporate ties or to the big city via corporate merger or recruitment," Martin Sklar has indicated, the large corporation "offered opportunities of social mobility for middle-class people."[51] That young Edwin Holter, educated in an eastern law school, should find his niche in a large corporate legal firm should come as no surprise, nor should we wonder, therefore, that he would adopt the ideological trappings of that environment.

Eighteen ninety-six was an auspicious year for the freewheeling Samuel Hauser. Sixty-three years old, his financial world in eclipse, and his personal reputation ostensibly in ruin, the old man seemingly had little to look forward to save advancing age, declining health, and a mere semblance of his once vast fortune. But where the more cautious and less energetic feared to venture, the intrepid Hauser never hesitated. In the next few years he linked arms with Henry H. Rogers of Standard Oil, which held controlling interest in the Anaconda Copper Company, for financial assistance in a series of hydropower developments on the Missouri River. As it turned out, that relationship was Hauser's last fatal attraction to eastern capital. The same personalized management habits and shifty bookkeeping practices that worked to his advantage in an earlier age eventually brought his final ruin.

Still, the aging Hauser maneuvered his hydropower enterprises through Montana's emerging corporate world with the skill of a buccaneer quartermaster. For a time he successfully stroked the vanity of William A. Clark, whose financial backing and prestige were critical to the Missouri River power venture. He urged Helena friend John S. M. Neil to compliment the copper baron publicly to entice him into furthering his Montana investments. Hauser claimed that Clark gave greater attention to personal puffery than most public men: "In my opinion that is his best trait. He loves [the] flattery and admiration of his fellow man. With most monied men cupidity absorbs all other passions or traits." When it became obvious that the Standard Oil and Anaconda sharks were circling his second great business enterprise, the United Missouri River Power Company, Hauser repeatedly sought Clark's financial support and his assistance in fending off forced consolidations.[52]

For a few short years, however, Hauser's relations with Standard Oil's Rogers gave the Montana capitalist a bit of independent financial leverage in expanding the Missouri River hydropower system. In a larger sense, Rogers and Hauser represented a rapidly diminishing generation of entrepreneurs who conducted business on a paternal basis, men who had dictated directorships of firms, personally elected company officials, and otherwise functioned as sole proprietors of their enterprises. (Unlike Hauser, however, Rogers had long since successfully accommodated himself to the reorganized world of corporate capitalism.) When Hauser completed both a loan agreement with Rogers and an arrangement to sell electrical power to Amalgamated in 1905, he informed Norman Holter that "all contracts and negotiations . . . have been strictly individual between Mr. Rogers and myself." He asked Holter to regard the agreements with Rogers "as *strictly confidential.*"[53]

With Rogers in failing health and John D. Ryan's star in the ascendant, Samuel Hauser's difficulties began to mount well before his dam gave way in the spring of 1908. When the shrewd Ryan (managing director of Amalgamated operations in Butte by 1905) manipulated the terms of the agreement between Hauser and Rogers to the company's advantage, Hauser went directly to Rogers for redress. And when Ryan began his move to gain control of the valuable power site at Great Falls and to consolidate electrical power production on the Missouri River, Hauser again appealed directly to Rogers, warning that such a move would depreciate stock in the United Missouri River Power Company (in which Amalgamated owned sizable shares). Hauser proposed to develop the power "through our Company on some plan that will be satisfactory to you and of mutual benefit."[54] But a changing of the corporate guard, the emergence of new and different forms of business enterprise, and the rapid consolidation of capital in certain lines of activity (such as hydropower development) brought an end to Samuel Hauser's financial world. He simply failed to recognize that Amalgamated was quickly consolidating its Montana industrial empire into a fully integrated operation that eventually would control raw materials, energy supplies, smelting, and refining under one corporate enterprise.

When abnormally high Missouri River waters burst through Hauser Dam in April 1908, Sam Hauser stood again at the brink of financial catastrophe. Although the destruction of the dam and the losses incurred from downstream damage were severe, Hauser's real difficulties lay with Amalgamated, purchaser of 75 percent of United Missouri hydropower and owner of more than $1 million of its securities. Moreover, within the year Henry H. Rogers was dead and John D. Ryan was on the move to consolidate hydropower development on the Missouri River. For Hauser, the habitual optimist, the next two years would prove the maximum challenge. From New York City, where he was spending most of his time, Hauser directed the financial-relief effort. When his business associates, especially chief hydropower engineer and resident manager M. H. Gerry, accused the copper trust of taking Hauser for a ride, the old man urged caution and cooperation. Though Hauser recognized that the power company faced a "desperate situation," he sent a message to Helena friend John Neil to "buy the ice to keep Gerry's head cool and make him cooperate and realize . . . that business is business and demands the suppression of personal feeling to the end of success."[55]

Still, Hauser struggled on, discussing the potential for an irrigation project in the Helena valley "to help develop the country." If he could get the cooperation of W. A. Clark in the venture it would "make success certain." At the same time, he told John Neil, "our power properties are in a very critical situation and in more danger of being swallowed up by our enemies than ever before." Always the optimist, Hauser reflected, "if Clark will stay with us and cooperate as he has up to date, we . . . will be . . . in better shape and condition than ever before." As late as November 1910 Hauser held out hope that Clark would "press the contemplated swindle to a halt"; he continued to believe that the Missouri River properties could "easily be saved" despite "our competitors' efforts" to swallow us up."[56] By that time, however, Clark had made peace with Amalgamated and was positioning himself for the failure of Hauser's enterprises.

The newly emerging corporate order of the Amalgamated Copper Company and its allied trusts was a world beyond Samuel Hauser's comprehension. Amalgamated held large shares in the United Missouri River Power Company, and when its own subsidiary at Great Falls began producing electricity in the fall of 1910, the company canceled its power contracts with Hauser's firm, thereby driving the latter into receivership. Deserted by personal friends and financial backers, including Henry Seligman and W. A. Clark, the United Missouri directors formed a new executive committee and removed Hauser from effective control of affairs. While Seligman carried on negotiations with Ryan and Amalgamated's interests, Hauser quietly turned to personal and family affairs, attending to complications involving Ellen Hauser's estate and perhaps contemplating his own death.

From the ashes of the failed Hauser enterprise, the Montana Power Company emerged (the legal work was completed by 1913).[57] Meanwhile, Hauser's old friends and associates were circling to trade or purchase preferred stock in the new company. From New York City, the aspiring Edwin Holter advised his brother to buy shares in Montana Power because "insiders here believe that it is going to be a wonderful company."[58] With the emergence of the hydropower giant, the largest market for electrical power, the Amalgamated Copper Company, and the producer of virtually all the state's generating capacity, the Montana Power Company, were now effectively one. Montana Power had a monopoly on the market, but as Carrie Johnson has indicated, "the market was itself monopolistic."[59] The new corporate environment had sharply restricted space for freewheeling proprietary entrepreneurs such as Samuel Hauser. The age of monopoly capital had settled firmly on the Big Sky country, and for the next forty years

Anaconda's stranglehold on Montana's economy would be the talk of writers and reformers everywhere.[60]

With the emergence of the new colossus and the disappearance of independent operators like Hauser, the state also lost a degree of autonomy. But events in Montana represented only a microcosm in the greater transformation of the American economy from the age of individual competitive capitalism to the modern bureaucratic corporate world of the twentieth century. The new environment socialized risk and diluted liability; it steadied and made more secure the business world for those who were shrewd in handling their securities like Edwin Holter; and it largely made obsolete Lone Ranger entrepreneurial types like Samuel Hauser. The decline of Helena's economy, the failure of Hauser's banking empire, and the collapse of his Missouri River hydroelectric ventures were part of a larger system of changes that revolutionized an entire economy.

The historical transformation of capitalism from the competitive to the corporate stage worked its way through the American West in different industries at different times. Owner-dominated, proprietary firms prevailed throughout most of Montana's rich silver-lode country at the onset of the 1890s, but in the world of copper the managerial revolution and corporate reconstruction were well under way with the emergence of the fully integrated Anaconda Copper Mining Company. Although the firm did not achieve monopolylike influence over the Montana economy until the onset of World War I, historian Michael Malone observes that the company had "steadily rationalized" its operations in the two preceding decades.[61] As it broadened and further integrated its business activities in the state, Anaconda was slowly destroying Montana's competitive atmosphere.

Samuel Hauser was no innocent victim of that larger and more powerful corporate world.[62] The record clearly indicates that he could be as ruthless as Henry H. Rogers and John D. Ryan in his business relationships. Unlike more restrained and conservative Montana entrepreneurs, Hauser always made the long reach for the brass ring. He failed, not because of altruism or sensitivity toward his business associates or sympathy for those who had placed their life savings in his bank; he failed because other individuals, better attuned to the emerging corporate milieu of the time, were a step ahead of him. In that intensely competitive world of Hauser's mature years, the American myth of success proclaimed as gospel the ever-increasing accumulation of material wealth; indeed those enthusiasts who failed and those who succeeded operated from common business perspectives. Samuel T. Hauser was very much a part of that environment.

CHAPTER SEVEN

An "Equilibrium of Chaos": External Control and the Northern West

> The West of my grandparents . . . is the early West, the last home of the freeborn American. It is all owned in Boston and Philadelphia and New York and London. The freeborn American who works for one of those corporations is lucky if he does not have a family, for then he has an added option; he can afford to quit if he likes it.
>
> —*Wallace Stegner*[1]

Norman Best grew up in the small northern Idaho community of Coeur d'Alene.[2] The famous mining district of that name, the center of protracted industrial warfare and labor radicalism before the turn of the century, lay more than forty miles to the east. Émigrés from the agricultural country around Prairie Farm, Wisconsin, where his paternal grandfather had helped form the Farmers' Equity to combat extortionate railroad rates, Best's parents arrived in Coeur d'Alene in 1907 (when Norman was a year old). By that time lumbering already had surpassed mineral production as the area's key enterprise. Best's father and an uncle worked in the woods at first, using family-taught skills in horsemanship to skid heavy logs to a loading site. Two other uncles, engineers for the Great Northern Railway, worked out of Hillyard, a suburb of Spokane.

The sounds of sawmill whistles and stories about the woods, the failures and successes of railroad workers, and the struggles of the Industrial Workers of the World (IWW) in the mills and logging camps filled Norman Best's childhood. Equally significant in his memory was the Nonpartisan League campaign in northern Idaho in the 1920 election. His father, Best later recalled, learned that farmers "were having hard times because of the low prices they received for their products and the high cost of everything they had to buy." As a consequence, his father actively supported the league's program and even loaned his automobile and his son's services to chauffeur candidates through Idaho's three northern counties. After that experience Best worked at several semiskilled jobs until early fall 1926, when he left northern Idaho to enroll as a student at the University of Washington. His schooling ended abruptly in spring 1930 when the family bank in Coeur d'Alene failed, and Best returned home to the life of a wage laborer.

Why is this sketch of Norman Best's life pertinent? Precisely because his boyhood and youth (indeed, his entire life) illustrate a fundamental reality about the instability and uncertainty of economic life in the northern West. And Best's experience also brings to mind one of Lewis Mumford's favorite aphorisms, which likened the kind of stability achieved under the capitalist system to the "equilibrium of chaos." Beginning in the 1880s and with increasing momentum throughout the succeeding decades, the northern tier of territories and states stretching from the Dakotas westward to the Pacific was integrated into the disorderly and tumultuous world of industrial capitalism. The process economists conventionally refer to as economic development came to the northern West with the building of the great transcontinental railroads that linked the natural abundance of the region to the industrial centers of the eastern United States. The transforming influence of the new transportation technology reverberated from the wheat country of the Dakotas and eastern Washington to the copper mines of Montana and the timbered slopes along the Pacific Coast.[3]

The history of the northern West in the last decades of the nineteenth century is a story in the exercise of power and influence, of decisions made in faraway places, of chicanery and hucksterism, of limited local autonomy, and of grass-roots suffering when the bets were called in banking centers in New York, Boston, London, Paris, and Berlin. Simply put: the transformation of the northern West was always part of a wider arena of activity in which events and circumstances in distant lands and continents influenced local conditions. In that sense, an understanding of the wide-ranging relationships associated with modern capitalism provides a way to bring organization and structure to an explanation of historical change in the region.

Joseph Kinsey Howard, acclaimed by some scholars as one of the most perceptive observers of the modern West, was fond of the appropriate metaphor. With an insurgent's feel for the jugular, Montana's most celebrated journalist/historian crafted an enemies' list, one easily recognizable to his fellow Montanans: The Anaconda Copper Mining Company, the intercontinental railroads that traversed the state, and the promoters who gulled would-be settlers into taking up marginal land.[4] But Howard's observations also applied to the great resource-rich region across western North America beyond Montana's borders. For that vast geographic area encompassed some of the richest mineral deposits and timber stands on earth, and it embraced broad alluvial valleys suited to a variety of agricultural pursuits. In truth, during the years following the Civil War, eastern and foreign investors viewed the country between the

Great Lakes and the Pacific as a magnificent source for profit-taking, a promoter's paradise.[5]

Emigrant newcomers from the East, having pushed out the Native American population, had already resettled parts of the northern West before 1880—Oregon's Willamette Valley, Washington's Puget Sound and Walla Walla Valley, the Red River Valley in Dakota Territory, and the isolated mining districts scattered across the region. But the coming of the transcontinental rail system brought the most dramatic change. As business enterprises surpassing anything the northern West had previously known, the heavily capitalized railroads brought the world of industrial capital to the region and initiated the full-scale exploitation of natural resources.[6] In the words of historian Carlos Schwantes, the emergence of industry in the interior West was largely the "child of the steel rail."[7] Within two generations the voracious appetite of the nation's burgeoning industrial centers in the East had transformed the subsistence economy of the interior northern West into an integral and largely extractive source of sustenance for eastern capital. Those structural alterations to the regional economy give substance to Bernard DeVoto's observation that the West "was born of industrialism."[8]

Between the slaughter of the buffalo on the high plains and the end of World War I, relationships were established between the metropolitan East and the expanding extractive economy of the northern West that would persist well into the twentieth century. Neither the achievement of statehood nor the insurgent protests that periodically racked the region from the Dakotas to the Pacific altered that relationship.[9] Today the few remaining miners at Homestake and Butte, farmers in the Red River Valley and the Palouse, and loggers in northern Idaho and the Grays Harbor district in Washington are even more closely linked to national and international systems of investment and exchange. The explanation for those ties rests in the historical circumstances of an expanding national and international economy and in the integration of the resource-rich northern West into the broader network of that system.

A friendly federal government provided much of the incentive for the expansion of commercial capitalism that occurred after 1870: (1) federal troops reduced the ability of native people to present a threat to settler occupation of the northern plains and effected the taking of Indian lands; (2) the federal government provided generous subsidies to spur transportation and mineral development; (3) it exercised great restraint in the face of obvious entrepreneurial transgressions against the public trust; and (4) its policies ensured that common citizens, not the corporate class itself, would suffer the social costs of those forms of economic piracy.[10] Joe Howard's reference to Montana as a subject colony, "the end of the cracked whip," is a fitting metaphor for the broader region.[11]

In addition to the extractive nature of the economy of the northern West, other liabilities hampered its political and economic autonomy: distance from markets (especially at the turn of the century when railroad transportation costs often spelled the difference between success and failure); dependence on the vagaries of a transportation system controlled from eastern banking establishments; the absence of indigenous capital; remarkably few cities; and a thoroughgoing dependence on resources such as mining, agriculture, timber, and fishing, activities that were volatile and highly competitive, prone to cycles of boom and bust. Hence, to protect themselves from financial ruin, employers in labor-intensive industries customarily shifted the costs of competition to workers in the form of wage reductions and faster-paced production processes. Those practices immediately gave root to the militant forms of industrial unionism that appeared in the region.[12]

The steel rails that linked the northern West with Chicago and points east helped fashion the region's most enduring historical themes: external control and perpetual, even revolutionary, change. In a biographical sketch of Nannie Alderson, an early settler in southeastern Montana, William Bevis underscored the one constant in an otherwise mythic West—change: "In Nannie's ten years of ranching, the buffalo disappeared, the Indians starved, the railroad and the barbed wire came, and the market crashed. Her old West was wild and free, but much of the wilderness was in the market, and the free were often left alone."[13] Yet Nannie Alderson's experiences on the Northern Plains mirrored developments west of the Continental Divide, where the railroad enabled farmers to move to the rich loess soils in the upland areas surrounding the Columbia Basin.

When U.S. Superintendent of the Census Robert P. Porter declared that the era of open western land had come to a close, the vast sweep of territory extending west from St. Paul to the Pacific was alive with activity.[14] Oblivious of the census report, the *Settler's Guide*, a Northern Pacific promotional pamphlet, applauded the prospects of the region for common people, where "the poor man . . . can earn a living easier than in the East, as labor is in demand, wages are good, and provisions are cheap."[15] Like so many bees clustered about the honeycomb, most of that recently arrived population hovered near the expanding rail network that progressively linked the region to metropolitan centers in the East and on the Pacific Coast. That was a world rife with the energy of venture capitalists, some large, others small, some shrewd, discerning, and artful, others lacking in judgment and easily gulled. But the newcomers to the northern West were not the primary movers and shakers in remaking the demographic landscape of the region; instead, the catalyst for change was to be found in the distant constellations of power, money, and influence.

Regardless of one's view of the development of the northern West and its ties to the greater realm of global capital, no person looms larger during those years of frenetic activity than Canadian-born James Jerome Hill.[16] From his Summit Avenue command post in St. Paul, high atop a bluff overlooking the Mississippi River, Hill could gaze westward to an ever-expanding empire of steel rails, timber, farming, and mining enterprises that defied the imagination. Like a giant octopus with its head centered in St. Paul, Hill's principal vehicle to power, the Great Northern Railway Company, had extended its financial tentacles to Washington's Puget Sound as early as 1893. For the next fifteen years, Hill and the Great Northern (and its financial backers in New York and London) jostled with other railroad barons for strategic positioning in the resource-rich northern West, a struggle the calculating Canadian would not lose.

Hill emerged from the depression of the early 1890s with a greatly enhanced financial reputation. He shrewdly manipulated the advantages of unique geographic and marketing opportunities through ties to impressive eastern and European financiers. A soundly financed and efficiently operating line, Hill's Great Northern was in a position to deal on more than equal terms with its principal rival, the less efficient and financially troubled Northern Pacific Railroad. In his effort to gain control of the Northern Pacific, Hill locked horns with the Wall Street financier, J. Pierpont Morgan, who attempted to negotiate a reorganization scheme favorable to his own interests. For more than three years the Hill and Morgan factions proposed and broke agreements and attempted to find a competitive middle ground; finally, Hill and his London associates and Morgan and the Deutsche Bank (representing a syndicate attempting to reorganize the Northern Pacific) signed the London Agreement, a compromise whereby Hill effectively gained control of the older company by the turn of the century, and Morgan bankrolled Hill's purchase of controlling stock in a third competing line, the Chicago, Burlington, and Quincy. For its part, the Northern Pacific emerged from bankruptcy court in a strengthened position with capital reserves. When Hill announced in 1901 plans to build a railroad from Great Falls to Billings, thus linking the Great Northern with the Northern Pacific and the Chicago, Burlington, and Quincy at Billings, the move indicated the practical influence of the Hill-Morgan alliance. Like other entrepreneurs of the time, James J. Hill wielded enormous power.[17]

Although the famous Northern Securities case in 1904 denied a formal legal merging of the two properties, the spirit of the London Agreement meant the cessation of competition between the two roads with the intent of "protecting the common interests of both companies." In practice, Hill and his backers continued to dominate rail transportation in the region, according to W. Thomas White. But whether the "friendly and harmonious working of the two systems" would redound to the benefit of the common people of the northern West was another issue. Although Hill is billed as the Empire Builder by some, others have described him as the Empire Wrecker, a hint of the acrimony in the region that still persists.

The actions of the great railroad buccaneer and his financial bagmen in New York, London, and Paris typified the pattern of the investment-money trail during those years. John S. Kennedy, the New York–based railroad financier, worked closely with Hill, especially during the 1880s, in weaving together the web of smaller lines that became the Great Northern. Another of Hill's lifelong business associates was George Stephen, Canadian immigrant, former president of the Bank of Montreal and of the Canadian Pacific Railroad, and a person with established ties to London bankers who subsequently became a British baronet.[19] There were other financiers, some with links to the House of Morgan, involved with financial decisionmaking that affected even the tiniest of settlements in the northern West.

For his part, Hill kept his New York and overseas backers informed of Great Northern activities, the financial health of the line, business prospects from the Dakotas west to the Pacific, and other bits of confidential information regarding competing roads. Hill was confident when it came to the Great Northern's chief competition, the Northern Pacific. When the House of Morgan moved slowly to implement the London Agreement, Hill informed Stephen that if the Great Northern were "forced into a fight with the Northern Pacific, there would be no doubt as to the outcome." Because the properties were "so intimately connected," either one or the other would "pitch the key and dominate policy," he told Stephen, "and I do not think there is any room for doubt as to which that one will be." He was equally blunt with the Morgan interests, criticizing the expansion plans of the Northern Pacific, enterprises that would "bring about a contest which will not have any doubtful result."[20]

Hill was equally sanguine and no less forceful in his dealings with the powerful Canadian Pacific. He negotiated with its president, William C. Van Horne, a general strategy covering all Canadian Pacific and American matters west of Lake Superior. He suggested to George Stephen a "permanent and safe settlement on territorial lines" that "would remove all cause for friction in the future." Then he informed Van Horne of his desire to "quietly discuss the matter of a territorial arrangement." Hill told the Canadian executive that he wanted an agreement where "both you and ourselves can make the fullest and greatest use of our respective railways in traffic going or coming from either side of the International boundary between Lake Superior and the Pacific." In a letter to T. G. Shaughnessy, Van Horne's successor, Hill wrote that he saw no "reason why we cannot work together for mutual protection . . . so as to give each other the least trouble and expense."[21] Removing the sources of friction with the Canadian Pacific was similar to Hill's effort to gain control of the Northern Pacific—to eliminate the destabilizing influence of competition.

The record clearly shows that the jurisdictional disputes between Hill's lines and those of Edward H. Harriman's Union Pacific were, if anything, even more volatile. The working alliance with the Morgan interests enabled Hill to outbid Harriman in 1901 for control of the Chicago, Burlington, and Quincy Railroad, a line originating in Chicago with a connection extending from Nebraska to Billings; the road also would provide Hill with the opportunity to extend his influence to the Southwest. In a long and complicated struggle for control that sent the stock market into a frenzy, Hill won a victory of sorts over the Harriman interests. Hill and Morgan thus controlled nearly all of the great rail lines to the west of the Mississippi River. In the midst of those struggles, Charles H. Coster, a Morgan representative, spoke of establishing "an armed truce" between their competing investment interests. "If we can get matters in shape," he suggested to Hill early on, "we shall have done a great deal towards insuring that peace and harmony we are all striving to maintain." Putting the best light on the role that he and Hill played in the matter, Coster observed: "I am glad to read in the Good Book that peacemakers will be rewarded in the next world."[22]

Throughout those years, Hill paid close attention to the fluctuations of the political world. He used his influence with politicians in the northern West to lower tariff barriers, especially those with Canada where much of his traffic originated. Hill also enjoyed a cooperative working relationship with several corporate point men in strategic locations such as Great Falls, where Paris Gibson did his bidding, and in Spokane, where Hill benefited from the great builder of feeder railroads, Daniel C. Corbin. He corresponded frequently with business-oriented presidents McKinley and Taft; with others of his class he worked tirelessly to finance and direct the political process.[23] But entrepreneurs such as Hill who could deal on equal terms with presidents of the United States and with J. Pierpont Morgan, Edward H. Harriman, and the Canadian Pacific could be even more arbitrary with those who were less powerful.

At the other end of the geographical and social spectrum, in the small towns and farming communities scattered across the northern West, a different scenario was unfolding, and it was less than flattering to the great manipulators of capital in St. Paul, New York, and London. It is important to remember that the prototypes of James J. Hill's fellow capitalists—those individuals who followed the rails west to invest in lumbering, mining, shipping, and other lucrative, resource-based enterprises—were the advance guard in shaping life in the region. By the early twentieth century the names of Rockefeller, Guggenheim, Weyerhaeuser, and Hearst controlled much of the significant economic activity that transpired in the countryside beyond the rail networks. Theirs was a world that had little in common with the people who were making their homes in Montana's mining country or along the timbered slopes of western Washington. As the holders of power, they saw an environment and a people who presented opportunity for exploitation and personal gain. In that sense, the northern West mirrored developments in the mineral-rich country of the American Southwest and in California's great Central Valley.[24]

When Frederick Pope and William Talbot sailed north from San Francisco in 1852 and built a sawmill at Port Gamble, they set in motion export-based commercial practices that have dominated lumber production in Washington, Oregon, and parts of Idaho and Montana for more than a century. Although the trade flourished from the beginning, rudimentary forms of ocean transport, distance from markets, and a limited technology for moving the huge logs to mill sites restricted production. With the onset of the 1880s, however, the industry underwent a technological revolution of sorts, a transformation that vastly increased production and provided manufacturers with readier access to markets. Capitalists, first from San Francisco and then from the Great Lakes and the East, pioneered in blocking-up large timberland holdings on the northern Pacific slope. Railroads were important, not only for the transportation they provided to production facilities and distant markets but also for their huge land grants, some of them embracing the finest timber stands in the region.[25]

A group of Great Lakes lumber capitalists—witnessing the end of the extensive pine stands in Michigan, Wisconsin, and Minnesota—led the way when they brokered a deal with the Northern Pacific Railroad, purchased 80,000 acres of the railroad's grant lands, and established the St. Paul and Tacoma Lumber Company on Commencement Bay in Puget Sound. But the biggest deal—made during the frenzied speculation in Northwest timberland—involved Frederic Weyerhaeuser's purchase of 900,000 acres of prime Douglas fir timber from the Northern Pacific on January 3, 1900. Weyerhaeuser and other Great Lakes lumbermen maneuvered around federal and state land laws, engaged in myriad illegal title transfers, and negotiated territorial deals with the railroads, thereby dramatically concentrating timberland in the hands of a few operators.[26]

The lumber industry was undoubtedly the primary force behind the expanding economic activity and the increase in population from western Montana to the Pacific Coast. Washington led the nation in lumber production by 1910, a position it held until the onset of World War II. Its economy west of the Cascade Mountains, where the lumber industry employed two-thirds of the state's wage earners in 1912, was also highly specialized, with the value added to lumbering usually occurring in San Francisco or Chicago, St. Paul, and other points in the East. Some lumber industrialists came to that cutthroat competitive environment, with its productive capacity far in excess of demand, "quite deliberately to capitalize, extract, export, count their money, and get out."[27]

The lumber manufacturing town of Everett, Washington, provides one of the best settings in the northern West to observe the influence of industrial capital between 1890 and 1920. Situated twenty miles north of Seattle, Everett has two fronts—one to the markets of the Pacific Rim through the waters of Puget Sound and the other to the industrial heartland of the United States via the transcontinental rail link. Its strategic location would appear to place the coastal community in a favorable situation, yet Everett has enjoyed little sustained prosperity since its establishment in the early 1890s. An export terminal for the timber and mining resources in the surrounding hinterland, Everett is a prototype of the extractive manufacturing towns in the northern West. The community's financial history is sprinkled with the names of some of the great entrepreneurs of the turn of the century: Hill, Rockefeller, Guggenheim, Weyerhaeuser, and the agents who did their bidding. Those individuals benefited through their investments in the region, and some, such as Rockefeller, pulled out and still cleared several million dollars.[28]

Norman Clark has likened conditions in Everett during the first twenty years of this century to "competitive plunder," a system in which the capitalist class was at war with itself and with the wage earners who made their wealth possible. Although the struggles in the industry were not as glamorous to newspaper editors as Montana's "war of the copper kings," conditions in the lumber trade produced a mercurial and destructively competitive economic environment that rivaled the cycles of instability and turbulence that afflicted the copper towns in the Big Sky State and in the Southwest.[29] That system, in the case of Everett and other lumber towns, according to Clark, "was constantly at war with rationality and order."[30] But it also reflected the ever-changing character of capitalism in the twentieth century, swaying oftentimes wildly in concert with cycles of prosperity and depression. In truth, the lumber industry during the twentieth century has functioned as a fully integrated component of the American economic order.

Until the great construction boom following World War II altered competitive conditions, the lumber trade on the Pacific slope provides the classic example of easy access to timber, an overbuilt manufacturing capacity, and little concern for the future. That system, in which profit and loss were the major criteria for decisionmaking, both created and impoverished communities in the timbered regions of the northern West. Investors in New York, Chicago, St. Paul, and Tacoma made the decisions to build new mills, to move on to fresh stands of timber, or to close operations when the market was tight, but the men and women in the small lumber towns suffered the social costs of those actions.[31]

Even in the best of times before Pearl Harbor, overproduction was the great nemesis to lumber capitalists. Because many of them had overextended their investments in timberland and manufacturing facilities, it was necessary to operate the mills, even under the worst of conditions, to defray bonded indebtedness, taxes, and fire-protection costs. Robert Ficken has illustrated how the Weyerhaeuser firm's profit and accounting ledgers forced decisions that further contributed to overproduction. To generate cash to pay the taxes on its great timber estate, the company built several new sawmills—at Longview, Washington, and Klamath Falls, Oregon—and purchased other existing mill sites in the late 1920s. In the year of the stock market crash, the Weyerhaeuser facilities at Longview, Snoqualmie Falls, and Everett produced by far the largest volume of lumber in the region. Even George Long, the shrewd manager who directed the company's timber operations, admitted that the new plants had come on line "at an unfortunate time for market conditions."[32]

The market-related circumstances that drove down the price of lumber wrought havoc in the woods, indeed even rewarded wasteful practices. Those competitive conditions placed a premium on cutting, hauling out only the best logs, and then moving on to the next stand. There was no incentive to conserve, to implement sustained-yield practices, or to reforest the cutover timberlands. Although those circumstances were more pronounced in western Washington because of the industry's early beginnings and the huge productive capacity in the region, similar conditions prevailed in the ponderosa pine country of eastern Oregon and Washington and in northern Idaho's white pine districts.[33] The restraints on private timberland harvests paralleled corporate behavior in market-oriented resource economies elsewhere. The need to satisfy the profit requirements of distant investors and the availability of markets, not a social commitment to local communities, guided the liquidation of timber.

It was no accident that western Washington lumbering communities faced their day of reckoning in the 1930s. Two market-related calamities brought distress and misery simultaneously to the region: the Great Depression and greatly reduced stands of private timber. A Forest Service study of the Grays Harbor area at mid-decade reported that "excessive sawmill installations" had been constructed "with no consideration of permanent timber supplies, but only as to a timber supply adequate to depreciate them." That the industry had lasted for fifty years could not be attributed to "planning on the part of the timber industry but rather to the huge . . . original timber supply and the restrictions on production imposed by general market conditions."[34] In brief, the market system had functioned in classic manner and to the detriment of the communities that were left with the social costs.

As for Everett, it survived into the depression years amid the rusting hulks of empty, aged, and silent mills, the remnants of an earlier period of industrial enterprise. Only the Weyerhaeuser Company, Norman Clark has pointed out, with its huge financial resources, was able to "thrive on the misfortunes of its competitors." As a harbinger of the future, the firm constructed a state-of-the-art electrically powered mill in 1923, a plant that established precedents for technological efficiency. Its streets named to remind its citizens of an earlier age of entrepreneur (including Rockefeller), Everett has continued to reflect the health of the forest-products market, even in the best of times during the post–World War II era.[35] In recent years, the defense establishment has anointed Everett with a naval shipyard, an event that some observers describe as an economic savior for the community. In the larger sense, however, that development may prove as economically risky and turbulent as did its earlier dependence on the lumber industry.

Even though the treasure-hunt aspect of western mining seldom brought riches to the rank-and-file who discovered mineral deposits, no romance looms larger in the chronicles of the American West than the prospector's solitary quest for mineral wealth. As it did in other matters, California played center stage and provided the premier performance: entrepreneurs purchased the early claims, invested in mill equipment, constructed cheap housing in the immediate vicinity, and began to export both the minerals and the wealth they produced to distant parts of the continent. Those circumstances applied to the emerging centers of mining activity in the northern West after 1880, a time when both railroad companies and eastern U.S. and European investors began to capitalize on the region's rich mineral lodes. From the Homestake venture at Lead, South Dakota, to the Monte Cristo district in Washington's Cascade Range, mining investments provided the basis for family dynasties—Hearst and Guggenheim—and augmented the wealth of other investors who already had amassed great fortunes.[36]

The long arm of the Wall Street investor is more apparent in western mining than in any other industrial undertaking. Despite the critical role of financing in shaping the region's social, political, and economic order, the manipulations of distant capital have made mining a "notoriously unstable and cyclical industry," according to Michael Malone. To historian William Lang, the story of the great mining enterprises evokes images of power, "the classic stuff of the Gilded Age political economy when corporations manipulated commonwealths at will and justified muckrakers' vitriol."[37] Contemplate Montana without Butte, northern Idaho without Wallace and Kellogg, or Colorado without its Telluride district, communities where mining as a working-class culture permeates the historical mosaic. Those circumstances and conditions resulting from distant financial maneuvering were especially true for the northern Rockies where mining has been the bellwether, along with agriculture, for the region's political economy.[38]

And the stakes were high, sufficient to invite collusion early on between Jim Hill's Great Northern Railroad and Montana's copper brokers. Marcus Daly, one of Butte's two great mining developers, informed Hill in 1893 that the sizable Anaconda and Great Northern properties in Montana suggested that "there will hardly be a Legislature meeting in the future that we will not be interested in some way." He hoped that Hill would give the subject "the importance that it deserves." Daly need not to have worried because the astute railroad entrepreneur took care of such matters as he would his daily business activities. Although Hill and the copper magnates differed over monetary policy, on most issues they worked in concert. It can be said that Hill's agents were sprinkled everywhere in the states and territories of the northern West.[39]

Over the course of the twentieth century, the presence that Montanans and others refer to as the Company has loomed even larger in the state's affairs than the personage of James J. Hill. The Anaconda Copper Mining Company, which emerged victorious from the entrepreneurial jousting for control of Butte's rich copper lode, casts a greater shadow over the state's history than the Great Northern Railway. At the corporate level, according to Malone, the "battle for Butte [was] a classic instance of raw, unrestrained frontier capitalism." And like the frontier, Butte has held the public's interest: "[It] was rich, unabashedly exploited, turbulent—and endlessly fascinating."[40]

Yet Butte was even more. Arnon Gutfeld, who has studied the influence of the company during World War I, referred to Montana as "the ultimate example of economic colonialism in the American West." Early in his own professional career, Ross Toole concluded that by World War I

Montana "was a one company state." Joseph Kinsey Howard was even less restrained (though more imaginative) in his indictment of Anaconda:

[The Company] owned the city of Butte—its mines, public services, some of its stores, its press, usually its government. It controlled, though less obviously, half a dozen other major cities in Montana, and still does. It owns most of the state's daily newspapers, including Butte's two and the two in Helena, the state capital, and because of its dominant business position it usually is able to dictate to the few it does not own.

One might quibble that Howard's role as Montana's conscience may have colored his assessment of the company, but no one has yet stepped forward to plead, "Say it ain't so, Joe."[41]

Although Anaconda dominated Montana's industrial economy until after World War II, it did not bring stability to the region. Linked through capital ties to world economic fluctuations in metal prices, the industrial work force—like its Arizona counterparts in Bisbee, Morenci, and Ajo—periodically suffered through periods of unemployment, especially when new sources of copper entered the scene in the 1920s or when the price of ore plummeted on the international market. Eventually Anaconda itself moved heavily into Third World copper mining in Chile, thereby weakening the competitive strength of its North American operations. "With the passing years," Malone concluded, "the mining industry went through cycles of boom and bust: up during the two world wars, down during the interwar period, and then into a slow decline after 1945."[42]

That scenario aptly portrays developments in the ore-metal industry beyond the great Butte copper district. To the east, where the Hearst syndicate first achieved its fortune, the great Homestake gold mine was a bit of an anomaly: from its beginning in 1877 and lasting until the outbreak of World War II, the Homestake venture generated great profits for its investors and regular paychecks for the miners. From its inception until 1935 the mine produced more than 80 percent of all the gold bullion taken out of the Black Hills.[43] Homestake truly has been the backbone of the mining economy of South Dakota and a dominant presence in the politics of the Black Hills and beyond.

According to company biographer Joseph H. Cash, however, Homestake was atypical of the mining districts in the northern West: Lead, South Dakota, the company town, "achieved and maintained a degree of stability unusual if not unique in the West." The nature of the ore being extracted, gold, and the size of the ore body precluded the kind of instability and turbulence that occurred in Butte. Nevertheless, in important respects the differences between Homestake and other mining districts blur into the familiar pattern: the Hearst syndicate crushed a union organizing effort in a winter lockout (1909–1910); it adopted a reactionary, antiunion stance in the aftermath; and, like other nonresident corporate owners, it directed mining operations from its offices in San Francisco and siphoned great profits from the enterprise, even after its control began to erode.[44]

As it did in other mining regions in the American West, gold also triggered the initial rush to northern Idaho's Coeur d'Alene district. The building of a transcontinental railroad through the area in the early 1880s transformed that early treasure hunt into heavily capitalized operations controlled by distant investors, including Andrew Mellon, the Union Pacific Railroad, Jay Gould, the Bank of England, and others. Indeed, if continuity is to be found in the Coeur d'Alenes between mining activity in the nineteenth century and that of the late twentieth century, it rests in the economic colonialism involved. When the multinational firm Gulf Resources announced the closing of its Bunker Hill mining and smelting facility in Kellogg in late 1981, the action was merely the most recent in a long series of decisions made in distant places that have affected the Coeur d'Alene communities.[45] Gulf Resources' announcement, which echoed similar corporate decisions through the years, implies that extractive economies in the world of modern capitalism function in concert with the profit-and-loss figures in the investors' accounting books.

The emergence of the Lewisohn- (and Rockefeller-) controlled American Smelting and Refining Company at the turn of the century established monopoly control over much of the lead-silver smelting operations in northern Idaho. The trust proved cumbersome to the Lewisohns, and within a year Meyer Guggenheim and his sons had assumed control. Through their expertise and efficiency in mining enterprises, ASARCO became an exceedingly profitable investment for those individuals who financed its operations. Amid the various corporate advances and strategic retreats, the largest investors made enormous profits. As for business propriety, Thomas Navin's judgment fits well: "The stakes were high and the ethics low."[46] But for resident workers and their families, a story emerges that is quite different from the one that unfolded in the executive boardrooms in New York.

Industrial activity offered little autonomy in most of the mining areas of the northern West. Tied to events and circumstances in a global context, the ore-producing districts of Idaho and southern British Columbia paralleled Butte in terms of the viability of life. During World War I investors in the lead-silver extracting business made great profits, production in the mines peaked, and employment was steady. But those peaceful labor relations ended with the armistice, when the workers struck. Their actions proved to no avail, for the owners closed the mines when the bottom dropped out of the metal market. Mine managers subsequently reestablished their own hiring halls and open-shop conditions prevailed. Operations opened when the price of lead rose and closed when it declined. John Fahey has observed that the 1920s passed "in cautious vigilance," and with the stock market crash of 1929 the mines closed one by one "to wait for better days."[47]

The influence of the corporate world was equally apparent in the expanding agricultural districts of the northern West. Both the Northern Pacific Railroad Company and (after 1893) the Great Northern Railway promoted the settlement of marginal agricultural areas including the arid lands of the Inland Empire. There the broadsides of railroad pitchmen and irrigation promoters drew large numbers of immigrants to the Columbia River's Big Bend country during the early 1890s. But that movement, exhilarating though it might have been for the promoters, was also deceptive. The price of wheat plummeted when the national depression settled across the land in 1893, a financial collapse that subsequently bankrupted railroad companies, including the Northern Pacific. Geographer Donald Meinig has argued that the hard times of the mid-1890s were a "severe reminder that wealth was not simply a local product, and that the region was merely a small corner of a national, indeed international, economic world." Yet market prices improved, refinanced and reorganized railroads added to their branch lines in the Big Bend country, and the weather cooperated in a series of abnormally wet years.[48]

Then in came the "honyockers" to the last of the open-range country: the western Dakotas, eastern Montana and eastern Washington, and the south-central Oregon high desert.[49] Promoters and developers of irrigation projects attracted still others to Montana's Yellowstone Valley and to developing irrigation districts in Washington's Yakima and Wenatchee valleys and to the Snake River plain in southern Idaho. "By 1900," Robert Athearn has pointed out, "the Indians were pretty well fenced in, and the cattle kings were fenced out."[50] Even as the cattle barons bewailed the passing of their species, other enterprisers, inspired with innovative scientific and technological perceptions, arrived on the scene to make capital out of the new circumstances. With their sizable real estate holdings and investments in rolling stock, the great transcontinental railroads once again played a leading role in promoting those would-be agricultural paradises.

At the onset of the twentieth century, agriculturalists had already taken up the best farmland in the northern West. Grain, hay, and row crops predominated in the Willamette and Puget lowlands, and wheat production had established itself in Washington's Palouse Hills and in the great Red River Valley of the Dakotas. Despite the new acreages already put to the plow, an equally impressive increase in cultivable land would occur between 1900 and 1920; in this instance, however, agricultural expansion took place in areas of much less precipitation. As in the earlier period (when settlers moved into the East River country in the Dakotas or to Washington's Palouse Hills), railroad officials actively promoted the settlement of marginal lands in the western Dakotas, in eastern Montana, and in the arid valleys between the Cascade Range and the Rocky Mountains.

Although the methods popularized as the dry-farming system were approved agricultural practices well before 1900, the aspect that changed with the turn of the century was the element of publicity. Developed in the Great Plains and promoted with evangelical fervor, dry farming, according to Donald Meinig, was viewed by its advocates "as the road to agricultural salvation for all who struggled to wrest a living from the earth."[51] Hired public-relations personnel for the railroads and the promotional schemes of land-settlement companies lured people to take up land in the arid regions of the West. For those who did, the hardships were many and immediate: summer drought, winter storms, grasshopper plagues, and a political economy that did not function in the interests of small farmers.[52]

Those settlers who attempted dry farming on the high plains between 1900 and 1920 were seemingly oblivious of the failures of an earlier age of agricultural expansion. Gilbert Fite has observed that although the first boom-and-bust cycle on the plains occurred between 1778 and 1896, it was not to be the last. During the first two decades of the twentieth century, settlers once again moved beyond what Walter Prescott Webb called the "line of semi-aridity," especially to the arid lands of the northern West. Spurred on by the likes of Hardy Webster Campbell, a dry-farming advocate who found lucrative employment with the railroads, the boosters initiated a series of dry-farming congresses whose successes in promoting settlement were truly impressive.[53] It is fair to say that the congresses served more as publicity forums rather than as educational ones.

The railroads, especially James J. Hill's lines, provided most of the financing for the dry-farming congresses, with the first one held in 1907. In Montana, where he controlled three major roads, Hill was in an excellent situation to reap the benefits of increased settlement. But dry farming was also promoted for eastern Washington and in south-central Oregon and the Deschutes River Valley. Thomas Shaw, the best-known proponent of dry farming in Montana and the Dakotas, began lecturing on the subject in 1907, initiated a demonstration project three years later, and by 1911 was the chief agricultural agent for the Northern Pacific and the Great Northern.[54]

The collective promotional work of the dry-farming congresses and Shaw's tireless lecturing and pamphleteering attracted sizable numbers of homesteaders. Many people settled in western North Dakota between 1900 and 1920, and the population of Montana's eastern counties grew by 220,000. The Great Northern Railway alone moved 135,750 new settlers to Montana and another 64,000 to North Dakota between 1909 and 1919. But that was only a small part of a larger movement of people onto the high Canadian prairies and into Oregon and Washington. In South Dakota's West River country, 100,000 newcomers arrived between 1900 and 1915.[55]

At first blush that repeopling of the last frontier would seem but another chapter in the wonders of the westward movement. And at least until the American entry into World War I, the financial backers of dry farming—James J. Hill and his son, Louis—might be termed the great industrial and agricultural statesmen of the northern West, empire builders of epic proportions, farsighted and social-minded with their investments. But the historical record tells a different story, one of abysmal failure everywhere in those submarginal lands. Joseph Kinsey Howard has noted that James J. Hill's grand scheme for settling the high plains with homesteaders "became a witless nightmare" as his rail cars "rattled empty through dying towns."[56]

Although the U.S. Department of Agriculture warned that the promoters of dry farming were interested chiefly in "exploiting the attractions and resources" of the arid West, a cycle of abnormally wet years put those premonitions of disaster to shame and gave the illusion of success.[57] Bumper crops and wartime demand kept prices high for most of the region through 1915 and 1916, but as Gilbert Fite has noted, that second boom period, like the one that preceded it, "ended in a bust." Recurring drought and blowing soil in parts of the region, faltering prices for crops, and rising production costs (primarily in mechanized equipment) brought ruin to many farmers.[58] Yet in a broader sense, the technological shifts that occurred in farming were in keeping with changes in the larger arena of agriculture: the trend toward eliminating labor as a factor in production; the introduction of ever more expensive types of mechanized equipment, and the move toward the consolidation of landholdings.

In her able study of efforts at dry farming in the little-known Fort Rock–Christmas Lake Valley area in south-central Oregon, Barbara Allen has illustrated the influence of natural and economic circumstances on the population exodus. Billed at first as "the promised land," it became in the end "a land of bondage," and the area's population, which peaked at 1,200 people in 1912, declined to 360 by 1920. Similar conditions on a much larger scale prevailed in South Dakota's West River country, where unpredictable precipitation, extremes in temperature and wind, and problematic farm prices brought a sizable out-migration. For the few people who remained, Paula Nelson has pointed out, theirs was a life based "on changed assumptions and diminished expectations," and, she added, one "of dreams and ambitions thwarted."[59]

The drought and hard times in the Dakotas and in Montana immediately following World War I were but a harbinger of the future. Depressed agricultural prices through the 1920s, recurring years of marginal precipitation, high interest rates, and the rising cost of manufactured goods brought depressed conditions to the region well before the stock market collapse at the close of the decade. A frontier boom had turned into a disaster. In Montana, as Michael Malone and Richard Roeder have observed, "the flood of immigration reversed itself and became an exodus to greener pastures elsewhere; and the dreams of the boosters soured into bitter memories." Karl Kraenzel has pointed out that the rural population for the Great Plains states was lower in 1950 than it had been in 1920 (during the 1920s the population of Montana actually decreased). The figures for South Dakota indicate even more persuasively the economic stasis that had taken hold in the region: between 1920 and 1985 the population increased less than 8 percent (637,000 to 687,000).[60] Need we wonder, then, about the popularity during the interwar period of radical protest movements such as the Nonpartisan League?

Natural calamities—searing drought and high, frightening winds—accompanied the Great Depression in the states to the east of the Continental Divide. Known as the Dirty Thirties on the Canadian plains, an area where the physical and economic realities are similar to those of its neighboring states, the depression wrought havoc on both sides of the border. In eastern Montana's wheat country, most of the counties applied for Red Cross relief in 1931. In neighboring North Dakota, where half the population was on relief, the economy was a shambles. In David Danbom's words, the state "had become a ward of the United States."[61]

Only the advent of another world war and a large out-migration of young people have helped maintain a semblance of social and economic stability on the Northern Plains. Occasional forays into petroleum development (in response to rising international prices) in eastern Montana and in the western Dakotas have brought the briefest flurries of prosperity to a few towns. There remains, however, what Karl Kraenzel has termed the "high cost of space" in the region. Public expenses for schools, highways, hospitals, and myriad other activities have escalated while the revenue to support those services has declined. A few years ago, before the farm foreclosures of the 1980s, Gilbert Fite warned, "As the population continues to decline on the farms and in the small towns, lack of support for institutions and essential services will bring a crisis in many communities."[62] Those tendencies, however, are consistent with the continued transformation of the countryside during the twentieth century.

While the high plains region, especially the western Dakotas and eastern Montana, provides the classic boom-and-bust story at the margins of American agriculture, there were more stable components to farming enterprise in the northern West. If the dreamers and the investor-promoters committed a cruel hoax in enticing the "honyocker" to the semiarid lands of the Northern Plains, in truth they had modest successes too: in the expansion of irrigated agriculture along the great sweep of the Snake River and its tributaries in southern Idaho, in Washington's fruit-growing areas in the Yakima and Wenatchee valleys, and on a lesser scale in Oregon's Hood River Valley. Still, the diversification of crops, small-scale, intensive-farming practices, large federal subsidies for reclamation projects, and relatively more stable markets were the most important factors in those achievements.

With considerable financial support and publicity from the Northern Pacific Railroad, private irrigation companies constructed a series of canals and ditches in the Yakima Valley during the early 1890s. Continued promotional efforts and the construction of additional irrigation waterways tripled the valley's population by 1910. By the middle of that decade, congressman and then senator Wesley L. Jones had worked effectively with lobbyists for the railroads to commit the Reclamation Service to fully developing the Yakima Valley as a federal project. With the onset of World War I, the valley sent forth a huge volume of apples to national and international markets.[63]

Following the Northern Pacific's example in the Yakima Valley, the Great Northern initiated its own private irrigation enterprise in the Wenatchee Valley to the north. For their part, the railroad companies did not offer the new farmland as a benevolent gift, as an exercise in generosity to would-be orchardists. One source estimated that it required about $3,500 for a beginning orchardist to purchase a forty-acre plot, build a small house and a few outbuildings, put in fruit trees, and pay irrigation fees. To make ends meet, heads of families had to seek seasonal work—as loggers, farmhands, or miners—to defray expenses while their orchards matured.[64]

Beyond that, there were the normal perils confronting small-scale enterprise: uncertain markets, the need to diversify crops, and the reality that malefactors frequently lurked behind some of the irrigation schemes. In a few instances, the courts sentenced overzealous speculators to prison terms for issuing fraudulent bonds and for bank pyramiding schemes related to canal and ditch ventures. There were also more powerful elements to deal with: the Great Northern Railway and the Northern Pacific Railroad, direct beneficiaries of the large volume of fruit production and row-crop agriculture in the Yakima Valley and elsewhere. "Beneficent, malignant, fickle," according to John Fahey, the railroads nevertheless provided the route to markets for people who had been lured to those new, would-be gardens. To confront the power of the railroads, the growers organized marketing cooperatives, established warehousing schemes, and lobbied Congress to gain more favorable rate structures. They fought equally hard in state legislatures to regulate the roads.[65] But not until the advent of the motorized truck and improved highways in the late 1920s did farmers have access to alternative means of transportation.

Nowhere in the northern West is the distribution of water more important to the success of agriculture than in Idaho. The beginnings of the state's reclamation projects date from the 1890s in the fledgling farming oasis on the western fringes of the Snake River basin and in the early Mormon cooperative settlements in the southeast. The construction of a transcontinental branch line across the Snake River plain in 1884 provided those agricultural communities with access to markets (and sparked the interests of still more investors).[66]

In an era of grand ventures, the New York Canal (with the backing of investors from that state) was the most imposing, but engineering problems and the lack of funds delayed the delivery of water. Not until 1890, and then under different management, did a successor firm complete a segment of ditching to the Nampa area, west of Boise. The New York Canal was not finished until after 1900, with the new Reclamation Service providing the funds. Even then it required the construction of three federally funded dams on the Boise River to provide sufficient water for the canal and its extensive system of ditches.[67] Elsewhere (again with the assistance of federal money) promoters were more successful in bringing water to the Snake River plain.

With the exception of its great water-diversion systems in Arizona and California, some of the largest and oldest Bureau of Reclamation operations are in Idaho. The Snake River's Minedoka Dam, which dates from the earliest years of federal reclamation projects, is an example. Despite the construction of several dams, canals, and ditches, Idaho remained a vicious battleground for its precious water resource (thirty irrigation districts and forty different companies were competing for the use of Snake River water by 1920). The state's tradition of mixing private enterprise with federal largesse contributed to that situation, and the result was chaos. After protracted deliberation, Snake River irrigators ultimately agreed to cooperate in the delivery of water and, most important, to demonstrate a common front in the quest for even larger storage facilities.[68]

But even those engineering successes tell only part of the story of southern Idaho's quest for more water: dam building displaced Native Americans from bottomland along the river; national economic dislocations drove farm prices down following the end of World War I; and an ensuing agricultural depression that lasted until 1940 put farmers in constant danger of failure. It is grand testimony to the functioning of much economic activity in the northern West that the venture capital and federal intervention that made possible the marked expansion in agricultural productivity also carried with it the curse of twenty years of overproduction. "Next to Montana," Ross Peterson notes, "Idaho had the highest rate of emigration of any western state during the roaring twenties."[69] The emergence in the postwar era of agribusiness giants such as Simplot and ORIDA on irrigated land in southern Idaho and in neighboring Oregon further eroded the agrarian dream of the small farmer.

And that brings this argument full circle—back to the experiences of Norman Best. During the course of his long life Best lived through much of the instability and uncertainty of economic conditions in the northern West. Although those volatile employment conditions existed everywhere in the United States prior to World War II, they were especially pronounced across the northern West because of the extractive, capital-poor, and colonial nature of the region's economy. "Walk the sad streets of Butte," the writer William Kittredge said recently, "a town mined and abandoned by Anaconda and ARCO and . . . see if you understand." For the last 100 years Montana and its neighboring states were exploited as colonies; "The money went East, and we were left with holes in the ground."[70]

Most scholars do not consider Montana the extreme example. K. Ross Toole, a Montana historian beloved for his subjectivity, put the case bluntly for his state and by extension for the northern West: "It is a raw materials area, not a fabricating area. Its wealth in terms of minerals, timber, grass, and abundant water is enormous. But by the very nature of things the largest percentage of this wealth is not kept at home." Clark Spence, another Montana historian, concurred: together with Idaho and Wyoming, he considered Montana "one of the last strongholds" of colonialism.[71]

Was there a real difference between the "nature of things" in Montana and in other extractive centers in the region? The argument I have presented in this chapter suggests not. The northern West from the Dakota farm country to the timbered slopes of Washington might serve as an exemplary case of exploitation in an advanced industrial nation. With the exception of the two great metropolitan centers at its opposite ends—the Twin Cities and the greater Seattle area—little happened in the region that did not have the sanction of external capital. Moreover, the persisting transformation of modern capitalism—from the corporate mergers of the turn of the century to the leveraged buy-outs and hostile takeovers of today—has reverberated across the northern West. For the people who have lived through those changes, the mark of success was simply the ability to endure.

PART THREE

Forces of Integration

CHAPTER EIGHT

The South and the West:
A Comparative View

The nature and extent of resources are of course meaningless apart from the social context within which they exist. And it is differences in social context that so strikingly set apart the West from the South.

—Douglas F. Dowd[1]

"Looking West," the writer Kevin Starr exclaimed, "is a persistent American habit." As a politically bounded place and "testing ground for the national experience," the West, he claimed, provided metaphor and symbol, a rationale and a forum for defining a larger sense of national purpose. The attributes of that mythical West were optimism, possibility, rejuvenation, a place where determination and human will could effect the good society, where freedom was unbounded and less shackled to tradition, and where the culture of abundance and opportunity burned like a bright and shining star. The West represented dynamic, cheerful, untethered enterprise, a paradise of riches, a land of limitless possibility, a place for nurture and refuge.[2] Wallace Stegner has captured that mythical geography of the mind in a "vagrant's vision of beatitude," a cryptic paraphrasing of Harry McClintock's 1928 hobo ballad: "a place where the bulldogs have rubber teeth and the cinder dicks are blind and policemen have to tip their hats, where there's a lake of stew and whiskey too, where the handouts grow on bushes and the hens lay soft-boiled eggs."[3] Although those lyrics unabashedly fantasize about and distort the Eden-like qualities of the West, they do more than amuse and entertain; they embody the dominant themes in the popular literature of the region.

If the legendary, imaginary West was the American success story writ large, the South was its antithesis, its failures emblazoned in Erskine Caldwell's *Tobacco Road* and William Faulkner's *As I Lay Dying*. Its writers have depicted it as a region with a deeply tragic sense of the past, with clearly institutionalized sins, with a pervasive and entrenched poverty, and with a ritual need to seek national atonement through a romantic defense of its mythical cultural attributes. Indeed the South appeared to be everything the West was not: it represented failure in both human and environmental terms; it was closed and insular while the West was

145

open; its economy, especially its agricultural sector, languished in a kind of postbellum, hand-labor torpor until the close of World War II; and its politics of race relations continued to be a national disgrace until recent times. That timeworn and static image of the South captured the attention of American presidents, social and cultural critics, Hollywood producers, and radio and television comedians alike. Just as in the mythical West, however, the stereotyping of southern regional attributes obscures more than it reveals and cloaks in generic rhetorical garb more than it illuminates.

According to the southern chronicler Jack Temple Kirby, progress and modernity spread from the North, "flowered most gloriously in the West,' and bypassed most of the population living south of the Mason-Dixon line and the Ohio River. If one associates "progress" and "modernity" with the transforming influence of industrial and corporate forms of capitalism, the concomitant mechanization of the production process, and the substitution of capital-intensive for labor-intensive production systems, then Kirby's assessment is on the mark.[4] Despite the newness of the West in terms of its annexation to an expanding American empire, there is little question that at the turn of the century the region was a more thoroughly integrated segment of national and international capitalist structures than was the former Confederacy. It is fair to say that the South generally stood apart in the years between 1880 and the onset of World War II, distinctively different in its economic and cultural worlds from the rest of the nation. For those several decades, Gavin Wright remarks, "the South was the largest and most cohesive region standing inside the country but outside the country's economic mainstream."[5]

Because the social, institutional, and material world of the West differed dramatically from that of the South, the capitalist transformation and integration of the former moved far more swiftly and in more thoroughgoing fashion. The explanation for the comparative differences in the structural realities of the South and the West rests in culture, economics, and legal structures: in the history of the nation-state; in modes of production; in patterns of landholding; in systems of labor; in the relations of class, caste, and race; and in the peculiarities attached to the encouragement of, or barriers to, capitalist innovation in those regions. Although there is a certain risk in treating either the West or the South as generalized monoliths, the substantial and significant structural differences between the two regions merit such a discussion. There are more penetrating and convincing explanations behind the popular myths and symbols associated with the West and the South, explanations that grow from a proper analysis of the differing economic cultures of the two regions.

"Being a Southerner," the journalist Joel Garreau has observed, "is the most fervent and time-honored regional distinction in North America." To the historian Dewey Grantham, a long-term coherence in southern distinctiveness helped to shape a region different from the rest of the nation; the South possessed "an exotic quality" of "mystery and mystique" that made it "an enigma, 'a kind of Sphinx on the American land.'" Although such descriptive southern lore emphasized romantic and mystic notions steeped in agrarian traditions, the conventional view of the West tended toward exceptionalist and triumphalist themes.[6] Neither regional description, however, offers critical insight into southern or western symbols and myths; indeed, in the absence of closer analysis, symbol and myth have often passed for reality.

Nearly twenty years ago the historical geographer Donald Meinig suggested that the West, specifically the West that emerged in the 1870s and 1880s, possessed a "persisting basis of identity." He argued that the region's economic growth was exceedingly complex because of its heavy dependence on the federal government for a variety of infrastructural requirements, especially the "revolutionary instrument" of the railroad. The completion of two major transcontinental railroads in the early 1880s—the Southern Pacific and Northern Pacific—according to Meinig, marked the emergence of that new, modern West. Now that we are more than a century removed from those unprecedented and revolutionary changes, what is most impressive is the striking rapidity with which that transformation took place, the dramatic repeopling of the western landscape, and the dynamics and turbulence associated with an expanding capitalist economic system.[7]

By any measure, the late nineteenth century was a remarkably tumultuous period in the development and expansion of worldwide capitalism. The United States itself was in the midst of the frenetic process of industrialization, moving rapidly toward core status among the nation-states of the world, and within a few short decades it would emerge as preeminent among the global capitalist powers. The integrative forces of market capitalism were reaching to the far corners of the globe, including the interior of western North America. Untimately, around the onset of World War I, the American West was transformed from a region dominated by preindustrial societies to a fully integrated segment of the modern world capitalist system. Under the set of relationships that emerged, western America provided the vital ingredients for the industrial development of the United States (and of western Europe): a rapidly expanding market, the necessary natural resources for the burgeoning industries of the East, and finally—once the human geography of the region had been redesigned—vast spaces to attract a new population thoroughly steeped in the values of the market culture.[8]

The process of military conquest and capitalist expansion was unusually brutal and violent, involving human and cultural genocide waged against the indigenous population, the subjugation and marginalization of Hispanic peoples, and, in the extractive industries that came to dominate much of the West, the ruthless exploitation of both environment and laboring people. Until recently, stories of adventure, individual success, and nation-building muted the dark and tragic side to much of the story told about the West. But issues of conquest and violence or success and growth provide only a partial explanation for the broader currents of change in the region.

In a sense, the history of the West—with its uneven development, its far-flung extractive economies, its turbulent community histories, and its highly mobile population—serves as a prototype for modern capitalism. The absence of capital in the region, a spare (albeit expanding) infrastructure, and distance from markets continued for some time to be western liabilities. And like the South, the West remained in a dependent relationship to the more powerful capital markets in the East, at least until the onset of World War II. Centers of influence in distant places and strategies worked out in corporate boardrooms in the East kept the West in a vulnerable position. And when the economy began to crack, when the price of precious metal plummeted in eastern U.S. and European financial houses, and when financiers decided to withdraw their securities, it was the underclass of residents in the West who suffered.

Yet the South endured those liabilities and more, difficulties and uncertainties that many scholars agree have set it apart from the rest of the nation. "The core of the development problem" of the South, Douglas Dowd observed in a penetrating essay four decades ago, was institutional. Differing social contexts, he believed, distinguished the West from the South: the West was linked to dynamic elements of the national and global economy, and the South stood in sharp contrast. With a historical legacy that included cash-crop monoculture, the plantation system, and slavery, the region remained the nation's "number one problem." Dowd argued that in contrast the West never had a development problem: its resources merely awaited "the needs of the vigorous East"; it was free from "vested interests and inhibited forms of economic and social organization"; and it was absent of the institutional constraints that would block development.[9]

Although scholars have vastly extended their research and continue to debate the larger complexities of capitalist development in the postbellum South, Dowd's study remains one of a kind in having raised some of the more significant comparative questions concerning the changing social and economic contours of the South and the West.[10] Jonathan Wiener carried the argument for southern postbellum distinctiveness a step further when he linked slavery to the development of the postwar economy. In a call for greater theoretical clarity on the issue, he characterized the region's sharecropping system as a persisting strain of bound labor that carried over into the modern era. The South, he said, perpetuated a system of unfree labor through a variety of debt-peonage schemes whereby a tenant's debt could be transferred from one landlord to the next, thus preserving the repressive nature of the system. Moreover, those regional trappings of various forms of involuntary servitude continued until World War II and, according to Wiener, "extended well beyond debt peonage" to embrace southern cultural and social traditions and the region's legal system, which imposed additional restrictions on a free-labor market. Therefore, it was "the formal and informal obstacles to the free market in labor" that set the region's repressive labor economy apart from the classical capitalism of the North and, he might have added, from the West.[11]

Wiener's argument that the South took a Prussian Road approach to economic development has been problematic, but his thesis about the peculiarities of the southern labor system between the end of Reconstruction and World War II is firmly grounded in the material forces of the region's history.[12] Steven Hahn, who posits an alternative to the Prussian Road assertion, disputes the notion that a newly emergent urban and industrial ruling class became ascendant in the postbellum South. Rather, he argues, the political and economic imbalances between the North and the South forced the latter into a "quasi colonial status" and restricted the "transition to wage labor and a more general reorganization of production." Sharecropping and tenancy emerged amid those limited options for economic growth.[13] Although Hahn's explanation of the evolving political economy of the new South takes a different approach, the result is the same: a largely land-bound, restricted labor force rooted in the structural peculiarities of the region.

The economic forces that were moving agriculture toward decidedly commercialized operations in many parts of the world encountered social and institutional obstacles in the South that inhibited the thoroughgoing capitalist transformation of certain sectors of its economy. It would not be too wide of the mark to say that the post–Civil War South remained largely precommercial in the sense that sizable segments of its population, both black and white, remained tied to subsistence forms of agriculture. In postserfdom Russia, as in the American South, the only fully capitalist and commercial constituents in the countryside were traders and merchants (many of them outsiders) and banking interests. "Neither abolition nor emancipation," according to E. J. Hobsbawm, "produced a satisfactory capitalist solution of the agrarian problem."[14]

The tendency to cling to precapitalist prerogatives and standards and to resist the incursions of commercial agriculture was especially widespread in the southern upcountry. Moreover, with its sizable reservoir of labor power, the region had not yet become the great supplier of workers to nonagricultural sectors in the North. With its overweening poverty, the rural South provided only the weakest of markets for manufactured goods produced elsewhere. The relative absence of capital accumulation in the region and its dependency on the industrialized North meant that the South also missed out on what John Agnew refers to as "the western bonanza."[15]

Because industrial employment was at best a limited option for most southerners, there were few opportunities for work beyond agriculture. For several decades following the Civil War, therefore, most farmers were forced to eke out a subsistence living on increasingly smaller parcels of land and on increasingly impoverished and eroded soil. Henry Grady's "New South," therefore, meant little to the great mass of southern farmers. Nor did the expansion of the textile industry, which provided some off-farm employment for white families, prove adequate to counter the appalling poverty among the rural farm population. For nearly sixty years following the Civil War southern agriculture was both labor-intensive and extremely low in productivity relative to the more thoroughly commercialized agricultural regions. Even for those farmers with the will and desire to modernize, the one great missing ingredient was capital or access to capital. To enlarge farms, to purchase mechanical pickers and tractors, and to diversify crops required investment capital, an element the region lacked. Additional and notable weaknesses prevailed in the region's economic infrastructure: poor educational and health services, deficient internal markets and banking and credit systems, and inadequate systems of transport.[16]

The labor market in the West differed remarkably from the tenant-dominated, sharecropping, debt-peonage system in the South. Indeed no distinction between the two regions stands in sharper contrast than the generally restrictive labor market in the one and the largely unrestricted, even anarchic conditions in the other. Free from structural and institutional constraints and more closely integrated with national and international capitalist relations, western conditions, albeit with some exceptions, were truly conducive to a free market in labor. Moreover, economic circumstances peculiar to the West aided and abetted a relatively unrestricted market for wageworkers: the scarcity of labor, the lure of higher wages elsewhere, the boom-and-bust nature of the region's extractive industries, and the tendency toward alternating periods of work and idleness.[17] Although some of those historical characteristics are true of the South, the particular combination of all those conditions in the West gave a unique cast to the nature of labor in the region.

Despite the revolutionary transformation in property relations that resulted from the defeat of the South in the Civil War, a convincing argument can be made that even more striking changes took place in the American West in the last thirty years of the nineteenth century. Those changes would include the final defeat and the social control of native people, the opening to commodity forces of vast acreages of the western landscape, the repeopling of the region with immigrant newcomers, and the great rush to exploit the mineral riches of the West. Nowhere was the rapidity of social and economic innovation more apparent than in western mining districts. In an extraordinarily brief period industrial towns replaced mining camps, and the long reach of eastern and corporate capital replaced the independent miner. In the South the slow transition from subsistence and handicraft activity to industrial forms occurred over a long period of time, whereas in the West those changes virtually accompanied the coming of the newly dominant social groups. Melvyn Dubofsky argues that in the mineral-rich districts of the West:

> Communities grew from villages to industrial cities, mining enterprises evolved from primitive techniques to modern technology, from the small business to the giant corporation, if not overnight, at least within a generation.[18]

But it is western labor that stands in sharpest contrast to the landbound labor relations that characterized much of the South. The one distinctive trait that best singles out the uniqueness of labor in the West between the end of the Civil War and the onset of World War II is its mobility. Miners, seasonal harvest hands, loggers, lumber-mill employees, and construction workers of all kinds were notorious for their willingness to "go down the road," to move to the next camp or "slave market" (hiring hall). The capricious and arbitrary power of bosses and supervisory personnel and the promise of higher wages elsewhere were the wage earners' main weapon against working conditions deemed unsatisfactory.[19] How else does one explain the relatively greater influence of the Industrial Workers of the World and other militant unions among the large agricultural and mining enterprises of the American West?

A major factor contributing to the scarcity of labor in the western United States was the isolated and backcountry character of many industrial activities. Unlike the South with its surplus work force, the people who employed miners, agricultural workers, and lumber-industry laborers were always hard-pressed to acquire and retain a full complement of skilled and unskilled workers. As a consequence wages for western laborers, miners in particular, were considerably higher than their industrial counterparts in the East. In virtually every instance western workers remained subservient to capital, but as individuals they always had the possibility and the option to move on: to the next camp, to the next town, or to an entirely new industrial setting. When John Quinn ran for an elective office in 1902 in the copper town of Butte, Montana, his work history included mining stints in Arizona, Utah, and in northern Idaho's Coeur d'Alene district. Another miner, who testified in a 1908 court case, accounted for his itinerary with a quip: "I was rambling a good deal during them years."[20]

Unlike the South after the Civil War, the West was a place where it was possible for the largely male, wage-earning work force to improve its circumstances and condition in life. "In the frontiersman's West," William Allen White remarked, "the poor man's case was really hopeful"; there existed a widespread sense that "things are changing for the better." As a consequence, the region attracted a welter of nationalities and races, especially to the mining districts. And with their great mobility, those male groups spread ideas of high wages and unionism throughout the region, a factor that also presented problems for organized labor in its effort to perpetuate itself. Regarding the work force in the West, however, Melvyn Dubofsky may offer the key to the argument: the region's most itinerant workers—harvest hands, coal and hard-rock miners, longshoremen, and loggers—"proved to be the most radical, militant, and class-conscious of working people."[21] Although recent scholarly research challenges the stereotype of docility among southern laborers between the end of the Civil War and the Great Depression, the pockets of worker insurgency in the South appear to be isolated and few in number.

To be sure, the industrial communities and camps of the West fell far short of a workers' paradise; they were exploitive, brutal, and violent in varying proportions. Corporate owners and absentee managers engaged in the full sweep of union-busting tactics, lockouts, strike-breaking, and other forms of labor intimidation. And because of the heavy influence of external capital in the region, workers were especially vulnerable to the mercurial price swings of ores and minerals in eastern and European financial houses. Yet in matters of degree, the western industrial towns differed markedly from the mill villages and textile towns that emerged in the South during the last thirty years of the nineteenth century.

In the years following the Civil War a disparate group of entrepreneurs began the slow process of undermining the premodern and precommercial southern economy through the introduction of corporate capitalism to the region. Perhaps the best representation of the new mode of production was the building of textile mills, especially in rural and upland areas. That process of "capitalizing the hinterland," according to Jack Temple Kirby, took several generations, and remote parts of Appalachia did not fully enter into market relations until well into the twentieth century. Thus did the South become part of the larger history of the textile industry, a system of capitalist production that historically has been exceedingly sensitive to labor costs. Cotton-textile production began spreading rapidly by the mid-1870s in the upcountry regions of the Carolinas, Georgia, and Alabama. The reason for the shift to the Piedmont was simple: cheap labor.[22]

The mill villages that increasingly dotted the southern upland landscape represented a cultural as well as a social and economic shift for the region's labor force. People who knew nothing of town life, of factory tasks, of working at the command of the mill whistle rather than by the natural rhythms of diurnal and seasonal change suddenly were cast into the structured world of industrial employment and all that it implied. The new people streaming into southern textile towns in the late nineteenth century were rural folk who were leaving behind a premodern world: they resented authority; they rebelled against imposed time constraints; and they disliked regulations of any kind. David Carlton, who has studied mill villages in South Carolina, refers to that newly recruited textile work force as a "cracker proletariat."[23]

But the industry spread, financed largely with indigenous capital savings and by hourly wage rates that by the 1880s were 30 to 50 percent lower than comparable levels in the North. In brief, the growth of textile manufacturing was linked firmly to advantages of locality: a large surplus, low-wage labor force and the emergence of small-town merchants as a dynamic new force in southern economic life. The mill villages themselves took on a life of their own, housing entire families but especially favoring those with large numbers of young females. Southerners who trekked to textile towns in the years following the Civil War were part of what Gavin Wright calls a "sorting equilibrium," a process whereby poverty-stricken and marginalized families from the countryside realized "that the family unit could do better in the mill village." By the turn of the century more than 90 percent of the textile workers lived in towns owned by the businesses that gave them work. "For these people, perhaps more than for any other industrial workforce," Jacquelyn Dowd Hall argues, "the company town established the contours of everyday existence." Although there were crosscurrents of movement from mill town to farm to mill town, the village often represented a social setting where people lived, worked, married, raised their children, and died.[24]

If the textile industry, then, provided the southern route to industrialization before World War II, it also reflected larger difficulties rooted in the region's past—the relative dearth of both entrepreneurial ability and industrial labor skills. Those town-based merchant/industrialists, according to David Carlton, embraced an industry that "required relatively few skills of worker or owner," and those protocapitalists did virtually nothing to advance work-force talents and adeptness. Moreover, as localities were increasingly integrated into national markets, the inability to influence in any significant way that larger world further hampered southern entrepreneurs. The combined weaknesses of that system, he concludes, were long-lasting and detrimental to the southern economy.[25]

Like the company-town in the West, especially the mining and lumbering communities, the mill village exploited all classes of employment; however, the experiences of most working people in those disparate regional settings were remarkably different. In the one, workers were much more likely to move on when wages were lowered or the conditions of employment became intolerable. In contrast, studies of mill-village demography in the South indicate conditions that fostered cultural isolation and limited movement among industrial settings.[26] The reformer Frank Tannenbaum summed it up: "Once a mill-worker, always a mill-worker. Not only you, but your children and children's children forever and ever."[27] Although Tannenbaum overstated the static nature of those communities, the evidence suggests that the mill-town atmosphere was often inward-looking, that it did little to widen horizons, and that it lacked much of the social dynamism of western industrial settings.[28]

Yet one should be cautious about overemphasizing the stark nature of the mill-village environment because the mill setting often was not exclusive in terms of an individual's employment; copious evidence shows that people moved back and forth between mill and agricultural work. Until the crisis of the Great Depression and the imposition of federal wage standards, however, textile earnings were ever so tenuously linked to the agricultural labor market.[29] And in an economic climate steadily devolving toward crisis, southern agriculture was certainly no bastion of relief for beleaguered mill hands.

Other structural problems and weaknesses in industrial activity existed in the post–Civil War South: technological advances were limited; the region was dependent on a low-wage, routinized, dead-end labor force; production centered on the manufacture of "cheap, standardized, low-skill commodities" and consequently little of value was added to the raw materials. Unlike the West, where industry-specific technological innovations abounded, in virtually every industrial sector in the South there was a general absence of an indigenous technology.[30] But as the national and international capitalist economy moved toward the crisis of the 1930s, wrenching changes were about to remake the demographic and social landscape of the South.

Despite the nominal inroads of industrialism in the South by the 1920s, ruralism still firmly set the tone for southern life. The federal census for 1920 listed only three major cities in the region: New Orleans (414,000), Atlanta (326,000), and Birmingham (310,000). Agricultural work continued to dominate employment, much of the region remained overwhelmingly rural and poor, and its urban population was well below the national average, ranging somewhere between Mississippi's 13 percent and Florida's 37 percent. Hence, if there is truth to Richard Hofstadter's famous aphorism that America "was born in the country and has moved to the city," then the majority of southerners did not fit that norm until World War II. Long after other sections of the country had lost their agrarian character, a majority of the southern population remained bound to the soil in a variety of agricultural enterprises.[31] Moreover, in the agricultural districts, the tenant-landlord relationship was more pronounced in the South than anywhere else in the nation, including the Midwest where tenancy was high. At the onset of the Great Depression, those distinctive features of the region's agricultural economy crowded too many people on too little land. As Jack Temple Kirby has observed, that aged system of labor-intensive production "teetered on the brink of catastrophe."[32] Indeed, it would not survive the 1930s.

Much of western agriculture stood in sharp contrast to that practiced in the early twentieth-century South. The pacesetter and the model for agricultural modernization was of course California, where machines had displaced people and animals and where corporate capitalism had come to dominate the production process. Long before 1920 California already had established the precedent for modern agriculture: heavy capitalization, vertical corporate organization, and mechanical innovation.[33] And in methods that were to become common practice elsewhere in the West and in the nation, California led all other states in reducing labor as a factor in agricultural production and in elaborating a political economy and corporate structure that would promote the welfare of a publicly subsidized, hydraulically based society. California agriculture was in one sense artificial, "a created industry" that was largely dependent on irrigation.[34] That system, which quickly distinguished California and other sections of the arid West from the rest of the nation, was the antithesis of the kind of productive system practiced in most of the southern states. The federal agricultural subsidies that were dispensed in the two regions beginning with the New Deal had contrasting effects: in California federal programs aided and abetted agricultural systems already well established; in the South the federal largesse destroyed the old labor-intensive, premodern system and replaced it with thoroughly commercialized operations.

The larger technological innovations of the modernizing world of capitalist agriculture, especially those methods used in California's sprawling Central Valley, placed the special and enduring agricultural production system of the South—with its labor surplus and continued reliance on animal and human power—at risk. Federally subsidized science and reclamation policies, crop-subsidy programs, the boll weevil, and the depression contributed to the transformation of agricultural modes of production but especially in the South. Moreover, the changes introduced in one region caused reverberations in the other. Government research programs had always spurred technological change in California's industry and agriculture, but nowhere was this more apparent than in the rise of irrigated cotton growing in the San Joaquin Valley and in the development of mechanical pickers.[35]

As the boll weevil waged war against cotton growers in the Old South, federally sponsored developments in California contributed to the emergence and rapid expansion of cotton production in the flat, dry acreages of the San Joaquin Valley. The establishment of a U.S. Department of Agriculture station near Bakersfield in 1917 and the transfer of a Clemson University–trained department of agriculture official, Wofford B. Camp, to head it provides the immediate background to the story of cotton-growing in the valley. The San Joaquin Valley—"an empire in itself," Carey McWilliams has called it—was ideally suited to the introduction of large mechanical cultivating and harvesting equipment, especially among farmers with capital and a willingness to experiment. Hence, with the federal government permanently fixed as an important part of a broadly coordinated production system, cotton-growing quickly expanded in the Central Valley. By the close of World War II, cotton was California's leading crop and manufacturers were turning out record numbers of mechanical pickers.[36]

As a symbol for the new corporate order for California cotton production, Wofford B. Camp stands alone. "The government cotton man," as he became known in the Bakersfield area, quickly linked hands with the .5-million-acre Kern County Land Company in cooperative cotton-growing experiments. Within a year after his arrival Camp was suggesting to the agricultural elite the value of single-variety planting as the route to efficient and profitable agricultural enterprise. When cotton cultivation in the San Joaquin Valley proved successful, Camp then signed on with A. P. Giannini's Bank of Italy (soon to be the Bank of America) as an appraiser of agricultural properties and to advise on matters having to do with agriculture. Finally, as his personal interests and investment strategies moved toward land purchases and cotton-growing, Camp became an early and active member of the Associated Farmers of California, the notorious union-busting organization that represented the emergent agribusiness fraternity in the Central Valley. When the National Farm Labor Union struck the giant DiGiorgio Farms, Camp, then president of the Associated Farmers, was active in providing police protection for strike breakers and in otherwise helping to break the union.[37] "The cotton man" had arrived.

With its inclination toward large-scale operation and corporate organization and its heavy reliance on migratory farm labor, California agriculture was a pacesetter for the emergence of agribusiness elsewhere. "Here," Carey McWilliams has pointed out, "a new type of agriculture has been created: large-scale, intensive, diversified, mechanized." Its methods of planting, harvesting, processing, and marketing were highly receptive to the most modern forms of technological innovation, placing the region at the forefront in the transformation of agriculture. In a larger sense, California farmers defined the modern world of agriculture because their practices set them, and segments of the arid West, apart from the rest of the nation.[38] It was that system—in conjunction with the economic crisis of the 1930s and the New Deal programs that followed—that wrought such dramatic change in the southern countryside.

There is little question about the transforming influence of the vast federal presence in the West during the 1930s. Making significant contributions to the region's economic infrastructure, the government funded the building of dams and hydroelectrical power facilities and the expansion of reclamation projects in addition to the general run of New Deal economic-recovery programs. Government assistance, Richard Lowitt observes, "subsidized free enterprise in the West on a grand scale," much of the funding channeled through the Bureau of Reclamation, the principal federal agency involved in the transformation and making of the modernized West. Because of those federal undertakings, Lowitt argues, the region "became less dependent upon the industrial East."[39]

New Deal programs in the western United States clearly served as a powerful attraction to people looking for work or otherwise wishing to escape the grinding poverty that existed, especially in the drought-ravaged, economically depressed states of the southern plains. That intraregional shift, the twentieth-century version of the mythical westward migration, was only one part of a much larger movement of people in the United States, one that gathered increasing momentum with the onset of World War II. The dramatic expansion of economic activity in the West during that two-ocean conflict greatly accelerated forces already in motion—both the growth of the western economy and internal demographic shifts.[40] Although these observations are not particularly new, especially on issues addressing East/West and North/South links,

scholars have paid far less attention to the reciprocal relationships between the West and the South. Those connections, though perhaps not
as significant to either region as the ties with the federal government,
nevertheless were substantial. Moreover, an understanding of the mass
exodus of people from the southern plains, the Old South, and Appalachia reveals the dynamic and integrated character of the capitalist transformation that took place in the West and the South beginning in the
1930s and that has continued into the 1990s. Improvements in agricultural technology and more efficient farming techniques have forced the
exodus of rural Americans from the land throughout the twentieth century. But that process—some economists prefer the bloodless term modernization—was more obvious in the South because a large percentage of
its rural population remained on the land until recent times.

"The great lurch forward" in the restructuring of the southern economy from its labor-intensive farming and mill-village life to the world of
the modern agribusiness and industrial corporation paralleled the somewhat different transformation of the economy of the American West into
more diversified production components, including expanded industrial
and technological systems. The West emerged from the war, in Gerald
Nash's words, "with a burgeoning manufacturing complex, a bustling
service economy, and a bevy of aerospace, electronics, and science-ori-
ented industries that heralded a new phase of economic development
with the rise of a postindustrial economy."[41] The South, on the other
hand, was experiencing a wrenching crisis that involved a massive demographic movement from rural areas to the North and West and to urban centers in the region.

In the wake of a problematic textile industry, a failing agricultural
production system, and a style of racial segregation that was becoming
an increasing national and international embarrassment, the South was
in the midst of a period of turbulent change. Either by choice or by necessity millions of rural southerners left the agricultural countryside after
World War II. Traditional forms of work culture in the region gave way to
mechanized production, the widespread use of chemicals in agriculture,
and the emergence of large corporate units. Changes in the mode of agricultural production, "in social organization, and in the nature of rural
life," according to Pete Daniel, "proved the most revolutionary in southern history."[42]

The economic transformation of the South differed in several respects from the process that was taking place in the western United
States, and nowhere do those differences stand in sharper contrast than
in matters relating to demography. If the postbellum planters had been
the locus of economic power in the South, then as a group they represented "the vanguard of change" during the period of great agricultural

modernization in the region. When the larger southern landholders turned to mechanized equipment and began to adopt the organizational and marketing tools of the corporate world, the South was convulsed. The consequence was the uprooting of more than 8 million farm people who moved to urbanizing areas in the South or to the cities of the North, the Midwest, and the Far West.[43] In essence, the region became the great exporter of human beings searching for a better life elsewhere. In terms of its larger significance the twentieth-century movement to the North is comparable in importance to the westward migration of the nineteenth century.[44]

Beginning with the decade of the Great Depression and then with gathering momentum during World War II a combination of circumstances drove people from the land: federal agricultural policies, newly emergent competition from the California cotton producers, the move toward mechanized operations, and a growing belief that the southern countryside was economically at a dead end. Yet those changes were not the only ones that the stark, productive efficiency of the new forms of capitalist agriculture imposed on the region. The "enclosure movement" that accompanied the structural shakeout also meant an end to a "traditional furnishing system" that had provided material for housing and fuel as well as hunting and fishing privileges; indeed the new commodity value attached to the land prohibited those customs that should properly be termed subsistence practices.[45] The revolutionary effects of those changes were far-reaching: the capitalization and enclosure of southern agriculture was widespread, dramatic, and compressed in time, the equivalent, according to Jack Temple Kirby, "of the principal phase of the English Enclosure Movement of the last decades of the eighteenth century."[46]

The New Deal programs, otherwise intended to alleviate agricultural and rural poverty, undoubtedly aided and abetted the social and economic restructuring of southern life. "Instead of reviving the old system, as it promised," Pete Daniel points out, "the New Deal in many areas destroyed that system's remnants more thoroughly than Sherman's troops had wrecked antebellum dreams." The larger thrust of the federal assistance that was designed to aid poor farmers in actual practice redounded to the economic well-being of the middle and upper classes. The intervention of New Deal economic programs was ambivalent in the sense that the internal dynamics of capital were not taken into consideration: its ability to continually revolutionize the means of production, in this case through mechanization. While "the science arm of the USDA worked to create a new mode of production," Daniel concludes, "its social agencies sifted through plans to prop up the old structure."[47]

Ultimately, federal programs combined with the modernizing forces of capital to revolutionize both the agricultural and industrial South. A rural and agrarian region, "caught by time" in 1940, was transformed into an "urbanized, postindustrialized Sunbelt." Moreover, federal intervention in the form of national wage and labor standards established during the 1930s diminished some of the distinctiveness of the southern labor market. With the advent of the Kennedy-Johnson administrations, the exodus of people from the region was reversed, and a "counterstream" movement to the South from elsewhere in the United States began. Heavily capitalized forest-products corporations, employing the most advanced form of mechanized equipment on the relatively even terrain in the region, consolidated woodland holdings throughout the South.[48] Federally subsidized reforestation programs aided the industry's reemergence as a significant factor in wood-products output in the United States.

Although southern economic life has slowly converged with that of the rest of the country, the region's fundamental distinctiveness continues to persist in some ways: depressed wage structures, the relative absence of unionization, a generally lower per capita income than the national average, and a similar lagging behind in levels of literacy. Even the Atlanta Miracle has its obvious downside in the persisting marginalization of most black workers, who moved into the core of the city as whites moved out and whose employment chiefly depends on providing services for metropolitan showplaces.[49] James Cobb provides, in my view, the most appropriate summary for understanding the transformed South:

A century after Henry Grady's New South speech the fundamental elements of what manufacturers describe as the South's good business climate are still policies that promise cheap labor, low taxes, and stable, conservative government.[50]

As they did in the American West, changing world and national economic conditions played a critical role in forging what we know as the modern South. The transition from subsistence farming to manufacturing, from labor-intensive agricultural production to agribusiness operation, from rural-dominated social arrangements to urban metropolis brought the South full circle, or in the words of Jack Kirby, "from undercapitalized colonial dependency to complex, well-capitalized dependency." And some of the more notable subregions in the South, especially Appalachia, remain bound to the national economy through the absentee ownership of its wealth of resources, a fundamental characteristic of the relationship between advanced centers of industrial capital and resource-dependent areas. With its natural abundance in coal, minerals, and timber, Appalachia provides an excellent example of the manner in which corporate and increasingly multinational conglomerates gain access to land and resources and drain a region of its wealth.[51]

While the West lacked the South's structural and institutional constraints in regard to farming, its rural population suffered with the rest of the nation the wrenching transition to industrial, mechanized agriculture in the mid-twentieth century. The new, tractor-centered technology eroded the social- and economic-support systems in hinterland communities, depopulated the countryside, and thereby accelerated the disintegration of the ideals and values associated with the land and with preindustrial agriculture.[52] Just as in the South, the machine's capacity to restructure life in the West was pronounced. But there were major differences: the region's most productive sector, California, led the nation in reducing labor as a factor in agricultural output; the West lacked an isolated, surplus-labor market; and for much of the area from the Great Plains west to the Pacific, corporate capitalism already had made significant inroads in shaping systems of agricultural production. The agricultural West also led the nation in modern forms of labor struggles as field hands and food-processing workers confronted the power of the agribusiness corporations and the state in their efforts to control events and conditions in the work place.[53]

Beyond the rural farming sector, the West presented special opportunities for capital that were absent in the South. Because its conquest and its annexation to the expanding American empire were relatively recent and because of its vast wealth in space and resources, the West presented few obstacles in the way of capital to work its will. Most important, the structural and institutional restraints that slowed the pace of the capitalist transformation in the South did not exist in the West. In contrast to the South, economic enterprise in the West was both expansive and dynamic during the seventy-year period following the Civil War. The relationship between the development of capitalism and the transformation of the American West was immediate and direct; in the South the tempo of economic and social change did not gain significant momentum until the 1930s.[54] The West therefore offers a more clearly delineated and unbridled example of capitalist development, unencumbered by ties to a feudal past or to historically institutionalized restraints. Its earlier integration into national and international economic relationships reflects the diversity of the integrative forces of modern capital.

CHAPTER NINE

Of Country and City: The Metropolis and Hinterland in the Modern West

History, when it transcends chronicle, romance, and ideology—including "left-wing" versions—is primarily the story of who rides whom and how.
—*Elizabeth Fox-Genovese and Eugene Genovese*[1]

West of Omaha, Nebraska, the landscape opens, the distance between towns lengthens, and except for east-west traffic, the intensity and volume of human activity noticeably lessens. Somewhere toward the middle of the state the air becomes markedly less humid; here, the Nebraska Chamber of Commerce informs travelers, is "the place where the West begins." Ian Frazier's best-seller *Great Plains* reminds readers of another reality about the land reaching toward the western horizon: "Money and power in this country concentrate elsewhere." In a "spiritual geography" of the Dakota's West River country, Kathleen Norris calls the region "a school for humility," where "our inability to influence either big business or big government is turning all Dakotans into a kind of underclass." The area has always been sparsely settled, a place with few urban and metropolitan centers, and thus the relationship of that West to the rest of the nation has been strikingly colonial.[2]

But the Great Plains stretching from the Canadian prairies to the Mexican border is of a piece with the Intermountain region, the Southwest, the Columbia and Snake river plains, Alaska, and sizable portions of other western states—an area that Joel Garreau has termed "the Empty Quarter." Carey McWilliams's remark of forty years ago that California has served as the urban center for the other western states strikes close to reality. The Far West and the continental West were different, another writer insists: the former "eventually found its own resources and developed them, and the money stayed at home."[3] Yet with the large exception of its Pacific and southern perimeters, most of the West lacks that which the word metropolis brings to mind: images of power, a centeredness to things, and for students of political economy, seats of industrial and financial organization. But the enormous distances and seeming emptiness across that sometimes harsh and rugged landscape belie its significance in the larger arena of national and world affairs. There is an essentially different quality to much of the West.[4]

With respect to the dynamics of population, therefore, the Empty Quarter is an appropriate metaphor for large sections of the region. A richly endowed wealth of natural resources, a sparse and scattered people, and great distances to markets characterize its hinterland areas. The decennial census reports portray the West in cold statistical terms, but those percentage figures and averages reveal little about the dynamics of its population configurations. Although some scholars ascribe progress and success to the region because of the great urban centers that concentrate on its perimeters, another less flattering, even tragic, reality better describes its vast hinterlands.[5]

Begin with Kellogg, Idaho, where more silver has been mined during the last century than in any other place in the world. The famed Silver Valley, with its ribbon of mining towns extending from Smelterville to Wallace, was once alive with the vital stuff of working-class life. Today, the barren hillsides around Kellogg and the huge slag heap at one end of town are the singular reminders of those industrial successes. Abundant evidence throughout the valley indicates that the great wealth produced during the exploitation of those mineral riches did not remain with the mining communities. Indeed, the current efforts of local promoters to refashion Kellogg into the Aspen of northern Idaho, complete with Bavarian motifs, suggest the desperation that has settled on those towns in the wake of several mine closures.[6]

Despite its once plentiful mineral ores and its location astride Interstate 90, the old Coeur d'Alene district is at one with other hinterland regions in the American West—areas that have contributed enormously to the successes of industrial capitalism in the United States and elsewhere. In that sense, Kellogg is a stark example of exploitation in the modern capitalist state: the extraction of great wealth through the exploitation of resource-rich areas and its appropriation by metropolitan bases of capital. The example of Kellogg also points to a major historical feature of economic relations in the United States: the flow of investment capital has been one of unequal exchange in which financial and industrial centers persistently draw resource-rich peripheral regions within their spheres of influence. Hence, colonialism, as many scholars have argued, is both an external and an internal phenomenon; the dividing line between dominant economies and dominated ones runs both between and within nations in the capitalist world. In that respect, the history of regional relationships in the United States, especially as the twentieth century has advanced, is complex and contradictory, resembling a mix of the imperial and the colonial at the same moment. In the years since World

War II, the older, stark delineations between an exploiting East and an exploited West no longer hold true.[7]

In western North America those circumstances cross international boundaries. Despite its large size, Canada's population is geographically concentrated into a chain of city-states, with each link dominating a vast hinterland, especially in the western reaches of the continent. At the onset of the twentieth century the basis for regional underdevelopment and metropolitan dominance of the hinterland was set by a greatly overbuilt rail system heavily indebted to British capital and to an American-controlled manufacturing sector. The sociologist Patricia Marchak has clearly stated the case as it applies in the Canadian West, where the metropolis has exploited the backcountry, a process that has contributed to the underdevelopment of the latter. In that set of relationships, she points out, hinterland areas find it impossible to reverse exploitation and hence become "poorer and less powerful." For the great timbered backcountry in British Columbia, writer Ken Drushka observes, "There has always been a tendency for resource decision-making to occur in the urban centres of Victoria and Vancouver." Historian Carlos Schwantes has called the long history of worker protest against the metropolitan control of the resource-rich rural West an "ideology of disinheritance."[8] Although the rural sectors of neither the Canadian nor the American West are unique, the distinctive configuration of urban-rural relations in those two Wests raises larger questions associated with change in the modern world. Because today's circumstances build cumulatively upon those of the past, they deserve historical explanation.

As a methodology for the study of western American history, the urban/hinterland dichotomy suggests a certain ambiguity and crudeness. It may be true, as Karl Marx observed, that the urban/rural distinction was an expression of the division of labor. Hence, to regard it as fundamental was to focus on an irrelevant phenomenon because the real issue rested in the problem of the division of labor. Marx's insight about specialization and the division of labor is appropriate; still, there is an undeniable utility in the urban/rural concept as a general way of understanding power relationships both within the West and beyond. There is little question that the great motive force of modern economic life has been centered in the metropolis. Fernand Braudel expressed it well when he drew a distinction between center and more distant peripheral areas in which the latter "in the division of labor . . . are subordinates rather than true participants." There were, he said, "increasingly fewer advantages as one moves out from the triumphant pole." Braudel pointed to a powerful truth—the lack of autonomy in the countryside, no matter the degree of radical insurgency involved. Indeed, the intensity of struggle in the hinterland gives legitimacy, in my view, to the ideological power of the rural/urban distinction.[9]

The use of urban/hinterland or core/periphery relations in the larger context of capitalist expansion and development is not meant to set up static, unchanging categories, which, I think, lead nowhere. Nor do I subscribe to a stark victim/victimizer dichotomy but rather to a continuum with dynamic categories of the relatively more powerful and the relatively less powerful. Ivan T. Berend and Gyorgy Ranki, in *The European Periphery and Industrialization*, propose that discussions of core/periphery be treated as "historical categories with ever-changing references." Based on the notion of a series of spatial zones, with each a complex functional part of the international division of labor, world-systems analysis offers a central truth in which aggregate decisions of individual capitalists assume a larger logic that transcends political boundaries in the quest for capital accumulation. In that sense I believe there is utility in using core/periphery, urban/hinterland relations as a general model for analysis. The intention here is not to test or to prove but to seek a strategy for framing new questions about power relationships in the American West.[10]

Scholarly discourse on metropolitan/hinterland, core/periphery relations (or dependency theory) has proliferated in the last two decades. The more notable debates have revolved around Third World dependency issues and the theoretical works of Immanuel Wallerstein, Fernand Braudel, Leften Stavrianos, Andre Gorz, and Andre Gunder Frank, but scholars have paid little attention to those questions within the United States. For the American West, only in the last decade or so have there been hints and suggestions about the potential for such a line of inquiry: Richard White's *Roots of Dependency*, John Thompson's *Closing the Frontier*, Thomas D. Hall's *Social Change in the Southwest*, and Sarah Deutsch's *No Separate Refuge*.[11]

But with the publication of William Cronon's *Nature's Metropolis*, a brilliant tour de force and an exhaustive inquiry into the city-country dichotomy in a mid-American setting, the theoretical framework and the symbiotic relationship between metropole and hinterland have been given convincing narrative form. In the matter of Chicago's amazing growth in the nineteenth century, Cronon observes, city and country "were hardly isolated":

Chicago had become "urban," spawning belching smokestacks and crowded streets, at the same time that the lands around it became "rural," yielding not grass and red-winged blackbirds but wheat, corn, and hogs. Chicago's merchants and workers had built their warehouses and factories in the same decades that farmers had plowed up the prairie sod and lumberjacks had cut the great pine trees of the north woods. City and country shared a common past, and had fundamentally reshaped each other.

The central theme to nineteenth-century western history, according to Cronon, "is that of an expanding metropolitan economy creating ever more elaborate and intimate linkages between city and country."[12] As for the expanding urban centers in the Great West beyond Chicago, the power relationship between city and country was even more striking; with the exception of the Far West after World War II, most western cities continued to exercise unchallenged control over immense tributary regions. The western experience during the last century or more gives substance to geographer Michael Conzen's judgment: "The larger the city, the wider its horizons, and the more elaborate its set of hinterlands."[13]

The argument presented here will examine the evolution of urban/ hinterland relations in the American West, the expanding power and influence of metropolitan centers, and the corresponding increase in dependency of its rural sectors. I am particularly interested in the way in which the metropolis, as an expression of strategic and powerful elements within the world of a modernizing capitalist system, conditioned life in the countryside. Richard White refers to "a syndrome of social, political, and economic characteristics" that contributed to conditions of subserviency. He suggests the examination of an interrelated series of phenomenon as the most fruitful empirical approach to understanding differences in associations that are essentially relationships of power: "the extent to which economic activities within a region only reflect factors essentially controlled outside the area; the lack of economic diversification and choice; and domestic distortions—social and political, as well as economic—within affected societies."[14] In essence, a constellation of these factors and others would appear to hold rich potential for assessing the intimate relationship between change in the modern West and the dynamics of modern capitalism.

The insights of critical urban theorists also have much to contribute to an understanding of urban/hinterland relations. Money represents the concentration of social power, David Harvey has argued, and financial markets, like money, "embody immense powers of centralization." That centralizing tendency under capitalism, accordingly, has contributed to the concentration of decisionmaking in urban centers and to the "hierarchical geographical ordering of financial centers into a system of authority and control."[15] It follows, therefore, that those highly centralized control and command functions (in the realms of both government and finance) embody great power to order the world about them. First centered in the eastern United States, and then in the emergent San

Francisco and other growing urban bases in the region, the influence of the metropolis has always loomed large in the American West.

Ann Markusen has pointed out that the United States provides a unique opportunity for examining regionalism in "a more purely capitalistic setting, with relatively fewer cultural complications."[16] In that respect, the North American continent (but especially its western portions) offers a fascinating physical environment for the study of the dynamic, sometimes wrenching changes that have accompanied the expansion of modern capitalism. As it did elsewhere, the extension of the market economy from the Atlantic-based metropolitan world revolutionized conditions in hinterland regions around the globe.[17] Perhaps nowhere have those changes been so striking as in the American West where the market system made inroads at a relatively late stage in the evolution of capitalist social relations. The point may seem trite, but in the West things happened fast.

As the most newly settled of the Euro-American dominated regions in the United States, the American West has experienced dramatic and recent metropolitan development (in comparison with urban centers elsewhere). And yet the most persisting themes in western literature are centered primarily on symbols and images of rural, backcountry life. The protagonists in regional fiction, urban historian Carl Abbott contends, represent the broad spectrum of hinterland occupational and folk characters, who experience life "in the land of wind and storm." Moreover, there is a prevailing tendency to recognize as legitimate writers "only those artists who deal with small towns and open landscapes." The major author in this context, of course, is Wallace Stegner.[18]

But beyond the realm of western cultural myth—in the larger context of political and economic power—the urban West was from the very beginning at the center of a burgeoning capitalist expansion with a commercial reach that extended well past the boundaries of the nation-state. The tumultuous circumstances and the dynamics of change in the region paralleled the emergence of the United States as a global power and the larger transformation of the modern world: population increases, expanding urban networks, industrialization, and the rise of corporate capitalism. In the new global geography, western cities such as San Francisco and Denver served as conduits, facilitating the distribution of foreign capital, developing the necessary infrastructure to service regional markets, and arranging the transshipment of local resources to places of manufacture. In that sense, the repeopling of the West with new and dominant forms of settlement paralleled the establishment of what Walter Nugent calls the "metropolitan mode."[19] With its vast hinterland, abundant resources, and rapid urban growth, the West affords an ideal setting and pattern of relationships for reflecting upon those issues.

The expansion of market capitalism outward from Atlantic-centered metropolitan communities has attracted the attention of numerous scholars during the last fifty years. Yet even before the turn of the century a few shrewd observers were aware of the influence of the metropolis on the countryside. And some of them, such as David Wasson, a Unitarian minister, expressed concern about issues other than the old bugaboo of industrial blight on the growing urban populations. Wasson remarked in an 1874 essay in *North American Review* that the countryside had become little more than a suburb of the city; the "autonomous life" of rural America, he noted, had "as good as disappeared."[20] What some writers today refer to as the "death of the countryside," had its North American beginnings in the nineteenth century and on the Atlantic side of the continent.

Another late nineteenth-century observer who recognized the effects of urbanization on rural areas was Adna Weber, whose *Growth of Cities in the Nineteenth Century* is one of the early and authoritative classics on the subject. "In the surrender of the small producer to the corporation and trust," he cautioned, "lies . . . the explanation of the decay of village or local industries." Using census data, Weber indicated that the rural population of the Northeast and the upper Midwest had declined between 1880 and 1890, a phenomenon that he attributed directly to an agricultural system languishing under the competition from Western farms.[21] Following the pattern in Europe, the successes of western agriculture contributed to the impoverishment of the countryside in the northeastern United States. Like Wasson and Weber (the latter was just beginning his professional career when his book appeared), few late-nineteenth-century Americans reflected on the larger question of eastern metropolitan influence on the trans-Mississippi West.

In a series of essays and in one important book, Walter Prescott Webb was the first prominent historian of the American West to bring scholarly attention to the reciprocal relationships between metropolis and hinterland. Webb's vision was all-encompassing; he likened western Europe at the onset of the Columbian voyage to a metropolitan center poised to take advantage of the vast continents beyond its shores, areas with resources in abundance that he dubbed the Great Frontier. It was to the success and glory of the metropolis that it lay proprietary claim to that wealth. But the Texas historian's focus on the metropolitan plunder of hinterlands had its limitations: capitalism was not the centerpiece of Webb's critique, even in his strident denunciations of the American establishment for treating the West as a mercantilist province of eastern capital.[22]

Henry Nash Smith also noted the pull of the metropolis although his argument was more sharply focused than Webb's. The most significant forces directing the course of American life following the Civil War, according to Smith, were "the machine, the devices of corporation finance, and the power of big business over Congress." The metropolis loomed large in determining configurations of influence in the industrial age, he contended, and made agrarian theory (adherence to the homestead myth) irrelevant; industry, urbanization, and international events provided a more adequate forum for understanding the modern West.[23]

In his influential study of the Far West, *The Pacific Slope*, Earl Pomeroy also emphasized the power of the metropolis in shaping the course of western development. Boston and New York, "the first cities of the coast," were principal determinants in directing commercial and financial traffic with Pacific ports, even long after the emergence of San Francisco as the preeminent urban center of the West. With the extension of the United States to the Pacific, cities developed "both because distance required them and geography invited them."[24] Yet Pomeroy's emphasis on urbanness and continuity in the West did not fully embrace the larger issue of the world of capitalism and relations between the region's urban centers of power and the surrounding countryside. Moreover, a casual perusal of historical scholarship on the American West reveals the obvious: the real West was not urban. And yet, as John Findlay points out, the "inauthentic" urban West has been at the center of regional development; it is time, he concludes, for a more inclusive story, one that embraces western "city-dwellers more on their own terms, rather than as a by-product of some defunct 'true' West."[25]

Although there are obvious strands of continuity in the focus on metropolitan development in both the East and the West, there are also parallels in the relative impoverishment and lack of power in their respective rural sectors. In both regions, as elsewhere in the world of modernizing capitalism, the expanding mechanisms of exchange have favored commercial centers. But the area beyond the metropolis was vital to the development and growth of industrial capitalism: as a market, as a provider of cheap foodstuffs, as a source of labor, and—especially in the West—as a storehouse of valuable raw material. The function of the countryside in that set of arrangements, according to one scholar, was "to remain a backwater, to remain dependent."[26]

The American West was unique in two additional respects: in the recentness of its dominant forms of settlement and in its geography—distance, vast spaces, far-flung settlement patterns—which conferred great advantage to those powers who controlled strategic locations such as the confluence of rivers, natural coastal ports, or convenient places adjacent to the Rocky Mountains. It is also important to recognize that conscious decisions made in the larger metropolitan centers dictated the allocation of investment capital in specific places in the West. Capitalists, after all, work as assiduously to shape the world according to their interests as do those individuals who oppose them. It follows, then, that urban environments were not a consequence of free-market forces; rather, they reflected the conscious decisions of influential private *and* public individuals.[27]

Metropolitan centers in the West did not develop, therefore, as isolated and autonomous islands—nor did the countryside. Capital linkages to eastern and transatlantic investment houses heavily influenced urban development west of the Mississippi River and directed the course of the exploitation of resources in the countryside. Older centers of capital accumulation provided the large infusions of financing required to bring into being infrastructures of transportation, manufacturing enterprises, and the other accoutrements of the larger built environment. Primary command centers in the East and in Europe funded the development of the initial western metropolitan power bases of San Francisco and Denver. Earl Pomeroy indicates that even after San Francisco became an imperial city in its own right, its business sector continued to pay homage to larger and more distant capital agglomerations. Nor do international boundaries appreciably alter the development of metropolitan areas; Seattle and Vancouver, British Columbia, prospered and suffered in concert with railroad booms, depressions, mining rushes, immigrant movements, and world wars.[28]

The American West serves as a prototype for examining urban/hinterland relations under capitalism in still another way. Because the most powerful elements in capitalist social relations derive their authority from the ability to control allocative resources, it follows that the most significant places of capital accumulation would be the locus for decisions affecting the tiniest of hinterland outposts.[29] In Appalachia, John Gaventa found that the forces "which propelled the development of a capital-intensive, resource-extractive" economy "lay *not* in Appalachia but in the economic and energy demands of the British and American metropolis."[30] That observation also fits the history of eastern U.S. and European investment in mining activity, railroad construction, reclamation projects, and other ventures in the effort to gain access to western resources. Urban areas thus grew in accord with the degree and volume of capital invested in the adjacent countryside.

Eventually, as accumulations of surplus capital emerged in western metropolitan centers, the ultimate decisionmakers sometimes were closer to the scene of action. That did little to alter the basic power configurations between city and countryside, however. Western cities and towns, themselves subordinate to eastern capital, "thickened" their own regional networks of domination through the extension of transportation and communication links to their contiguous hinterlands.[31] At the local or subregional level that relationship replicated larger continental, even intercontinental, associations. The relationship between San Francisco and the Central Valley, Portland and the Willamette Valley, or Denver and the central Rocky Mountains reflected the influence of Chicago and its vast reach throughout the rural West. In the latter instance, William Cronon observes, although western towns competed fiercely for railroads, "the eastern terminus was never in doubt. All roads led to Chicago."[32]

With only a few exceptions, most of the important urban centers in the western United States originated as Pacific coastal ports or railroad towns. Rail transport, because it was largely liberated from the strictures of geography, was critical in linking sources of raw materials in the broad expanses of the West with urban processing and manufacturing centers and ultimately with distant markets. The railroads also illustrated the propensity of capitalism to repeated technological innovation in the interests of greater profits: they accelerated the commodification of nature (making raw materials economically accessible); they inflated values in real estate; and they represented an agglomeration of capital "designed to make more capital." The new mode of transportation was also revolutionary in another sense; it aided and abetted the development of larger metropolitan areas to the detriment of smaller ones. Although the expanding network of rails brought countless new small towns into existence, in the larger scheme of things those networks confirmed Adna Weber's observation that commerce "favors the great centers, rather than the small or intermediate ones."[33]

The railroad was also the catalyst for the mining boom that occurred in the central Rocky Mountains during the 1870s and 1880s. Although other rail lines were involved, William Jackson Palmer and the Denver and Rio Grande Railroad were the most active in pushing new lines in the mountains south and west of Denver. The sudden emergence of the new mining camps and supply towns made the Rocky Mountain area remarkably urban, especially given the region's small population. The federal census for 1880 indicated that more than two-thirds of the population of the territories of Colorado, Wyoming, and Montana lived in urban settings or within a short reach of a mining town.[34]

Although the railroad redirected the demographic makeup of the West, its most significant long-range effect was to centralize population, financial and banking houses, federal offices, and other decisionmaking institutions. The new roads bound the urban-service infrastructures, the vast hinterland beyond, and distant markets and industrial centers into a cohesive system. In the set of relationships that emerged, the countryside became ever more closely integrated into the fabric of an urban-based capitalist network. "Not only did the railroad system make modern technology visible, intruding it as a physical presence in daily life," Alan Trachtenberg contends, "but it also offered means of exercising unexampled ruthlessness of economic power." The railroad symbolized the influence of great financial interests and the power of the metropolis over the countryside. Rails meant speed, predictable schedules, the ability to move goods in any season; they also were great centralizing forces. Earl Pomeroy argues that for a time and within their realms "the lords of the rails ruled as probably only the DuPonts have ruled in Delaware or the copper magnets in Montana."[35]

One of the more striking examples of the influence of the railroad on regional geography is the rise of Dallas, Texas, in the last quarter of the nineteenth century. Serving as the transportation crossroads for a surrounding extractive economy, Dallas developed both as a distribution center for its own hinterland and as the center point for transport arterials reaching north, east, south, and west. Until the oil rush that began with the strike at Beaumont in 1901, Dallas was an integral link in a colonial relationship—shipping raw materials to the industrialized world and transshipping incoming manufactured products to its own countryside.[36]

Yet not all railroad towns enjoyed endless years of economic boom. When the profit-and-loss margins on their ledger books dictated, the financial magnates who underwrote the great rail ventures in the West could take away as easily as they had given earlier. In the aftermath of the panic of 1893 Jacob Hunsaker, mayor of the demoralized lumber town of Everett, Washington, lamented: "Our city is built upon the heads of corporations, by them conceived and rocked in the cradle of their nursery . . . their interest and that of the humblest citizen cannot but be identical." Hunsaker, himself a speculator in town lots, lost everything when James J. Hill's Great Northern Railroad ceased all construction activity and other distant financiers (notably the Rockefeller interests) withdrew investment promises.[37] Moreover, the effects of those distant corporate decisions were not unique to Everett, nor were such actions confined solely to the 1890s.

Some emerging transportation hubs moved quickly to consolidate tributary relationships with adjacent regions. With the powerful pull of Chicago to their east, Saint Paul and Minneapolis capitalists worked diligently to extend their economic and political influence west into the Dakotas. As the rail lines pushed farther onto the northern plains and the acreage planted to wheat expanded, the functional capital of North Dakota during its early statehood years was Saint Paul rather than Bismarck. Because of regional control of the great continental lines—the Northern Pacific and Great Northern—and because the grain and milling industry resided in the Twin Cities, North Dakota remained subservient to outside financial influences. "It has always been true, and it is still true today," two scholars argue, "that the major agricultural products of North Dakota are marketed outside the state's borders by corporations headquartered outside the state."[38] Although geography and the logic of capital may have contributed to those circumstances, it is also reasonable to assume that those same forces also helped foster the state's historic tradition of insurgent politics.

The control of strategic locations confers great power in determining the allocation of resources and access to markets and in the ability to expand economic activity. Fundamental to the social relations of capitalism—and this was especially true of the American West—was a fiercely competitive global struggle for superior positioning in transportation, trade, and in the processing of raw materials. Because the great mass of capital and social expenditures has traditionally been directed toward urban environments, merchants, bankers, manufacturers, and others who established themselves in the more important western metropolitan centers enjoyed great advantage. Nowhere was favorable location more apparent than in San Francisco, the prototype for the rapid development of an urban power base in the nineteenth-century West. The Queen City, in Pomeroy's words "was first in time and for long first in power."[39]

Virtually with the discovery of gold San Francisco emerged as the imperial heart of a vast trading network that extended the length of the Pacific Coast and inland as far as the Rocky Mountains. The gold rush, Carey McWilliams has argued, established the burgeoning bay metropolis for fifty years as the capital of the western empire: "It drew the first transcontinental railroad directly to San Francisco. And, above all, it got California off to a flying start, decades ahead of the other western states." By the time the United States entered World War I, Wallace Stegner points out, San Francisco was already a global city: "worldly, rich, energetic, violent, wicked and used to the exercise of power and influence."[40] Indeed, San Francisco was an entrepreneur's dream, especially for those who supplied goods and services to the area and who equipped and outfitted the treasure seekers swarming through the backcountry.

As the preeminent "city-state" on the Pacific slope, San Francisco dominated trade relations from Panama north to Alaska until late in the nineteenth century. John Agnew includes San Francisco with New Orleans and Minneapolis as gateway cities, peripheral centers in resource regions linked by rail and sea to the manufacturing core of the East. Already the fifteenth largest city in the United States at the onset of the Civil War, it ranked ninth in 1880 (and was the only sizable city west of St. Louis) with a population of 233,959. At that point, San Francisco numbered more people than the combined population of Oregon and Washington, and its local traders controlled 99 percent of all imports on the coast and 83 percent of all exports. Using data from the 1880 census, William Issel and Robert Cherny have described that statistical dominance:

> For thirty years after the discovery of gold, San Francisco stood virtually unchallenged as the economic capital of the Pacific slope. . . . The city had more manufacturing establishments, more employees in workshops, greater capitalization, larger value of materials, and higher value of products than all the other twenty-four western cities combined.[41]

The rapidly growing metropolis attracted capital and enterprising capitalists from all points and all at once (and it continued to do so into the twentieth century). Like Portland and Seattle to the north and Los Angeles to the south, San Francisco benefited from the increased economic activity in its hinterland. Gold flowed to the Bay Area and helped turn San Francisco into a major center for the colonization of the interior West, enabling the city to gain a degree of autonomy from the constraints of eastern capital. Federal land grants, public funding for harbor improvements and other forms of support for its infrastructure aided San Francisco's development; those public subsidies also reflected the close ties between finance and politics. Powerful capitalists exercised political influence at all levels and played to the natural advantages of geography to enhance and expand certain locations to the detriment of others. San Francisco Bay (Oakland, to be precise) became the rail terminus for the first transcontinental railroad because of the conscious activities of powerful and prominent individuals. In that respect, San Francisco was the first western metropolitan center to benefit from that form of political activism.[42]

According to William Issel and Robert Cherny, only New York and San Francisco among major late-nineteenth-century American cities enjoyed a semblance of economic autonomy. Although the city's business activities enjoyed a broad geographic spread and ranged through a wide variety of industrial pursuits, decisions were made mostly in the corporate boardrooms of San Francisco. Issel and Cherny are blunt about the influence that San Francisco's entrepreneurs exercised over the Pacific slope: "They operated on an imperial scale." By the early twentieth century the city's economic tentacles extended from Alaska to Panama, from Hawaiian sugar plantations to the mining districts of northern Idaho. San Francisco pioneered the establishment of California's historic satellite relationships with Alaska, Washington, Oregon, Idaho, Nevada, Arizona, and Hawaii.[43] And with the emergence of the Bank of America and the Bechtel Corporation by the time of World War II, San Francisco's reach became truly global.

Although the 1980 census for California reported that San Francisco's population had dropped to third place behind Los Angeles and San Diego, the city presently occupies an even more important position in the world capitalist system; it ranks only behind New York as a primary center for international banking houses. Because of their changing corporate structures and the variety of services they offer, New York and San Francisco mark the emergence of "global cities," centers of international business decisions and places for formulating corporate strategies. Moreover, San Francisco's major firms, the Bechtel Corporation still among them, cast their plans on a worldwide scale, and presidential administrations have periodically selected the city's business executives for national and international political and banking leadership positions.[44] The city thus continues its historic tradition of serving as the dominant urban center for northern California and the surrounding hinterland.

Two other West Coast port cities, Los Angeles and Seattle, also grew rapidly when local capitalists successfully attracted railways to their communities (the Santa Fe and the Great Northern). Similar developments unfolded in the interior where convenient location and collusion between local and distant capitalists brought rail lines to places such as Spokane, Denver, El Paso, and Albuquerque. Each of those emerging communities, in turn, serviced (and dominated) an expanding agricultural, lumbering, and mining hinterland.[45] Subsidies and other forms of support for the construction of the railroads demonstrate the formidable federal presence that has aided and abetted capitalist expansion in the vicinity of each of those settlements.

Situated in a rather nondescript high plain on the eastern front of the Rocky Mountains, Denver is a bit of an anomaly in western urban development because it enjoys none of the conventional and strategic advantages of natural location. Good fortune and the zealous activities of local promoters (with appropriate links to powerful eastern capitalists) contributed to the phenomenal growth of Denver into what Gunther Barth has dubbed the most striking example of an "instant city" in the nineteenth-century West. William Gilpin, the effusive railroad and town promoter, proclaimed the geographic potential of the budding township: Denver was the "isothermal axis," the point where the worlds of the Atlantic and Pacific met; "We consent to face about! The rear becomes the front! Asia in the front; Europe in the rear!"[46]

Railroad trunk lines constructed during the 1870s centered on Denver, triggering the community's growth. The city's population leaped from 4,759 in 1870 to 106,713 in 1890, turning the "paper city" of the gold rush at the juncture of South Platte Creek and Cherry Creek into the dominant metropolis in the central Rocky Mountain region. In the process, Denver quickly surpassed other front-range towns—Leadville and Cheyenne the most conspicuous—with similar aspirations. During Colorado's major period of mineral development, Denver served as the central distribution point for eastern investment along the Rocky Mountain cordillera. The growing metropolis emerged as the geographic nexus and regional command post for the extraction of wealth that added to the great fortunes of such families as the Rockefellers and the Guggenheims. The authors of Colorado's centennial history describe Denver as a conduit, an agency for channeling external influence: "If Colorado and other western states have been economic colonies of the East, as numerous writers have complained, then Denver has been one of the colonial capitals."[47]

Denver's position as a preeminent commercial, manufacturing, transportation, and administrative center continued to gain strength with the twentieth century. Moreover, in the city's growing hegemony over its vast hinterland, the role of the state—heavily influenced by the most important capitalist actors—loomed large. An active chamber of commerce, cognizant of the importance of federal influence in the building of an urban power base, strove to keep old military bases open and to gain funding for the construction of a rehabilitation center for military personnel during World War I. Its successes merely prefaced the chamber's activities in the following decades.

During the Great Depression, the Denver Chamber of Commerce launched a Little Capital of the United States campaign designed to expand existing federal bureaucracies and to attract new ones. The increasing number of federal employees in the greater urban area testifies to the successes of that effort and to the growing influence of the Mile High metropolis. At the onset of the Great Depression the federal government headquartered more than 2,000 employees to administer its programs in the Rocky Mountain region. After Denver's intensive lobbying in the 1930s and during World War II, the number of federal civilian employees had grown to 16,456. Because the federal government had made large land purchases in the area, it was deemed economically prudent to build a huge regional center in greater Denver after the war. Hence, more than 33,000 federal employees worked in the greater Denver area in 1980, a larger number than in any other urban center with the exception of Washington, D.C. Denver's power structure, Lyle Dorsett has argued, was more active and successful than its competitors in attracting an expanded federal presence to the region.[48]

The federal infrastructure present in metropolitan Denver has made the area an ideal location for a variety of defense-related development activities in the last few decades. As a consequence, Colorado's preeminent city has emerged as a major center for the defense industry and as the regional headquarters (or as the location for important branch operations) of high-technology aerospace and electronics firms. In an innovative study of the new American West, Peter Wiley and Robert Gottlieb have raised questions about the extent of the city's autonomy in an age of global capitalism: "Despite the population growth, despite the energy boom, and despite the emerging 'professionalism' of its business elite, Denver remained, as it entered the 1980s, a city 'under the influence.'" Its leaders, they argue, continued to look eastward and westward "for leadership and direction" from companies and financial centers that dominate the interior West: "Ultimately, Denver remains a secondary center of power whose major role consists of dominating other, more exploited regions of the interior."[49]

The historic circumstances of two cities at the northern and southern reaches of the West, El Paso and Spokane, provide still other examples of secondary urban power centers in the West. The development of the two urban enclaves suggests the multiple meanings of the city-country relationship: the role of external capital, the domination of an extensive hinterland, the emergence of a sizable federal influence, and the intimate ties between local and distant entrepreneurs. For El Paso, situated at a historic and ultimately strategic international trafficway and commandeering an extensive hinterland on both sides of the U.S.-Mexican border, railroads provided the transportation infrastructure so vital to early economic expansion. Linked to both the Southern Pacific and the Santa Fe roads in 1881 and with connections to Los Angeles, Denver, New Orleans, and the Midwest, El Paso grew apace as the preeminent crossroads and trade center on the U.S.-Mexican border. The completion of the north-south Mexican Central Railroad in 1884 enhanced El Paso's position as an international trading entrepôt. Ciudad Juarez, its counterpart on the Mexican side of the Rio Grande, evolved as the northern outpost of a developing country, but El Paso emerged as the most important southwestern metropolis of a highly developed modern industrial power.[50]

With its rail ties to the surrounding countryside, El Paso quickly took on the appearance of a regional satellite. Linked to eastern capitalists who financed the ventures, who developed the marketing arrangements for the raw materials, and who provided the engineering and accounting skills and manufactured equipment necessary to exploit the region's resources, El Paso dominated economic activity in western Texas, southern New Mexico and Arizona, and northern Mexico, especially the state of Chihuahua. One of the oasis towns in the American Southwest, El Paso symbolized an urban enterprise that exercised an imperial presence over the vast spaces of a sparsely populated region. Moreover, as one of the spearheads of development in the southwestern desert country, the rapidly growing city served as the principal accounting hub for relations between its own hinterland and more distant centers of capital and population.[51] As investment capital flowed into regional agricultural and mineral enterprises, El Paso quickly became part of a larger commercial system that involved both rural development and metropolitan expansion.

Yet in the larger, perpetually changing world of a modernizing capitalist system, El Paso was a lesser satellite, a point of transfer, a subsidiary to more powerful industrial and banking centers elsewhere. Its singular strategic importance for most of the twentieth century has rested in its location as a convenient port of trade and distribution point for the region's extractive economy and as a service center for American investments in Mexico. El Paso was a central outpost for incredibly profitable economic enterprises, with the great bulk of that wealth accruing to distant investors. The huge ASARCO facility there symbolized the colonial and exploitive nature of its economy. Beginning as a processing company with most of its profits coming from the smelting and refining of lead and silver, the Guggenheim- and Lewisohn-controlled El Paso operation was for many years the area's largest employer. In that capacity the firm further integrated the region into the larger network of national and international economic relations.[52]

But El Paso was more than an ASARCO town. International events—a decade of revolution in Mexico and World War I in Europe—deeply influenced its social and public life. Indeed, the city became the way station for revolutionary and counterrevolutionary maneuvering and the command post and supply base for the U.S. punitive expedition into Mexico in 1916. And even though El Paso was the regional outpost of one empire, serving as the headquarters for the financial and industrial infrastructure that extended through an extensive tributary region on both sides of the border, it also harbored a deep attachment to Mexico. Culture and politics intersected (especially during the revolutionary decade) to make El Paso something less than a stronghold for Anglo values, despite the influence of American-based capital after the arrival of the railroads in the 1880s.[53]

The clock tower from the original Great Northern Railway station is the center of attraction in a beautiful urban park adjacent to the high-rise office and shopping district of downtown Spokane. The old tower is a stark reminder that the sizable and attractive setting was once laced with railroad tracks, the very symbols of the city's rise to prominence in the late nineteenth century. The builders of the Northern Pacific Railroad chose the easy grade of the Clark Fork River to complete their rail line from the Missouri to the Columbia rivers, thus accentuating the importance of the tiny village. That decision resulted in Spokane's becoming the largest metropolitan center between Minneapolis and Puget Sound south of the forty-ninth parallel. Spokane's rather unlikely setting gives substance to William Cronon's remark about the factors that determine the location of cities: "Geographical arguments do not explain. . . . Only history and culture can do that." Until competition from truck transportation grew in the 1920s, the city was the principal rail hub for the vast Inland Empire, an area extending into western Montana and southern Canada and embracing the entire Columbia basin. By serving as the strategic link for points east, west, north, and south, Spokane was the nexus binding those disparate extractive regions into a single unit.[54]

When gold discoveries triggered a rush to the Coeur d'Alene mining district in the early 1880s, newly arrived entrepreneurs in Spokane found a ready-made arena for profitable activity: providing the trade services in goods and supplies necessary to mining enterprise. Daniel Chase Corbin, with ties to Northern Pacific capital, forged a rail and water link to the Coeur d'Alene district in the late 1880s and followed that in 1893 with another line extending to Nelson, British Columbia, thus fixing those two mining regions in Spokane's metropolitan orb. When the ambitious Corbin extended his route into British Columbia and linked it with the Canadian Pacific in 1904, Spokane commanded an empire that reached into parts of four states and into one Canadian province.[55] The city's tributary area also included an expanding agricultural base to the south and west, an area around the perimeter of the Columbia plain destined to become one of the great wheat-producing regions of the country.

Spokane's entrepreneurs made lasting fortunes during the years of the great boom. Corbin garnered his wealth building feeder railroads from Spokane and then selling them to the major transcontinentals—the Northern Pacific, the Great Northern, and the Union Pacific. Other individuals profited by trading in mining stocks; still others, such as the Cowles family, published newspapers and invested in real estate property, thereby fixing themselves as permanent scions of the Spokane establishment. In the mining region to the east a few indigenous, self-made millionaires emerged, but by the turn of the century in most cases control of the mines had passed to stockholding syndicates and trusts whose boardrooms were located in places as distant as New York City. Just as in El Paso, ASARCO and the Guggenheims exerted great influence over mining activity in the Coeur d'Alenes, operating the production capacities of their smelters to synchronize with the international price of ore. ASARCO's presence ensured that real control over life in the Coeur d'Alenes resided far from the mining district.[56]

Carlos Schwantes uses the term "wageworkers' frontier" to describe that early period of industrial activity in the late-nineteenth- and early-twentieth-century West. Centered largely in the extractive industries and with a predominantly male work force, the wageworkers' frontier, according to Schwantes, "was a fragile entity forever at the mercy of the outside world's pricing of its basic commodities—coal and nonferrous metals, timber, fish, wheat, fruit, and other agricultural produce." The lack of a sizable home market in the West, at least until World War II, meant that the great bulk of that production was shipped out of the region. Moreover, as a functioning part of a greater global capitalism, the western industrial workers' environment was in a state of constant change, expanding and contracting to match the whim and fancy of distant economic forces and decisionmaking.[57]

As for Spokane, volatile class relations, both within the city and in the land beyond, paralleled the frenzied economic expansion in the Inland Empire. The dramatic worldwide expansion of capitalist agriculture affected wheat-producing areas such as that of the Palouse; similar international fluctuations in the prices of metal ores created chaotic conditions in the mining districts; and a persistent glut on the lumber market beginning in the first decade of the twentieth century periodically brought hard times to northern Idaho's logging and lumber camps. In times of unemployment or labor troubles and during the slack seasons, out-of-work miners and harvest hands drifted into Spokane for social discourse, to obtain information about jobs, and to listen to the appeals of union organizers, especially those of the IWW.[58]

Like El Paso, Spokane served as a crossroads labor market, servicing the production-oriented needs of the mining, agricultural, and lumber industries in the interior northern West. The rapid industrialization of the region, the extractive nature of its economy, and its boom-and-bust character undoubtedly exacerbated the normal tensions between capital and labor.[59] The celebrated class warfare that occurred during the 1890s in the Coeur d'Alenes is but the most notable and well-known part of the story. As the principal metropolis for that resource-rich hinterland, Spokane serves as a mirror for class relations in the region. A generally stagnant economy in the Inland Empire between 1910 and 1940 ensured that the early friction between owners and managers and workers would persist.

Labor contractors, a group derisively referred to as sharks by the workers, haunted the streets of Spokane, El Paso, and other industrially based western cities. One of the favored stopping-over centers in the northern West for workers seeking rest and social discourse after the long harvest summers or a season of railroad construction, Spokane was the scene of one of the IWW's more celebrated free-speech fights in the winter of 1909-1910. Although the Wobblies won a victory of sorts, effective and more lasting labor organization in the Spokane area had to await another day. But the city would remain through two world wars as the center of labor activism in the region.[60]

In El Paso the fortunes of world war and revolution had a striking influence on class (and race) relations. Thousands of Mexicans fled across the border to El Paso to escape the fighting in northern Mexico between 1914 and 1916, and Anglo observers warned of epidemics and a glut on labor markets. Yet, when Congress restricted immigration in 1917 and war-related manpower shortages in the United States created a demand for labor, those conditions were reversed. Employers in El Paso and the Southwest eventually succeeded in persuading the government to suspend the ban and to allow Mexican workers to enter the country to work in the mines, on railroads, and in agriculture. Mario Garcia points out that El Paso served as a vital entry station for cheap unskilled labor to serve the needs of southwestern enterprises. That system, he concludes, "produced profits and privileges for the region's employers and their managers, while limiting wages for all workers and, unfortunately, dividing them along racial lines."[61]

Spokane and El Paso provide models for the study of urban/hinterland relations in still another way. Because they developed as isolated urban centers servicing sparsely populated sections of the West, the growth of the two cities stands as striking testimony to the influence of the central state in subsidizing urban development. As case studies, their histories are instructive: in the dialectic between city and country the role of the state should not be underestimated, or as one scholar put it, "in the real world of the twentieth-century metropolis, the economy and the state are integrally related." Federal subsidies included support for the building of a transportation infrastructure (especially railroads in the nineteenth century); liberal public-domain entry requirements for mining companies over vast areas; federal land policies that promoted private real-estate ventures; federal investment capital for roads, schools, and government buildings; federal assistance for scientific and research support pertinent to the region's major forms of economic activity (mining and agriculture); and in the case of El Paso, federal management of traffic across the international border.[62]

In more recent times, the largest federal infusions of capital to the economies of Spokane and El Paso have centered on defense-related matters. Due largely to the construction of two U.S. Air Force installations and the building of Kaiser's huge aluminum facilities, Spokane's population, which had languished between 1910 and 1940, grew sharply during and after World War II. And a bit of historical irony conspired to send Spokane through a second great boom: the earlier federal transportation subsidies that had made the city a major railroad hub convinced defense officials at the onset of World War II to develop an air-defense perimeter to protect that web of rail lines. War-induced change in El Paso was even more dramatic: once the principal cavalry-training post in the United States, Fort Bliss was the nation's largest army base by 1942, and at the end of the 1950s the government designated it as headquarters for the U.S. Army Air Defense Center. The simultaneous expansion of Biggs Field into a strategic-weapons center tripled El Paso's population between 1940 and 1960 (96,810 to 276,687) and made the military the area's largest single employer. Although Phoenix had surpassed El Paso as the preeminent city of the Southwest by 1960, defense-fueled activity continued to power the Texas border community's economy.[63]

If, as Stephen Hahn and Jonathan Prude argue, "American history was launched from the countryside," then it also follows that its metropolitan sectors ultimately prevailed in determining the direction and circumstances of daily life everywhere. As a metaphor in the broadest sense, a city has no fixed physical being, but its reach—economic, political, cultural, and social—has been pervasive. Despite America's present circumstances as one of the most urban nations in the world, a powerful rural mythology continues to mold the public consciousness in the United States. Eric Monkkonen rightly points out that Americans still cling to a "rural sense" of their own history.[64]

The historian's affection for that mythical, rural-centered world, much of it attributable to Frederick Jackson Turner's thesis, has dominated the literature about the American West, at least until recently. But the Turnerian convention, as Earl Pomeroy and other critics have noted, grants too much agency and autonomy to western conditions and circumstances and far too little to metropolitan centers of primary capital accumulation (whether it be Paris, New York, or later, San Francisco). The view that change originated in western environments ignores the fact that many newly established communities owed their existence to the decisions of the railroad locators, to financial investments in mineral exploitation, and to myriad other activities associated with the dynamic centers of an expansive global network of capitalist relations.

Competitive advantage and initiative under the volatile economic conditions that have prevailed over much of the trans-Mississippi West always have rested in the larger arenas of capital accumulation. When powerful urban enclaves emerged in the West, as they did in San Francisco early on and then during World War II in southern California, it meant simply that the banker had moved closer to the scene of action. Whether it was the San Francisco-based Hearst syndicate appropriating the riches of the great Homestake Mine in South Dakota or New York's ASARCO gleaning immense wealth from Idaho's Coeur d'Alene district, the consequences signified enormous successes for industrial capitalism on the one hand and persisting change and struggle in the resource-rich hinterland on the other. Little has happened since James Marshall plucked that first nugget of gold from northern California's American River to redirect those structured inequalities.

PART FOUR

Forces of Disintegration

CHAPTER TEN

Epilogue: Recycling the Old West

If America is the land where the world goes in search of miracles and re-demption, California is the land where Americans go. It is America's Amer-ica, the symbol of raw hope and brave (even foolish) invention, where an-cient traditions and inhibitions are abandoned at the border. Its peculiar culture squirts out—on film and menus and pages and television beams—the trends and tastes that sweep the rest of the country.

—*Time*, November 18, 1991

Mark Taper, Ben Weingart, and Louis Boyar may lack the heroic qualities of the empire-builder James J. Hill, the late-nineteenth-century railroad baron, but in many respects their activities have contributed in equally significant ways to the story of change in a more recent West. Developers of the planned community of Lakewood, California—"Tomorrow's City Today"—Taper, Weingart, and Boyar were on the move in the years fol-lowing World War II to take advantage of California's booming economy. The three entrepreneurs purchased a sizable acreage of farmland adja-cent to the government-subsidized McDonnell Douglas plant and subse-quently advertised the grand opening of the proposed 17,500-home tract in April 1950. Grander in conception than Long Island's famous Levit-town, plans were made to build 900- to 1,100-square-feet homes on each of the 50-by-100-foot lots. Sales of the Lakewood homesites subsequently exceeded even the wildest dreams of the developers, with 30,000 people showing up on opening day. Nearly two decades later Mark Taper ob-served: "Everything about this entire project was perfect. . . . *Things happened that may never happen again.*"[1]

As Joan Didion points out, Lakewood was the product of "the per-fect synergy of time and place": World War II, the onset of the cold war and the expansion of defense-related industry, government-funded housing loans through the GI bill, and U.S. involvement in a series of Pacific basin and global crises from the Korean to the Vietnam wars. With its 250-acre regional shopping mall—Lakewood Center—the complex of planned homes, thirty-seven playgrounds, twenty schools, and seven-teen churches provided living space for the nation's growing middle class. It was, in short, the California dream writ large. Generally veterans of World War II and the Korean conflict, the people who bought most of those homes were often young, usually hailed from the Midwest or the border South, and typically worked in blue-collar or low-ranking white-collar jobs. "Their experience," Didion argues, "tended to reinforce the conviction that social and economic mobility worked exclusively upward."[2]

Lakewood, however, signified even more. It was part of an incredibly expansive postwar economy that touched every metropolitan area on the Pacific Coast from Seattle to San Diego as well as urban centers in the mountainous interior from Spokane to Denver, Phoenix, and Albuquerque. Indeed, the transformation of southern California—with its growing urban infrastructures, its booming home-building industry, and its expanding defense sector—dwarfed changes taking place elsewhere. The historian Gerald Nash has likened the postwar West, but especially southern California, to a futuristic theme park, a model, a pacesetter for the rest of the nation. "The West today," he remarked in 1973, "was America tomorrow." A decade earlier, the writer Neil Morgan observed that newcomers to the West had developed "a sense of having discovered the life of tomorrow."[3]

The trend-setting, metropolitan West—especially its archetype in California—may have dazzled the world with its freeways, its space-age industries, its informality and outdoor living, and its experimentation in the sciences and education, but its performance at center court has been very short-lived.[4] The end of the cold war and cuts in defense expenditures, especially in aerospace programs, have been particularly stressful to corporations such as McDonnell Douglas and their dependent communities. With its once pacesetting economy now in the doldrums, with its politics and race relations in gridlock, and with the flight of white middle-class Californians to small towns elsewhere in the rural West, the Golden State is beginning to look much like older resource centers in the region, places that have long since taken their "turn in the bucket."[5] Joan Didion's assessment of Lakewood, I submit, may well be appropriate for much of the once-booming California economy:

> Lakewood exists because at a given time in a different economy it seemed an efficient idea to provide population density for the mall and a labor force pool for the Douglas plant. There are a lot of places like Lakewood in California. They were California's mill towns, breeder towns for the boom. When times were good and there was money to spread around, these were the towns that proved Marx wrong, that managed to increase the proletariat and simultaneously, by calling it the middle class, to co-opt it.[6]

It turns out that times were good in the aerospace, defense-dependent mill towns (and Marx wrong) only in the face of the Big Evil out there, the Soviet Union, and only because of the series of international crises (Berlin, Korea, Vietnam, Central America) that fueled industrial production in the defense-related sector of the American economy. Hence, communities such as Lakewood may well become anachronisms, much like the once booming resource-based industrial towns of the interior West, where capital flight to more lucrative investment arenas has been a fact of life at least since the great silver bust of 1893. If McDonnell Douglas becomes history, as an aircraft-industry executive remarked in April 1993, or if the company follows through on another rumor and shifts some of its production overseas, then the Lakewood experience will be but another component of the western story, one that Patricia Limerick has called an "unbroken past" of short-lived and uncertain enterprises.[7]

California has not been the centerpiece of this book, but its story provides a fitting illustration and symbol for the continuing instability of economic life throughout the American West, even in the once seemingly most buoyant and spectacular sector of the region's economy. Its special promise worn thin amid choking smog, crumbling urban communities, clashes among its citizenry, and an economy suddenly gone wrong, its dream literally imploding, the postindustrial malaise plaguing California is sending reverberations across the West. More than .5 million people left California in 1990, half of them settling in adjacent states. And while the state gained nearly 300,000 new residents between 1992 and 1993, the number leaving during the same period was even greater—377,000. Such statistics moved the journalist Foster Church to observe: "The West as Westerners have known it is changing. It will never be the same."[8] What appears to be emerging in the post–cold war era, then, is a New West, a region characterized by dramatic demographic movement, the persistent restructuring of local economies, and a future that promises more of the same.

But that emerging New West is at one with the past. Success and failure, prosperity and misfortune, expansion and decline, boom and bust, after all, were components of the broader development and evolution of capitalism at the local and regional, national, and global levels. To grasp the essence of the transformation of the American West during the last century and a half, therefore, one must look to the mainstays of material relations in the region: the perpetually changing, even revolutionary character of its political and economic culture; the inherent instability of its resource sector and its relation to larger centers of capitalist decisionmaking; the dynamic and always-changing dialectic over time between country and city; and the larger mosaic of global conditions and circumstances.

The historical experiences of communities such as Lakewood (and Montana's historic copper-mining town, Butte) suggest that both industrial and postindustrial societies share common characteristics in their ability to revolutionize production, in their failure to bring a sense of permanence and the good life to their residents, and in their reliance on a large underclass of workers. Moreover, those communities also reveal that despite the impressive economic growth in the West since World War II, there has been no corresponding leveling in the distribution of wealth. The spectacular urban expansion, the installation of new, innovative, and highly productive manufacturing facilities, and the explosive growth of the high-tech sector have been accompanied by growing urban and suburban poverty as well as by increasing economic hardship in the countryside.

Yet indications throughout the interior West suggest that some of those once-blighted rural communities are taking on a different hue in recent years as people and the more mobile corporations take flight from socially problematic and tax-expensive metropolitan settings. Many farming and ranching communities and resource-dependent areas that had once been slipping down the wrong side of the economic roller coaster are in the process of being refurbished as centers of business activity for information-age entrepreneurs, as recreational playgrounds for the mobile middle and upper classes, as up-scale retirement locales, and as large, landed private preserves for the super rich. The circumstances responsible for that remaking of the countryside are found in the special tensions and conditions of material life in the metropolis and in the ability of capital to exercise its will on a money-poor hinterland. From New Mexico north to Montana, from Idaho through Nevada and Arizona, a sizable demographic shift is reshaping both property relations and the social dynamics of life in the countryside. Still, if the story behind previous population movements is any indication, the present circumstances represent flight from high land prices and taxes (and labor costs for entrepreneurs) as well as social problems. Thus, as land and labor costs in the outback reach parity with those in San Jose or southern California, the rate of flight will probably slow.

Middle- and upper-class Californians, fleeing to sparsely populated, rural areas in the West (or to the more desirable metropolitan settings of Seattle, Portland, and Boise) are the most noticeable group in what is becoming a sizable migratory stream. Even though some of the newcomers hail from the crowded cities of the East and Midwest, the bitterness, opposition, and resentment of longtime residents is directed toward the mythical California lifestyle and especially toward California money.

There is a telling reality to this new juncture in the ever-changing face of the region; as one writer has observed, "California numbers, trends, attitudes and ways of life are changing the look, feel and culture of the West."⁹ But above all, and this is especially true in the hinterland, it is big money—outside capital—that is the most prominent feature in the remaking of that rural New West.

Until ten years ago, St. George, Utah, was a quiet Mormon community in the high desert country of the southern part of the state. Andrew McArthur, whose grandfather served baked goods to workers building the community's large Mormon temple in 1871, recalled a local aphorism from his youth: "The elevation is 2,800, the population is 2,800, and it seldom gets below 28 degrees." The 1990 census listed the population of St. George at 28,000, twice the number of people living in the community ten years earlier, and there is little question that California refugees supplied much of the growth. The newcomers, who are responsible for the opening of five non-Mormon places of worship, are diluting the town's social and religious base, a change exemplified in part by the construction of the striking state-operated liquor store. Although fewer newcomers are flooding other small western towns, their money—much of it garnered from real-estate sales in the overheated California market during the late 1980s and early 1990s—is skewing hitherto traditional lifestyles and otherwise disrupting local economies in a number of ways.¹⁰

More than any other factor, the staggering flow of cash in recent years is the driving force behind the changing face of the rural West. Floundering communities, whose livelihoods were once dependent on mining, agriculture, or fishing, are especially vulnerable to newcomers with ready capital to invest in home-building real-estate deals, small-business enterprises, or resort and recreative developments. Rural towns are being commercialized and their natural settings commodified by new and ingenious methods; indeed, the transformation of some of those hinterland communities reminds one of the way the entrepreneurs of snow remade Aspen from a small and faded mining town into the glitz and glamour of Colorado's most famous and pretentious ski resort in the years after World War II.

Park City, Utah, albeit not on the scale of Aspen, is a more recent example of the new face being put on many old mining communities. Situated in a small, high-mountain valley in the Wasatch Range, Park City was victim to escalating production costs and a corresponding worldwide depression in metal prices; that is, until the United Park City Mines Company built Treasure Mountain Resort, the immediate predecessor to the Park City Ski Area. In the process the character of the old working-class community was destroyed; in its place, recreation developers built condominiums, extravagant contemporary homes, and up-scale restaurants and littered the commercial district with imitation decor to give the town an exotic presence. Raye Ringholz, a local historian, also notes that in the wake of those changes, "we have almost lost our funky little town" with its "home-grown rodeo," its colorful local personalities, and its ability to laugh at itself. "Becoming citified," Ringholz observes, "is making us take ourselves too seriously."[11]

Park City, and the specter of growth that the resort community continues to confront, reflects similar conditions being played out elsewhere in the Intermountain West, where old resource-dependent settlements are being wrenched into a strikingly different social and cultural world. Places such as Jackson Hole, a seasonal playground for the wealthy dating back to the beginning of the century, have become thoroughly gentrified, a setting for gated residential subdivisions, expensive condominiums to house affluent snow birds, and equally costly resorts to cater to winter-sports enthusiasts and summer tourists. In the twenty-year period between 1970 and 1990, the permanent population of Teton County grew from 4,823 to more than 13,000. The largest town, Jackson, lost most of its old dignity and charm as "the last and best of the Old West." Franchise operations and chains replaced small family groceries, restaurants, and mercantile operations. "The major issue now," according to Bob McConaughy, who operates one of the few surviving guest ranches in the area, "is how much growth can the valley take and do the people want. And what should we do about that?"[12]

The transformation of Jackson Hole—from a cattle ranching area that catered to seasonal, middle- and upper-class recreational and leisure activities to a community of part-time and permanent homes for the self-consciously rich—reflects the influence of wealth from both the United States and overseas and a group of people who can live anywhere and conduct business with clients via telephonic and computer networks. Because they are security-conscious, many of these residents live in walled enclaves that provide twenty-four-hour protection. The source for their livelihoods lies elsewhere; their social circles remain exclusive; they represent, according to longtime residents of Jackson Hole, the antithesis of neighborliness and community.

Jackson and Aspen are merely the most ostentatious and conspicuous examples of the redesigning of the landscape beyond the great metropolitan places in the West. The driving force contributing to a large segment of that transformation appears to be centered in California, its huge population, and increasingly, the multiethnic character of its citizenry. The Los Angeles basin alone, with 14.5 million residents in 1990, surpasses in numbers every American state except Texas and New York. A federal demographer, Calvin Beale, describes the population movement into California in terms of a ripple effect: "People hit the coast in such large numbers that they begin to go the other way." Urban-affairs scholar Louis Masotti characterizes California as the "staging ground for the dispersement of population."[13] Yet the move from the Golden State to other places is selective, white flight some observers have called it, involving mostly middle- and upper-class whites with capital.

The population increases during the decade of the 1980s for the eight western-most contiguous states reflect the dynamics of those demographic changes:

State	Percentage Increase
Arizona	34.8
California	25.7
Idaho	6.7
Montana	1.6
Nevada	50.1
Oregon	7.9
Utah	17.9
Washington	17.8[14]

Beyond the realm of cold statistics, however, there is a material world that explains far more. Although certain sectors of the California economy are in a state of free-fall from cuts in defense expenditures in the early 1990s, there remains a vibrant, global, borderless component to its economic life centered on exports (electronics, computers, biotechnology, and aerospace), transnational business alliances, and overseas-partnership relations. These primary activities are propelling the changes occurring in California and in adjacent states. Even in the midst of a fierce and deep-seated depression, California continues to attract new people, with nonwhites constituting more than 80 percent of the newcomers.[15] The counterpart to that sizable in-migration is the out-migration, the white flight of modestly affluent and wealthy Californians to less densely settled urban and rural areas in adjacent western states. *High Country News* listed the familiar litany of reasons given by those people who were leaving: "crime, the congestion, the smog, the economy, the high cost of living."[16]

And that is the substance of the New West, a region in transition with rising and declining sectors, both in the metropolis and in the hinterland. Once-bustling centers of resource production, places linked to eastern U.S. and western European capital through investment and market relations, are being remade in the face of new forms of capital ventures. Except for those agricultural areas where a low-wage, surplus labor force is deemed important to production and profits, most of the population shift to the hinterland is made up of the educated and affluent. And whether they are retirees, active, information-age business people, or trekkers to recreational and resort areas, the combined effect of their presence is revolutionary. The New West taking shape beyond the city is considerably removed from the resource- and production-oriented industrial world of the mining, logging, and milling communities of yesteryear. The values of the newcomers and their opposition to local and state taxes—especially among the newly arrived retirees living on fixed incomes—promise to wreak havoc with social-service infrastructures. The writer William Kittredge observed that "these good folk don't seem to give a damn about the welfare of our next generation. They want to buy into our functioning culture on the cheap."[17]

Yet it is a mistake to assume, as one contemporary Republican consultant suggests, that the jobs of the new migrants to the hinterland West are dependent on the global economy rather than on what happens at the local level.[18] The implication is that the New West is unique and different (from the old West) only in its infinitely closer ties to the world economy. The form of capital remaking the hinterland may be different, the ensuing pace of change may be more immediate, and the remapping of regional landscapes may be on a much greater scale, but in terms of external influences on local conditions, little has changed. Events in the West today differ only in scope and magnitude from the events of 1893, when decisions made in distant transatlantic boardrooms brought immediate chaos and suffering to the tiniest of industrial communities in the western outback.

The influx of capital that is triggering the creation of the New West is also leaving in its wake a two-tiered society: (1) on one level the "equity refugees" or "equity bandits," well-to-do newcomers with sizable capital savings or independent sources of income; and (2) on the other, low-wage service workers and longtime residents dependent on relatively fixed incomes.[19] The juxtaposition of new money and dying industries on such a scale is relatively new to the West, but it is a specter that will probably continue to haunt smaller communities. In terms of real income, service-sector jobs bring a poor return in comparison with older forms of industrial work. The consequence is a sharpening of class divisions on a scale never witnessed in the older, more traditional West with its agricultural and industrial base.

Northern Idaho, an area in transition from primary employment in mining and lumbering to a retirement, information-age, tourism-based economy, illustrates the timeworn dichotomy between the haves and the have-nots; it is also a striking example of the two-tiered society, with mining and industrial jobs still paying an average of $24,000 and hotel and restaurant workers earning an average of $7,500. The town of Coeur d'Alene, located at the north end of Coeur d'Alene Lake and once a thriving sawmill town, is at the center of the northern Idaho boom. A new $60-million resort, opened in 1986 on the shores of the lake, employs as many as 1,000 people during the peak of the tourist season; however, as the head of the local chamber of commerce points out, "a $5-an-hour job parking cars is no substitute for sawmill work that pays $15."[20] But Coeur d'Alene, like other towns of its kind, is at the cutting edge of change in the New West, communities in transition from resource-based production to information-based tourist enclaves with new displays of wealth apparent on every hand. With convenient travel by automobile and air and with ease of communication through facsimile machines and computers, the outside world is readily accessible to the rural West. From Kalispell, Montana, to Bend, Oregon, and southward to St. George, small towns in the interior West are becoming part of a larger constellation of capital and business relations linking rural areas with the great metropolitan centers on the coast and with the global community beyond.

There is yet another twist to the remaking of the countryside in the American West. With a relatively low tax base and a work force being marginalized through declining industrial jobs, rural areas are providing unique opportunities for mobile, capital-intensive, computer-age companies. Stevensville, Montana, a small town in the Bitterroot Range, is the recent home to Nick Granny's Niche Engineering, a development engineering firm formerly operating out of San Jose, California. Although Granny found Stevensville a great place to live, there was a certain lack of business drive in the local work force, a "strong work ethic and a lack of hustle ethic," he calls it. But the California transplant sees the emergence of a new economy, one in which companies such as his own can help reverse the flow of jobs and capital to Latin American countries and assist in the rebuilding of the rural West. Granny is blunt and optimistic about that unique, strikingly different New West he sees in the making: "What we are doing is promoting Montana as the newest North American emerging nation."[21]

In the central Oregon town of Bend—once a bustling center of pine sawmilling—a winter-sports boom following World War II has mushroomed into an incredible growth spurt. Retirees, monied refugees from inflated real-estate markets elsewhere, and affluent and active business people have created the driving force behind the booming land and home-building sales occurring in the greater Bend area in the last few years. The director of the Central Oregon Economic Development Council, Leland Smith, acknowledges that the relocation of smaller California businesses is a significant factor in reshaping the local economy, sufficient enough to make central Oregon almost "a suburb of the San Francisco Bay area." Smith sees companies moving to Deschutes County to allow for expansion "without isolating themselves from all the things in California that make their company work—just like Santa Barbara is a suburban enclave of Los Angeles."[22]

Tom Pickell, a Bay Area transplant who is a partner in a development and consulting firm, is convinced that cities such as Bend are the business centers of the future: "For people like myself, it's the next frontier. I want to be in economic development, and there are tremendous opportunities." Set free and footloose by money, easy air travel, and the telecommunications revolution, Pickell and other people like him are independent of the traditional requirements of a centralized work place (and, it might be added, free of the conventional notions of a sense of commitment to community and place). For rapidly growing Washington County, west of Portland, county administrator Charles Cameron—himself a 1985 transplant from northern California—expresses the kind of confidence that some of the movers and shakers hold for the future:

> I am not enough of a historian or clairvoyant to predict how it is going to work out. But it will be a unique experience for us. I am an eternal optimist. It promises a lot of tremendous opportunities, and to me that is what is gratifying. *It is our time.*[23]

The creation of the still-emerging New West of recent years has wrought the obvious—open opposition in many communities, especially among older residents suddenly hit with crowded traffic conditions, escalating taxes, sharply rising real-estate prices, and the other distortions that large infusions of outside capital bring to local economies. In a letter to the *Portland Oregonian,* one disgruntled resident of Bend observed that the newcomers have meant "gaudy ostentatious houses, big cars, pseudo-Italian suits, soap-opera tart dresses, and deals, deals, deals." And, as the writer openly acknowledged, a sometimes overblown chauvinism has resulted, directed in most instances at the euphemistic Californian:

> The locusts of our time, the Californians cut a swath of destruction wherever they go, always in search of that lifestyle that only exists in Hollywood movies.[24]

Before 1945, before it became home to hands-on fantasy in the form of Disneyland and Knotts Berry Farm, Orange County's primary attraction was its good farmland and its energy resources. Within two decades the region had emerged as an important center of industrial manufacturing. And by the mid-1980s Orange County was the sixth most populous political unit of its kind in the United States; it was a major center of high-technology production; and its work force included "technologically skilled and specialized occupations" and a large unskilled, low-income, and unorganized group of laborers. The county had also emerged as a power base for conservative, even reactionary, politics.[25] Although the special circumstances surrounding the transformation of Orange County during the last half century will probably not be replicated elsewhere in the future, in other respects the experiences of the county might suggest some insight into understanding change beyond southern California.

As Orange County progressively became a more closely integrated segment of the global community of capital, Spencer Olin points out, the "ideology and aspirations" of a cosmopolitan and international corporate world replaced local political ideologies that formerly had spoken for local interests and local constituencies.[26] In the county's transition from an agricultural base to regional networks of production and exchange, it became more an investment arena for mobile capital and less an autonomous political entity. In effect, the county had lost control over the terms of its relations with the wider world. And now that Orange County is in the midst of a profound and deep recession with no immediate relief in sight, it offers yet another example of the play of capital in constructing and deconstructing local economies. But, as a friend has cautioned, "Don't be too quick to count California [and Orange County] out." It has an abundant pool of qualified, educated workers and a "relatively new infrastructure." California, according to this line of argument, may be "in transition, rather than decline."[27]

Even though places such as St. George, Utah, and Bend, Oregon, are far removed in kind, distance, and size from Orange County, they function in a broad global theater of market-exchange relations, industrial strategies, and investment decisionmaking that is linked to the great mobility of capital in the late twentieth century. Moreover, as capital increasingly disperses itself across the hinterland West as the close of the century approaches, it will leave in its wake a local autonomy more diminished than ever before. There is an old populist cartoon portraying a cow with its feeding end sprawled across the West and with its immediate production apparatus in New York City. The illustration still suggests the exchange relationship that links western communities with the investors of capital and the outside world. For many people, only the financial dexterity and the mobility of those doing the milking have changed over the course of the last century.

NOTES

PREFACE

1. Quoted in Louis P. Masur, "In Retrospect: Bernard DeVoto and the Making of *The Year of Decision: 1846,*" *Reviews in American History* 18 (1990): 441.
2. See Ann Markusen, *Regions: The Economics and Politics of Territory* (Totowa, N.J.: Rowman and Littlefield, 1987), 11.
3. Martin J. Sklar, *The Corporate Reconstruction of American Capitalism, 1890-1916: The Market, the Law, and Politics* (New York: Cambridge University Press, 1988), 2, 6. Joseph A. Schumpeter posited essentially the same argument although he believed that capitalism would eventually devolve to a point at which it would no longer be identifiable as capitalism. He spoke of a "civilization of capitalism," a "social value system [in which] all the conditions of life are mirrored" (see Schumpeter, *The Theory of Economic Development: An Inquiry into Profits, Capital, Credit, Interest, and the Business Cycle* [1934; Cambridge, Mass.: Harvard University Press, 1959], 56, and Schumpeter, *Capitalism, Socialism, and Democracy* [1942; New York: Harper and Row, 1976], 121-29).
4. See Spencer C. Olin, "Free Markets and Corporate America," *Radical History Review* 50 (1991): 213-15.
5. This discussion is based on my reading of Sklar, *Corporate Reconstruction of American Capitalism*, 1-20.
6. For North America, there may be different forms of adaptation under the capitalist system, but as Donald Worster argues, capitalism is *still* a mode of production with "a recognizable identity" that transcends immediate environments (see Worster, *The Dust Bowl: The Southern Plains in the 1930s* [New York: Oxford University Press, 1979], 6; emphasis added.)
7. For a discussion of this point, see William Appleman Williams, "Confessions of an Intransigent Revisionist," *Socialist Review* 17 (September–October 1973): 93–94, and Williams, "A Profile of the Corporate Elite," in *A New History of Leviathan: Essays on the Rise of the Corporate Estate,* ed. Ronald Radosh and Murray Rothbard (New York: E. P. Dutton, 1972), 1-2.
8. Fernand Braudel, *Afterthoughts on Material Civilization and Capitalism,* trans. Patricia M. Ranum (Baltimore: Johns Hopkins University Press, 1977), 45.
9. See Sklar, *Corporate Reconstruction of American Capitalism*, 2-3.

CHAPTER ONE: IDEOLOGY AND THE WAY WEST

1. Norman Best, *A Celebration of Work,* edited and with an introduction by William G. Robbins (Lincoln: University of Nebraska Press, 1990), 8.
2. For Herbert Hoover's early career in international mining activities, see Joan Hoff Wilson, *Herbert Hoover: Forgotten Progressive* (Boston: Little, Brown, 1975), 12-17, 21-23; David Burner, *Herbert Hoover: The Public Life* (New York: Alfred A. Knopf, 1979), 24-44; and George Nash, *The Life of Herbert Hoover: The Engineer* (New York: W. W. Norton, 1983), 52-124. For a brief contemporary discussion of the global movement of people and capital, see Chris Raymond, "Global

Migration Will Have Widespread Impact on Society, Scholars Say," *Chronicle of Higher Education,* September 12, 1990, A1, A6.

3. This argument is expressed best in Arthur Power Dudden, *The American Pacific: From the Old China Trade to the Present* (New York: Oxford University Press, 1992), xvii–xx; Earl Pomeroy, *The Pacific Slope: A History of California, Oregon, Washington, Idaho, Utah, and Nevada* (New York: Alfred A. Knopf, 1965), 8–22; Rodman W. Paul, *California Gold: The Beginning of Mining in the Far West* (Lincoln: University of Nebraska Press, 1965), 20–35; and Carlos A. Schwantes, *The Pacific Northwest: An Interpretive History* (Lincoln: University of Nebraska Press, 1989), 38–46.

4. Ann Markusen points out that with the construction of the transcontinental railroads, purchasing and banking regions "had the upper hand" in those relationships (Markusen, *Regions: Economics and Politics of Territory* [Totowa, N.J.: Rowman and Littlefield, 1987], 91).

5. The most recent examples undermining the notion of an insular West are Walter Nugent, *Crossings: The Great Transatlantic Migrations, 1870–1914* (Bloomington: Indiana University Press, 1992); Donald W. Meinig, *The Shaping of America: A Geographical Perspective of 500 Years of History,* vol. 2, *Continental America: 1800–1867* (New Haven, Conn.: Yale University Press, 1993); Patricia Nelson Limerick, *The Legacy of Conquest: The Unbroken Past of the American West* (New York: W. W. Norton, 1987); and Donald Worster, *Rivers of Empire: Water, Aridity, and the Growth of the American West* (New York: Pantheon Books, 1985).

6. Henry Nash Smith, *Virgin Land: The American West as Symbol and Myth* (Cambridge, Mass.: Harvard University Press, 1950). Few historians, according to Donald Worster, have pursued Smith's criticism of the "isolation of western writing" (Worster to the author, July 9, 1990).

7. This argument is adapted from Dudden, *American Pacific,* xviii.

8. Loren Baritz, "The Idea of the West," *American Historical Review* 66 (April 1961): 618, 639, and William Appleman Williams, "Thoughts on the Fun and Purpose of Being an Historian," *OAH Newsletter* 15 (February 1985): 3.

9. Edward Pessen, "'A Historian Must Have No Country': John Quincy Adams' Standard for Historians," *OAH Newsletter* 15 (February 1988): 2–3; Thomas B. Hietala, *Manifest Design: Anxious Aggrandizement in Late Jacksonian America* (Ithaca, N.Y.: Cornell University Press, 1985), 272; and Frances FitzGerald, *Fire in the Lake: The Vietnamese and the Americans in Vietnam* (Boston: Little, Brown, 1972), 9. For an important elaboration of the attractions of mythical versions of American history, see James Oliver Robertson, *American Myth, American Reality* (New York: Hill and Wang, 1980), xv–xvii, 3–8.

10. David W. Noble, *The End of American History: Democracy, Capitalism, and the Metaphor of Two Worlds in Anglo-American Historical Writing, 1880–1980* (Minneapolis: University of Minnesota Press, 1985), 7, and Carl N. Degler, "In Pursuit of an American History," *American Historical Review* 92 (February 1987): 2, 9–12.

11. William H. Truettner, "Ideology and Image: Justifying Westward Expansion," in *The West as America: Reinterpreting Images of the Frontier, 1820–1920,* ed. Truettner (Washington, D.C.: Smithsonian Institution Press, 1991), 40.

12. Daniel Boorstin's comments are in *Time,* May 13, 1991, 79–80.

13. References to these comments are in Eric Foner and Jon Wiener, "Fighting for the West," *Nation,* July 29/August 5, 1991, 163, and the *Billings Gazette,* July 28, 1991. For a more favorable review, see the essay by art critic Robert Hughes in *Time,* May 13, 1991, 79–80.

14. Martin Ridge, "The American West: From Frontier to Region," *New Mexico Historical Review* 64 (April 1989): 138–39, and Donald Worster, *Under West-*

ern Skies: Nature and History in the American West (New York: Oxford University Press, 1992), 16. Donald Pisani finds a "confrontational tone" in some of the recent interpretation; he links the work of these scholars to the "New Left historians of the 1960s and 1970s" who showed far more concern "with ideology and the search for a 'usable past' than [did] earlier western historians" (Pisani, "Is There Life after Turner? The Continuing Search for the Grand Synthesis and an Autonomous West: A Review Essay," *New Mexico Historical Review* [July 1992]: 294).

15. Barrington Moore, *Social Origins of Dictatorship and Democracy* (Boston: Beacon Press, 1966), 522–23.

16. Baritz, "Idea of the West," 618; Robertson, *American Myth, American Reality*, 148–51, 258–59; and David Montejano, *Anglos and Mexicans in the Making of Texas, 1836–1986* (Austin: University of Texas Press, 1987), 1. See also William Appleman Williams, *The Contours of American History* (1961; Chicago: Quadrangle Books, 1966), 181–83.

17. The debate during the latter 1980s on the need for (or lack of) new syntheses in historical writing is one manifestation of this tendency. Among the more important contributions to the argument is Thomas Bender's, "Wholes and Parts: The Need for Synthesis in American History," *Journal of American History* 73 (June 1986): 120–36. For further comment on the issues raised in Bender's essay, see David Thelen et al., "A Round Table: Synthesis in American History," *Journal of American History* 74 (June 1987): 107–30. See also Eric H. Monkkonen, "The Dangers of Synthesis," *American Historical Review* 91 (December 1986): 1146–57, and Donald Worster, "New West, True West: Interpreting the Region's History," *Western Historical Quarterly* 18 (1987): 147. One widely acclaimed and important study that avoids the exceptionalist paradigm while presenting itself as a work of synthesis is Limerick, *Legacy of Conquest*.

18. For use of the term "economic culture," see Donald Worster, *Dust Bowl: The Southern Plains in the 1930s* (New York: Oxford University Press, 1979); and Peter L. Berger, *The Capitalist Revolution: Fifty Propositions about Prosperity, Equality, and Liberty* (New York: Basic Books, 1986), 7–8, 26–27.

19. Martin J. Sklar, *The United States as a Developing Country: Studies in U.S. History in the Progressive Era and the 1920s* (New York: Cambridge University Press, 1992), 13–18.

20. Only the American South, until World War II, stood as an exception to this statement.

21. Wilson is quoted in Martin J. Sklar, *The Corporate Reconstruction of American Capitalism, 1890–1916* (New York: Cambridge University Press, 1988), 391.

22. Again I am indebted to Martin Sklar for the genesis of these ideas (see Sklar, *United States as a Developing Country*, 141).

23. Herbert G. Gutman, *Work, Culture, and Society in Industrializing America* (New York: Vantage Books, 1977), xii.

24. Elizabeth Fox-Genovese and Eugene Genovese, *Fruits of Merchant Capital: Slavery and Bourgeois Property in the Rise and Expansion of Capitalism* (New York: Oxford University Press, 1983), x, 200–201; Paul Goodman, "Putting Some Class Back into Political History: 'The Transformation of Political Culture' and the Crisis in American Political History," *Reviews in American History* 12 (March 1984): 80–88; Spencer C. Olin, Jr., "Toward a Synthesis of the Political and Social History of the American West," *Pacific Historical Review* 55 (November 1986): 599–601; and Degler, "In Pursuit of an American History," 1.

25. Gene Gressley, speaker, "The Twentieth-Century West: A Retrospective

Panel Discussion," Western History Association, Twenty-seventh Annual Conference, Los Angeles, October 9, 1987.

26. "Twentieth-Century West: A Retrospective Panel Discussion," and Samuel P. Hays, "Theoretical Implications of Recent Work in the History of American Society and Politics," *History and Theory* 26:1 (1987): 17.

27. "Environmental History: A Panel Discussion," Western History Association, Twenty-seventh Annual Conference, Los Angeles, October 8, 1987.

28. Worster, *Dust Bowl*, 5; and Robert L. Heilbroner, *The Nature and Logic of Capitalism* (New York: Basic Books, 1985), 15–16.

29. Berger, *Capitalist Revolution*, 3 (emphasis added). Ian Tyrrell, an Australian critic of historical scholarship in the United States, notes only a "*belated* assertion of a serious Marxist presence" in the writing of American history (Tyrrell, *The Absent Marx: Class Analysis and Liberal History in Twentieth-Century America* [Westport, Conn.: Greenwood Press, 1986], 3). For a discussion of the "strongly anti-theoretical" strain in the historical profession in the United States, see Steve J. Stern, "Feudalism, Capitalism, and the World-System in the Perspective of Latin America and the Caribbean," *American Historical Review* 93 (October 1988): 836.

30. Studies that see capitalism in its broadest form as an integral force in western American history include in addition to Worster's *Dust Bowl* and *Rivers of Empire*, Peter Wiley and Robert Gottlieb, *Empires in the Sun: The Rise of the New American West* (New York: G. P. Putnam and Sons, 1982); John Thompson, *Closing the Frontier: Radical Response in Oklahoma* (Norman: University of Oklahoma Press, 1986); Sarah Deutsch, *No Separate Refuge: Culture, Class, and Gender on an Anglo-Hispanic Frontier in the American Southwest, 1880–1940* (New York: Oxford University Press, 1987); and Montejano, *Anglos and Mexicans in the Making of Texas*.

31. Frederick Jackson Turner, *The Frontier in American History* (1920; New York: Holt, Rinehart, and Winston, 1962), 330, 311; Alan Trachtenberg, *The Incorporation of America: Culture and Society in the Gilded Age* (New York: Hill and Wang, 1982), 17 (emphasis added); and William Cronon, "Revisiting the Vanishing Frontier: The Legacy of Frederick Jackson Turner," *Western Historical Quarterly* 18 (April 1987): 158.

32. See Walter Prescott Webb, "Ended: 400 Year Boom. Reflections on the Age of the Frontier," *Harper's*, October 1951: 25–33; "Windfalls of the Frontier," *Harper's*, November 1951: 71–75; and *The Great Frontier* (1951; Lincoln: University of Nebraska Press, 1986), 1–28.

33. Even in borderlands history, David J. Weber notes that no "explanatory device has replaced Turner's thesis." But social scientists, he observes, have been attracted to Immanuel Wallerstein's world-systems theory, "even if historians are embracing it timidly" (Weber, "Turner, the Boltonians, and the Borderlands," *American Historical Review* 91 [February 1986]: 81n). For a few select samples that focus on California and the Southwest, see the special issue of *American Historical Review* 4 (Winter 1981).

34. See Richard C. Wade, *The Urban Frontier: The Rise of Western Cities, 1790–1830* (Cambridge, Mass.: Harvard University Press, 1959).

35. Among the sources that underscore the rapidity of the resettlement of the West, see Arrell Morgan Gibson, *The West in the Life of the Nation* (Lexington, Mass.: D. C. Heath, 1976), ix, 3–9, and Williams, *Contours of American History*, 227.

36. Bernard DeVoto, "The West: A Plundered Province," *Harper's*, August 1934: 355–64; Walter Prescott Webb, *Divided We Stand: The Crisis of a Frontierless Democracy* (New York: Farrar and Rinehart, 1937); A. G. Mezerik, *The Revolt of the*

South and West (New York: Duell, Sloan, and Pearce, 1946); Wendell Berge, *Economic Freedom for the West* (Lincoln: University of Nebraska Press, 1946); Joseph Kinsey Howard, *Montana: High, Wide, and Handsome* (1943; Lincoln: University of Nebraska Press, 1983); and Ladd Haystead, *If The Prospect Pleases: The West the Guidebooks Never Mention* (Norman: University of Oklahoma Press, 1945).

37. Representatives of this group include Pomeroy, *Pacific Slope*, 297–305; Gerald D. Nash, *The American West in the Twentieth Century: A Short History of an Urban Oasis* (Englewood Cliffs: Prentice Hall, 1973), 233–34, 300; Nash, *The American West Transformed: The Impact of the Second World War* (Bloomington: Indiana University Press, 1985) viii—ix; and Nash, *World War II and the West* (Lincoln: University of Nebraska Press, 1990), 17. See also Carl Abbott, *The New Urban America: Growth and Politics in Sunbelt Cities* (Chapel Hill: University of North Carolina Press, 1981), 15.

38. For a historiographical discussion of these issues, see William G. Robbins, "The 'Plundered Province' Thesis and the Recent Historiography of the American West," *Pacific Historical Review* 55 (November 1986): 577–97. On the point of continuity for certain persisting features of western history, see Limerick, *Legacy of Conquest*, 18–19, 26–30.

39. Donald W. Meinig, "American Wests: Preface to a Geographical Interpretation," *Annals of the Association of American Geographers* 62 (June 1972): 170–75, 181, 179.

40. Cronon, "Revisiting the Vanishing Frontier," 174–75, and Richard White, *Roots of Dependency: Subsistence, Environment, and Social Change among the Choctaws, Pawnees, and Navajos* (Lincoln: University of Nebraska Press, 1983), xvii.

41. For a sampling of the now standard references to world-systems theory, see Immanuel Wallerstein, *The Capitalist World Economy* (New York: Cambridge University Press, 1979); Wallerstein, *The Politics of the World-Economy: The States, the Movements, and the Civilizations* (Cambridge: Cambridge University Press, 1984); Fernand Braudel, *Civilization and Capitalism, 15th–18th Century*, trans. Sian Reynolds (1979; New York: Harper and Row, 1984); Braudel, *Afterthoughts on Material Civilization and Capitalism*, trans. Patricia Ranum (Baltimore: Johns Hopkins University Press, 1977); Leften S. Stavrianos, *The Promise of the Coming Dark Age* (San Francisco: W. H. Freeman, 1976); and Andre Gorz, *Socialism and Revolution*, trans. Norman Denny (New York: Doubleday, 1973). For criticism of Wallerstein's work, see Theda Skocpol, "Wallerstein's World Capitalist System: A Theoretical and Historical Critique," *American Journal of Sociology* 82 (March 1977): 1075–90; Robert Brenner, "The Origins of Capitalist Development: A Critique of Neo-Smithian Marxism," *New Left Review* 104 (July–August 1977): 25–92; T. H. Ashton and C. H. E. Philpin, eds., *The Brenner Debate: Agrarian Class Structure and Economic Development in Pre-Industrial Europe* (Cambridge: Cambridge University Press, 1985); and especially Stern, "Feudalism, Capitalism, and the World-System," 829–72.

42. One fundamental characteristic of capitalism, according to Wallerstein, is its ability to work its way beyond the will of nation-states: "The capitalist world-economy has, and has had since its coming into existence, boundaries far larger than those of any political unit" (Wallerstein, *Politics of World Economy*, 13, and *Capitalist World Economy*, 19). There are, of course, national and regional peculiarities that limit the degree of the world-system's influence (see Stern, "Feudalism, Capitalism, and the World-System," 857. In defense of Wallerstein, it should be noted that in relative terms core nations, states, and regions did benefit greatly from events in the periphery.

43. For select studies that address these issues, see Wallace Stegner and Page Stegner, "Rocky Mountain Country," *Atlantic Monthly*, April 1978: 45–91; Worster, *Rivers of Empire*; Wiley and Gottlieb, *Empires in the Sun*; K. Ross Toole, *The Rape of the Great Plains: Northwest America, Cattle and Coal* (Boston: Little, Brown, 1976); John A. Young and Jan M. Newton, *Capitalism and Human Obsolescence: Corporate Control versus Individual Survival in Rural America* (Montclair, N.J.: Allenheld, Osmun, 1980); and Elvin Hatch, *Biography of a Small Town* (New York: Columbia University Press, 1972).

44. Stephen Cox has drawn attention to this fact: "The history [of the West] is the imposition of federal policy—federal Indian policy, federal lands policy, federal railroad policy, federal Air Force policy—and the exploitation of natural resources by the use of capital from somewhere else, and the way those two forces combine, in real estate development, to produce huge cities with very sparse hinterlands" (Cox, "Talking, Reading, and Writing Western History," *Journal of the Southwest* 29 [Winter 1987]: 377). There were limits to the power, even of capitalists; the resistance by the forces of labor and local intraclass collaboration often worked against the desires of distant banking houses and investment entrepreneurs. For other examples, see Stern, "Feudalism, Capitalism, and the World-System," 857.

45. Raymond Williams, *The Country and the City* (New York: Oxford University Press, 1973), 289, 293.

46. For sources that address this assessment, see Douglas F. Dowd, "A Comparative Analysis of Economic Development in the American West and South," *Journal of Economic History* 16 (December 1956): 570–73; Jonathan M. Wiener, "Class Structure and Economic Development in the American South, 1865–1955," *American Historical Review* 84 (October 1979): 991–92; Jack Temple Kirby, *Rural Worlds Lost: The American South, 1920–1960* (Baton Rouge: Louisiana State University Press, 1987), xiv–xv; James C. Cobb, *Industrialization and Southern Society, 1877–1984* (Lexington: University Press of Kentucky, 1984), 136–39, and Cobb, *The Selling of the South: The Southern Crusade for Industrial Development, 1936–1980* (Baton Rouge: Louisiana State University Press, 1982), 254–56, 265. See also Gavin Wright, *Old South, New South: Revolutions in the Southern Economy since the Civil War* (New York: Basin Books); and Stanley Aronowitz, "The End of Political Economy," *Social Text: Theory, Culture, Ideology* 1, no. 2 (1979): 12–17.

47. Kirby, *Rural Worlds Lost*, 14–16, and Young and Newton, *Capitalism and Human Obsolescence*, 75. On the development of cotton production in California, see William J. Briggs and Henry Cauthen, *The Cotton Man: Notes on the Life and Times of Wofford B. ("Bill") Camp* (Columbia: University of South Carolina Press, 1983).

48. See Noel J. Kent, *Hawaii: Islands under the Influence* (New York: Monthly Review Press, 1983), 4.

49. Gorz, *Socialism and Revolution*, 218–21.

50. On the emergence of new centers of power in the West, see Nash, *American West in the Twentieth Century*, 191–92, 213–14, and *American West Transformed*, 201–16, and especially Wiley and Gottlieb, *Empires in the Sun*, 77–216.

51. Norman H. Clark, *Mill Town: A Social History of Everett, Washington* (Seattle: University of Washington Press, 1970), 234. For a sampling of similar accounts, see Howard, *Montana: High, Wide, and Handsome*; John Fahey, *Inland Empire: Unfolding Years, 1879–1929* (Seattle: University of Washington Press, 1986); Arnon Gutfeld, *Montana's Agony: Years of War and Hysteria, 1917–1921* (Gaines-

ville: University Presses of Florida, 1979); Barbara Allen, *Homesteading the High Desert* (Salt Lake City: University of Utah Press, 1987); Neal R. Peirce, *The Rocky Mountain States of America: People, Politics, and Power in the Eight Rocky Mountain States* (New York: W. W. Norton, 1972); and Ivan Doig, "You Can't NOT Go Home Again," *Montana: Magazine of Western History* 35 (Winter 1985): 2–15.

52. In the case of the lumber industry, see William G. Robbins, *Hard Times in Paradise: Coos Bay, Oregon, 1850–1986* (Seattle: University of Washington Press, 1988), and Robbins, "Lumber Production and Community Stability: A View from the Pacific Northwest," *Journal of Forest History* 31 (October 1987): 187–96.

53. Wiley and Gottlieb, *Empires in the Sun*, 304–7, and *New York Times*, December 28, 1987.

54. Patricia Marchak, *In Whose Interest: An Essay on Multinational Corporations in a Canadian Context* (Toronto: Metheun, 1979), 100–105. Other Canadian scholars who focus on the hegemony of the metropolis include Leo Panitch, "Dependency and Class in Canadian Political Economy," *Studies in Political Economy* 6 (1981): 7–34; Mel Watkins, "The Staple Theory Revisited," *Journal of Canadian Studies* 12 (Winter 1977): 83–95; and Wallace Clement, *Class, Power, and Prosperity: Essays on Canadian Society* (Toronto: Metheun, 1983), viii–ix.

55. For studies that examine the power of the metropolis in the American West, see Wiley and Gottlieb, *Empires in the Sun*, 75–216; Bradford Luckingham, "The American Southwest: An Urban View," *Western Historical Quarterly* 15 (July 1984): 261–80; Joe R. Feagin, *Free Enterprise City: Houston in Political-Economic Perspective* (New Brunswick, N.J.: Rutgers University Press, 1988); William Issel and Robert W. Cherny, *San Francisco, 1865–1932: Politics, Power, and Urban Development* (Berkeley: University of California Press, 1982); and Nash, *American West in the Twentieth Century.*

56. For use of the term, see Nash, *The American West in the Twentieth Century*, 195.

57. Cronon, "Revisiting the Vanishing Frontier," 174–75.

58. *Portland Oregonian*, December 29, 1985; Spencer Olin, Jr., "The View from the Top: Orange County's Political Elites since World War II" (Paper presented to the annual meeting of the Pacific Coast Branch, American Historical Association, Seattle, August 21, 1984; copy in possession of the author). See also Rob Kling, Spencer Olin, and Mark Poster, eds., *Postsuburban California: The Transformation of Orange County since World War II* (Berkeley: University of California Press, 1991).

59. Aronowitz, "End of Political Economy," 12, 18, 43; Gorz, *Socialism and Revolution*, 221–22; and Wallerstein, *Capitalist World Economy*, 70–71. Aronowitz attributes changing demographic patterns to the movement of capital—in its quest for greater profit taking—from one industrial sector to the next or from one country to the next (Stanley Aronowitz, *False Promises: The Shaping of American Working-Class Consciousness* [New York: McGraw Hill, 1973], 178).

60. Peter F. Drucker, "The Changed World Economy," *Foreign Affairs* 64 (Spring 1986): 768–70.

61. Michael Malone, "The Collapse of Western Metal Mining: An Historical Epitaph," *Pacific Historical Review* 55 (August 1986): 455–64.

62. *Corvallis Gazette-Times*, October 14, 1985.

63. "American West Suffering from Shock," *Ogden Standard-Examiner*, April 14, 1987.

64. Lewis Mumford, *Technics and Civilization* (New York: Harcourt, Brace, 1934), 431.

65. Meinig, *Continental America*, 28, and Williams, "Thoughts on the Fun and Purpose of Being an Historian," 3.

66. White made those remarks at the session "What's Wrong and Right with Western History," Western History Association's Twenty-Ninth Annual Conference, Tacoma, Wash., October 13, 1989.

67. For a review of that critique, see George Wilson Pierson, "American Historians and the Frontier Hypothesis in 1941," *Wisconsin Magazine of History* 26 (September 1942): 36–60, 170–74; George Rogers Taylor, ed., *The Turner Thesis Concerning the Role of the Frontier in American History*, rev. ed. (Boston: D. C. Heath, 1956); Richard Hofstadter and Seymour Martin Lipset, eds., *Turner and the Sociology of the Frontier* (New York: Basic Books, 1968); Ray Allen Billington, ed., *The Frontier Thesis: Valid Interpretation of American History?* (New York: Holt, Rinehart, Winston, 1968); and Ray Allen Billington, *The Genesis of the Frontier Thesis: A Study in Historical Creativity* (San Marino, Calif.: Huntington Library, 1971). Other sources offering critical insights into the frontier thesis include Lee Benson, *Turner and Beard: American Historical Writing Reconsidered* (Glencoe, Ill.: Free Press, 1960); Jackson K. Putnam, "The Turner Thesis and the Westward Movement: A Reappraisal," *Western Historical Quarterly* 7 (October 1976): 377–404; Richard Jensen, "On Modernizing Frederick Jackson Turner: The Historiography of Regionalism," *Western Historical Quarterly* 11 (July 1980): 307–22; and David Noble, *The End of American History* (Minneapolis: University of Minnesota Press, 1985).

68. Fred A. Shannon, "A Post-Mortem on the Labor–Safety-Valve Theory," *Agricultural History* 19 (January 1945): 31–37; Smith, *Virgin Land;* and Earl Pomeroy, "Toward a Reorientation of Western History: Continuity and Environment," *Mississippi Valley Historical Review* 41 (March 1955): 579–600. See also Harry N. Schreiber, "Turner's Legacy and the Search for a Reorientation of Western History: A Review Essay," *New Mexico Historical Review* 44 (July 1969): 231–48; Jerome O. Steffen, "Some Observations on the Turner Thesis: A Polemic," *Papers in Anthropology* 14 (1973): 16–30; and Martin Ridge, "Frederick Jackson Turner, Ray Allen Billington, and American Frontier History," *Western Historical Quarterly* 19 (1988): 5–20. In addition to Cronon's excellent "Revisiting the Vanishing Frontier," readers should consult Michael Malone, "Beyond the Last Frontier: Toward a New Approach to Western American History," *Western Historical Quarterly* 20 (November 1989): 409–28.

69. Among the many critiques of the exceptionalist theme, see Laurence Veysey, "The Autonomy of American History Reconsidered," *American Quarterly* 31 (Fall 1979): 455–77; Michael Kammen, "The Historian's Vocation and the State of the Discipline in the United States," in *The Past Before Us: Contemporary Historical Writing in the United States*, ed. Kammen (Ithaca, N.Y.: Cornell University Press, 1980), 22; Robertson, *American Myth, American Reality*, 7–8; Warren I. Susman, *Culture as History: The Transformation of American Society in the Twentieth Century* (New York: Pantheon, 1984), 3–26; Loren Baritz, *Backfire: A History of How American Culture Led Us into Vietnam and Made Us Fight the Way We Did* (New York: W. Morrow, 1985), 9–34; Monkkonen, "The Dangers of Synthesis," 1146–47; and Ian Tyrrell, "American Exceptionalism in an Age of International History," *American Historical Review* 96 (October 1991): 1031–72.

70. William Howarth, "America's Dream of the Wide Open Spaces," *Book*

World, January 4, 1987, 4; and Peter Shrag, "Straddling the Fault," *Nation,* November 27, 1989, 638–40.

71. Elliott West, "A Longer, Grimmer but More Interesting Story," in *Trails: Toward a New Western History,* ed. Patricia Nelson Limerick, Clyde A. Milner II, and Charles E. Rankin (Lawrence: University Press of Kansas, 1991), 103–5.

CHAPTER TWO: THE U.S.-MEXICO BORDERLANDS

1. Quoted in Robert W. Johannsen, *To the Halls of the Montezumas: The Mexican War in the American Imagination* (New York: Oxford University Press, 1985), 217–18.

2. E. J. Hobsbawm, *The Age of Capital, 1848–1875* (1975; New York: New American Library, 1979), 128–30.

3. Otis A. Singletary, *The Mexican War* (Chicago: University of Chicago Press, 1960), 1–5; Donald W. Meinig, *Continental America, 1800–1867,* vol. 2 of *The Shaping of America: A Geographical Perspective on 500 Years of History* (New Haven, Conn.: Yale University Press, 1993), 151–52; and W. Eugene Hollon, *The Southwest: Old and New* (1961; Lincoln: University of Nebraska Press, 1968), 188–89. For an account of the boundary survey, see Robert V. Hine, *Bartlett's West: Drawing the Mexican Boundary* (New Haven, Conn.: Yale University Press, 1968).

4. The *Spectator* is quoted in David S. Painter, "Making Connections," *Reviews in American History* 21 (June 1993): 268.

5. Linda B. Hall and Don M. Coever, *Revolution on the Border: The United States and Mexico, 1910–1920* (Albuquerque: University of New Mexico Press, 1988), 3, 6, 8. Carey McWilliams is quoted in Joel Garreau, *The Nine Nations of North America* (Boston: Houghton Mifflin, 1981), 211. For differences in the scholarly works on the borderlands region, see David J. Weber, "Turner, the Boltonians, and the Borderlands," *American Historical Review* 91 (February 1986): 66–81.

6. For suggestions based on these insights, see Gerald E. Poyo and Gilberto M. Hinojosa, "Spanish Texas and Borderlands Historiography in Transition: Implications for United States History," *Journal of American History* 75 (1988): 393–416; Jorge A. Bustamante, "Demystifying the United States-Mexico Border," *Journal of American History* 79 (September 1992): 485; Elizabeth A. Johns, "A View from the Spanish Borderlands," *Proceedings of the American Antiquarian Society* 101, pt. 1 (1991): 78; and Lawrence R. Clayton, "The Southwest and Its Culture," *Journal of American Culture* 14 (Summer 1991): 7.

7. Bustamante, "Demystifying the United States-Mexico Border," 489–90.

8. Hollon, *Southwest: Old and New,* 152–74; John A. Hawgood, *America's Western Frontiers: The Exploration and Settlement of the Trans-Mississippi West* (New York: Alfred A. Knopf, 1967), 153–58; Kent Ladd Steckmesser, *The Westward Movement: A Short History* (New York: McGraw Hill, 1969), 260–75; Richard A. Bartlett, *The New Country: A Social History of the American Frontier, 1776–1890* (New York: Oxford University Press, 1974), 83–114; and Arrell Morgan Gibson, *The West in the Life of the Nation* (Lexington, Mass.: D. C. Heath, 1976), 334–57.

9. Meinig, *Continental America,* 17.

10. David J. Weber, *The Mexican Frontier, 1821–1846* (Albuquerque: Univer-

sity of New Mexico Press, 1982), 282; and Weber, "Turner, the Boltonians, and the Borderlands," 79. Patricia Nelson Limerick is even more blunt on the theme of the celebratory frontier: "Turner's frontier had no relevance to Hispanic borderlands history" (Limerick, *The Legacy of Conquest: The Unbroken Past of the American West* [New York: W. W. Norton, 1987], 253). For an essay on borderlands historiography, see Poyo and Hinojosa, "Spanish Texas and Borderlands Historiography in Transition," 393–416.

11. David J. Weber, "The Spanish Legacy in North America and the Historical Imagination," *Western Historical Quarterly* 23 (February 1992): 7–8.

12. This theme is addressed in William G. Robbins, "Laying Siege to Western History: The Emergence of New Paradigms," in *Trails: Toward A New Western History,* ed. Patricia Nelson Limerick, Clyde Milner II, and Charles E. Rankin, (Lawrence: University Press of Kansas, 1991), 195–200.

13. David Thelen, "Of Audiences, Borderlands, and Comparisons: Toward the Internationalization of American History," *Journal of American History* 79 (1992): 443.

14. Donald Meinig, "Continental America, 1800–1915" (Paper presented to the annual meeting of the Organization of American Historians, Reno, Nevada, March 26, 1988, p. 17; copy in possession of the author). See also Meinig, *Atlantic America, 1492–1800,* vol. 1 of *The Shaping of America* (New Haven, Conn.: Yale University Press, 1987), xv–xix.

15. Oscar Martinez argues this point in *Border Boom Town: Ciudad Juarez since 1848* (Austin: University of Texas Press, 1975), 4–5, and *The Mexican-American Border: Issues and Trends* (Notre Dame, Ind.: University of Notre Dame Press, 1989), 1.

16. John Phillip Santos, "Rio Grande: A Chicano's Berlin Wall," *Portland Oregonian,* December 19, 1989, and Joel Garreau, *Nine Nations of North America,* 211, 214.

17. Thomas D. Hall, *Social Change in the Southwest, 1350–1880* (Lawrence: University Press of Kansas, 1989), 5, 8, 12. For California, according to Albert Hurtado, the conquest meant a rapidly diminishing living space for Indians who had lived on the margins of white society. The objective of the Hispanic regime was to integrate native people, but U.S. policy resorted to the segregated reservation system (see Hurtado, *Indian Survival on the California Frontier* [New Haven, Conn.: Yale University Press, 1988], 213).

18. Alvar W. Carlson, *The Spanish-American Homeland: Four Centuries in New Mexico's Rio Arriba* (Baltimore: Johns Hopkins University Press, 1990), xiii–xiv, 67–68.

19. Richard L. Nostrand, "The Hispano Homeland in 1900," *Annals, Association of American Geographers* 70 (September 1980): 382–96.

20. Carlson, *Spanish-American Homeland,* 82–83, 88.

21. Ibid., 204, 212–18.

22. Richard L. Nostrand, *The Hispano Homeland* (Norman: University of Oklahoma Press, 1992), 169, 190–91, and John Nichols, *The Milagro Beanfield War* (New York: Random House, 1974).

23. Sarah Deutsch, *No Separate Refuge: Culture, Class, and Gender on an Anglo-Hispanic Frontier in the American Southwest, 1880–1940* (New York: Oxford University Press, 1987), 9–10, 200–201. For a parallel inquiry into the historical geography of the Hispanic settlements in northern New Mexico, see Nostrand, *Hispano Homeland.*

24. Deutsch, *No Separate Refuge,* 8–12.

25. Donald W. Meinig, *Imperial Texas: An Interpretive Essay in Cultural Geography* (Austin: University of Texas, 1969), 71–72.

26. Montejano, *Anglos and Mexicans in the Making of Texas,* 313–14.

27. Ibid., 108–14, 313.

28. Ibid., 118–25.

29. I use the term indigenous here to refer to both Indian and Mexican people residing in the borderlands region at the time of the conquest. For reference to definitions of the terms Hispanic, Mexicano, Mexican-American, and Chicano, see Juan Gomez Quinones, *Chicano Politics: Reality and Promise, 1940–1990* (Albuquerque: University of New Mexico Press, 1990), 6–8.

30. Sherburne F. Cook, *The Conflict between the California Indian and White Civilization* (Berkeley: University of California Press, 1976), 255–79, 351, and Albert Hurtado, *Indian Survival on the California Frontier* (New Haven, Conn.: Yale University Press, 1988). For the decimation of the Indian population in Oregon and Washington, see Carolyn M. Buan and Richard Lewis, eds., *The First Oregonians* (Portland: Oregon Council for the Humanities, 1991), and Eugene S. Hunn, *Nch'i-Wana, "The Big River": Mid-Columbia Indians and Their Land* (Seattle: University of Washington Press, 1990).

31. Marx is quoted in Hobsbawm, *Age of Capital,* 32.

32. Ramon Eduardo Ruiz, *The People of Sonora and Yankee Capitalists* (Tucson: University of Arizona Press, 1988), 26. For a discussion of the link between railroads and the expansion of capitalism to the far corners of the globe, see Hobsbawm, *Age of Capital,* 32–55.

33. Niles M. Hansen, *Border Economy: Regional Development in the Southwest* (Austin: University of Texas Press, 1981), 45.

34. Martinez, *Border Boom Town,* 22; Hansen, *The Border Economy,* 45; and Garcia, *Desert Immigrants,* 13–14.

35. Mario T. Garcia, *Desert Immigrants: The Mexicans of El Paso, 1880–1920* (New Haven, Conn.: Yale University Press, 1981), 3–5; Martinez, *Border Boom Town,* 6; and Hansen, *Border Economy,* 45–46.

36. Ralph Mann, "Frontier Opportunity and the New Social History," *Pacific Historical Review* 53 (1984): 484, and Limerick, *Legacy of Conquest,* 244.

37. Bradford Luckingham, "The American Southwest: An Urban View," *Western Historical Quarterly* 15 (1984): 263–65; and Luckingham, *The Urban Southwest: A Profile History of Albuquerque, El Paso, Phoenix, Tucson* (El Paso: Texas Western University Press, 1982), 35.

38. Michael Malone, "The Collapse of Western Metal Mining: An Historical Epitaph," *Pacific Historical Review* 55 (1986): 457; Robert Glass Cleland, *A History of Phelps-Dodge, 1834–1950* (New York: Alfred A. Knopf, 1952), 130–31; Rodman Paul, *The Far West and the Great Plains in Transition* (New York: Harper and Row, 1988), 275; and Hollon, *Southwest,* 337.

39. Leo E. Zonn, "The Railroads of Sonora and Sinaloa, Mexico: A Historical Geography," *Social Science Journal* 15 (April 1978): 1–4. For a description of the historical geography of northern Mexico, see Mark Wasserman, *Capitalists, Caciques, and Revolution: The Native Elite and Foreign Enterprise in Chihuahua, Mexico, 1854–1911* (Chapel Hill: University of North Carolina Press, 1984), 8–15.

40. Luckingham, "American Southwest," 266–67.

41. Martinez, *Border Boom Town,* 4–5, and Oscar Martinez, *Troublesome Border* (Tucson: University of Arizona Press, 1988).

42. Meinig, *Continental America,* 549; Eric R. Wolf, *Peasant Wars of the Twentieth Century* (New York: Harper and Row, 1969), 13–18, 33; John Mason Hart, *Revolutionary Mexico: The Coming and Process of the Mexican Revolution* (Berkeley: Uni-

versity of California Press, 1987), 6; and John H. Coatsworth, *Growth against Development: The Economic Impact of Railroads in Porfirian Mexico* (DeKalb: Northern Illinois University Press, 1981), 1–5.

43. Although I recognize that change was apparent throughout Mexico during these years, the most obvious and glaring manifestations of the capitalist transformation outlined here occurred in the north. See Wolf, *Peasant Wars in the Twentieth Century*, 22, 32–33; James D. Cockroft, *Mexico: Class Formation, Capital Accumulation, and the State* (New York: Monthly Review Press, 1983), 86–93; Hart, *Revolutionary Mexico*, 6; and Hall and Coever, *Revolution on the Border*, 3–12.

44. Hart, *Revolutionary Mexico*, 130–33.

45. Wasserman, *Capitalists, Caciques, and Revolution*, 6 and 153.

46. Ruiz, *People of Sonora and Yankee Capitalists*, 4–5.

47. Ibid., 26, 246.

48. Hall and Coever, *Revolution on the Border*, 7–8; and Montejano, *Anglos and Mexicans*, 109–14.

49. Ibid., 24–25, and Montejano, *Anglos and Mexicans*, 117. For a history of the Plan de San Diego, see James A. Sandos, *Rebellion in the Borderlands: Anarchism and the Plan of San Diego, 1904–1923* (Norman: University of Oklahoma Press, 1992).

50. Montejano, *Anglos and Mexicans*, 118–25.

51. Hart, *Revolutionary Mexico*, 373–78.

52. New Mexico Bureau of Immigration, *The Mines of New Mexico* (Santa Fe: New Mexican Printing Company, 1896), 1, *Santa Fe County, New Mexico* (1909), 1, and *Ho! To The Land of Sunshine* (1909), 1; Larry Schweikart, "Early Banking in New Mexico from the Civil War to the Roaring Twenties," *New Mexico Historical Review* 63 (1988): 17, 22; and Sigurd Johansen, *Population Changes in New Mexico*, Agricultural Experiment Station Research Report 191, New Mexico State University (n.d.), 3.

53. Lawrence Clark Powell, *Arizona: A Bicentennial History* (New York: W. W. Norton, 1976), 50–51; Odie B. Faulk, *Arizona: A Short History* (Norman: University of Oklahoma Press, 1970), 218–21; and Carlos A. Schwantes, "Introduction," in *Bisbee: Urban Outpost on the Frontier*, ed. Schwantes (Tucson: University of Arizona Press, 1992), 1–5.

54. Schwantes, "Introduction," 2, 5, and Lynn R. Bailey, *Bisbee: Queen of the Copper Camps* (Tucson, Ariz.: Westernlore Press, 1983), xi.

55. Raul A. Fernandez, *The United States–Mexican Border: A Politico-Economic Profile* (Notre Dame, Ind.: University of Notre Dame Press, 1977), 4, and Ruiz, *People of Sonora and Yankee Capitalists*, 247–48.

CHAPTER THREE: THE AMERICAN AND CANADIAN WESTS

1. Donald W. Meinig, "Continental America, 1800–1915: The View of an Historical Geographer," *History Teacher* 22 (February 1989): 199.

2. *New York Times*, October 26, 1992.

3. Meinig, "Continental America, 1800–1915," 201. A *Maclean's* survey taken early in 1989 indicates that although Americans know practically nothing about Canada, Canadians know a great deal about the United States (cited in Seymour Martin Lipset, *Continental Divide: The Values and Institutions of the United States and Canada* [New York: Routledge, 1990], xvi).

4. *New York Times*, October 26, 1992; Kenneth Coates, "Borders and Border-

lands: A Canadian Perspective" (Paper presented at the April 1992 annual meeting of the Organization of American Historians in Chicago, copy in the author's possession).

5. Donald Worster, *Under Western Skies: Nature and History in the American West* (New York: Oxford University Press, 1992), 226.

6. Meinig, "Continental America," 199–200.

7. Lipset, *Continental Divide*, 91.

8. Fernandez, *The United States–Mexico Border: A Politico-Economic Profile* (Notre Dame, Ind.: University of Notre Dame Press, 1977), 4.

9. Patricia Nelson Limerick, *The Legacy of Conquest: The Unbroken Past of the American West* (New York: W. W. Norton, 1986), 30.

10. This assessment is based on the comments of Susan Armitage, "Invisible People, Invisible Issues" (Paper presented at April 1992 annual meeting of the Organization of American Historians in Chicago; copy in the author's possession); and of Coates, "Borders and Borderlands." For two studies that bridge the international boundary, see Hana Samek, *The Blackfoot Confederacy, 1800–1920: A Comparative Study of Canadian and U.S. Indian Policy* (Albuquerque: University of New Mexico Press, 1987), and Carlos A. Schwantes, *Radical Heritage: Labor, Socialism, and Reform in Washington and British Columbia* (Seattle: University of Washington Press, 1979).

11. Paul F. Sharp, "Three Frontiers: Some Comparative Studies of Canadian, American, and Australian Settlement," *Pacific Historical Review* 24 (1955): 369–77; Timothy Egan, *The Good Rain: Across Time and Terrain in the Pacific Northwest* (New York: Alfred Knopf, 1990), 53; Norbert MacDonald, *Distant Neighbors: A Comparative History of Seattle and Vancouver* (Lincoln: University of Nebraska Press, 1987), 55, 100.

12. I use the term economic culture for its all-inclusive meaning, the supposition that capitalist societies are moved to action by widely accepted assumptions and values. See Peter Berger, *The Capitalist Revolution: Fifty Propositions about Prosperity, Equality, and Liberty* (New York: 1986), 7–8, 26–27, and Donald Worster, *Dust Bowl: The Southern Plains in the 1930s* (New York: Oxford University Press, 1979), 6.

13. Barry M. Gough, *Distant Dominion: Britain and the Northwest Coast of North America, 1579–1809* (Vancouver: University of British Columbia Press, 1980), 32–33, 41–51; according to Gough, Cook's voyage was truly significant: "It represented the initial penetration of the market system to the region, even though the initial exchanges of commodities were by accident rather than by design." Cook's *Voyages* is cited in Carlos Schwantes, *The Pacific Northwest: An Interpretive History* (Lincoln: University of Nebraska Press, 1989), 19.

14. Gough, *Distant Dominion*, 126, 147. As Ralph Mann has observed about the Southwest in the aftermath of the war with Mexico, "what was opportunity to one system was destruction to another" (Mann, "Frontier Opportunity and the New Social History," *Pacific Historical Review* 53 (November 1984): 468).

15. The literature on Lewis and Clark is vast. Those sources that have contributed to my assessment of the importance of the Corps of Discovery include Bernard DeVoto, ed., *The Journals of Lewis and Clark*, 2 vols. (Boston: Houghton Mifflin, 1953); DeVoto, *The Course of Empire* (Boston: Houghton Mifflin, 1952); John Logan Allen, *Passage through the Garden: Lewis and Clark and the Image of the Northwest* (Urbana: University of Illinois Press, 1975); William Nichols, "Lewis and Clark and the Heart of Darkness," *American Scholar* (Winter 1979–1980): 94–101; and James P. Ronda, *Lewis and Clark among the Indians* (Lincoln: University of Nebraska Press, 1984). In a recent essay on the resurgence of Lewis and Clark

studies, Gary E. Moulton cites the expedition as "one of the great adventure stories in American history." Excitement, "dangerous encounters," and "hair-raising" activities fill the journals. This western epic is set apart from others, he contends, because of "the true and undisputed evidence upon which it is based" (Moulton, "On Reading Lewis and Clark: The Last Twenty Years," *Montana: Magazine of Western History* 38 [Summer 1988]: 28).

16. Ronda, *Lewis and Clark among the Indians*, 202–3.

17. Allen, *Passage through the Garden*, 394. According to Bernard DeVoto, the publication of the journals removed the West from the realm of myth and fantasy: "Henceforth the mind could focus on reality. Here were not only Indians but the land itself and its conditions: river systems, mountain ranges, climates, flora, fauna, and a rich and varied membrane of detail" (DeVoto, ed., *Journals of Lewis and Clark*, lii).

18. Lewis to his mother, Fort Mandan, March 31, 1805, in *Original Journals of the Lewis and Clark Expedition, 1804–1806*, ed. Reuben Gold Thwaites, 7 vols. (New York: Dodd, Mead, 1905), 7: pt. 2, 310–11; Lewis to Jefferson, September 23, 1806, in Thwaites, ed., *Journals of Lewis and Clark*, 7: 334–37; and DeVoto, *Course of Empire*, 527–28.

19. DeVoto, *Course of Empire*, 528.

20. The literature citing the significance of the expedition to American expansionism is vast. See especially DeVoto, *Course of Empire*, xxx, 539; DeVoto, ed., *The Journals of Lewis and Clark*, 1; William Appleman Williams, *The Contours of American History* (Chicago: Quadrangle Books, 1966), 184; Richard Dillon, *Meriwether Lewis: A Biography* (1965; reprint, New York: Capricorn Books, 1968), xi–xii; and Ronda, *Lewis and Clark among the Indians*, 255.

21. The newspaper references are in Thwaites, *Original Journals of the Lewis and Clark Expedition*, 7: pt. 2, 347–49.

22. Ross Cox, *The Columbia River*, ed. Edgar I. Stewart and Jane R. Stewart (Norman: University of Oklahoma Press, 1957), 71, 80, 167, 256.

23. For a discussion of the larger factors in this argument, see Tzvetan Todorov, *The Conquest of America*, trans. Richard Howard (1982; New York: Harper and Row, 1984), 42–43.

24. Elliott Coues, ed., *The Manuscript Journals of Alexander Henry and David Thompson, 1799–1814*, 2 vols. (1897; reprint, Minneapolis: Ross and Haines, 1965), 1: 754, 776–77.

25. Ibid., 748. For praise of Thompson's cartography, see Gordon B. Dodds, *Oregon: A History* (New York: W. W. Norton, 1977), 47, and Schwantes, *Pacific Northwest*, 56. Donald W. Meinig points out that Thompson's great maps, almost unknown to outsiders during his lifetime, hung for many years on the walls of company headquarters at Ft. William (Meinig, *The Great Columbia Plain: A Historical Geography, 1805–1910* [Seattle: University of Washington Press, 1968], 39. Exploration and discovery have been central to Euro-American mythology in North America; in the material world, however, reality suggested quite the opposite: "The countryside was inhabited, explored, and crisscrossed with roadways" (James O. Robertson, *American Myth, American Reality* [New York: Hill and Wang, 1980], 36).

26. For the quotations, see Burt Brown Barker, ed., *Letters of Dr. John McLoughlin, Written at Fort Vancouver, 1829–1832* (Portland: Binford and Mort, 1948), 41, 57, 138, 185, 213, 236.

27. Frederick Merk, ed., *Fur Trade and Empire: George Simpson's Journal* (Cambridge, Mass.: Harvard University Press, 1931), 74.

28. Ibid., 40, 74, 87, 92.

29. Ibid., 94, 106.

30. Ibid., 108. White indicates that in some instances market relations "blended with other imperial, religious, or cultural aims" (Richard White, *Roots of Dependency: Subsistence, Environment, and Social Change among the Choctaws, Pawnees, and Navajos* [Lincoln: University of Nebraska Press, 1983], xv).

31. Merk, ed., *Fur Trade and Empire*, 298, 309–10.

32. In a provocative essay, Harold P. Simonson posits three stages in the elaboration of a regional literature: The first identifies place, its climate, geographical contours, its human inhabitants; the second builds upon the materials of the first and attempts to provide interpretation based on the evidence in the primary accounts; and the third moves toward a universality in which the region is placed in a larger context of all-inclusive issues and themes (see Simonson, "Pacific Northwest Literature—Its Coming of Age," *Pacific Northwest Quarterly* 71 [October 1980]: 146–51.

33. For the tragic element in the fiction and literature of the American West, see Harold P. Simonson, *Beyond the Frontier: Writers, Western Regionalism and a Sense of Place* (Fort Worth: Texas Christian University Press, 1989).

34. J. Russell Harper, *Paul Kane's Frontier* (Austin: University of Texas Press, 1971), ix, xii, 18, 74.

35. Ibid., ix, 74. Kane's description of the Chinook Indians followed in the tradition of Lewis and Clark, a people who possessed "filthy" habits, "their persons . . . abounding in vermin," and their language "horrible harsh, spluttering sounds which proceed from their throats, apparently unguided by the tongue or the lip" (93–94).

36. Elizabeth Johns, "Settlement and Development: Claiming the West," in *The West as America: Reinterpreting Images of the Frontier, 1820–1920*, ed. William Truettner (Washington, D.C.: Smithsonian Institution Press, 1991), 233.

37. For information on Kelley, the "Oregon prophet," see Malcolm Clark, *Eden Seekers: The Settlement of Oregon, 1818–1862* (Boston: Houghton Mifflin, 1981), 57–59; and Schwantes, *Pacific Northwest*, 78–79.

38. The quotations, most of them excerpts from speeches in the U.S. Senate, are from Thomas Hart Benton, *Thirty Years View* (New York, 1897), 2: 468–69.

39. Ibid., 470, 474–75.

40. See especially, Dodds, *Oregon*, 68, 95, 174, and Dorothy O. Johansen, *Empire of the Columbia: A History of the Pacific Northwest* (New York: Macmillan, 1968), 231–32. For a critical appraisal of the Donation Land Law, see William G. Robbins, "The Indian Question in Western Oregon: The Making of a Colonial People," in *Experiences in a Promised Land: Essays in Pacific Northwest History*, ed. G. Thomas Edwards and Carlos A. Schwantes, eds. (Seattle: University of Washington Press, 1986), 51–67.

41. Paul Tennant, *Aboriginal Peoples and Politics: The Indian Land Question in British Columbia, 1849–1989* (Vancouver: University of British Columbia Press, 1990), 3.

42. For studies that discuss the differences in violence toward Indians north and south of the border, see Robin W. Winks, *The Relevance of Canadian History: U.S. and Imperial Perspectives* (Toronto: Macmillan, 1979), 18; Robin Fisher, *Contact and Conflict: Indian-European Relations in British Columbia, 1774–1890* (Vancouver: University of British Columbia Press, 1977), 60–61; and Barry M. Gough, "The Character of the British Columbia Frontier," *BC Studies*, 32 (Winter 1976–1977): 32–33.

43. Gough, "Character of the British Columbia Frontier," 37–39, and Edgar W. McInnis, *The Unguarded Frontier* (Garden City, N.Y.: Doubleday, 1942), 306–7.

44. Wilson is quoted in Gough, "Character of the British Columbia Frontier," 49; see also MacDonald, *Distant Neighbors*, 43.

45. Lipset, *Continental Divide*, 1, 10, 218. For the remark about Canadian and Mexican counterparts to Frederick Jackson Turner, see David J. Weber, "Turner, the Boltonians, and the Borderlands," *American Historical Review* 91 (February 1986): 79. For a discussion of these issues in Canadian writing, see Dick Harrison, ed., *Crossing Frontiers: Papers in American and Canadian Western Literature* (Edmonton: University of Alberta Press, 1979). I have benefited greatly from an ongoing dialogue with Max Geier about American and Canadian historiography; scholars interested in an excellent comparative study of transnational rural communities should read his "Comparative History of Rural Community on the Northwest Plains: Lincoln County, Washington and the Wheatland Region, Alberta, 1880–1930" (Ph.D. diss., Washington State University, 1990).

46. See especially, Fisher, *Contact and Conflict*, and Tennant, *Aboriginal Peoples and Politics*.

47. George F. G. Stanley, *The Birth of Western Canada: A History of the Riel Rebellions* (1936; reprint, Toronto: University of Toronto Press, 1970), vii–viii.

48. Ibid., 380. While Stanley focused on Metis and Indians, J. Arthur Lower virtually ignored them in a later effort that emphasized natural-resource wealth to western Canada; see Lower, *Western Canada: An Outline History* (Vancouver: Douglas and McIntyre, 1983).

49. Gerald Friesen, *The Canadian Prairies: A History* (Toronto: University of Toronto, 1984), xiv, 4, 23. Friesen's argument about the erosion of native autonomy follows that of Richard White, who contends that subsistence systems, disrupted from without, contributed directly to varying forms of dependency (see White, *Roots of Dependency*, xix, 318).

50. Friesen, *Canadian Prairies*, 92–93. Issues of race and class have been at the center of the most innovative research on the American Southwest, but scholarship on the northern West has lagged in that respect. For the Southwest, see Oscar Martinez, *Border Boom Town: Ciudad Juarez since 1848* (Austin: University of Texas Press, 1975), 4–5.

51. See Vernon C. Fowke, "National Policy and Western Development in North America," *Journal of Economic History* 16 (December 1956), 461–79; Gerald Friesen, "Recent Historical Writings on the Prairie West," in *The Prairie West: Historical Readings*, ed. Douglas Francis and Howard Palmer (Edmonton: University of Alberta Press, 1985), 5–18; and Roger Gibbins, "Western Alienation in Canada and the United States: A Cross-National and Trans-National Comparison," circa 1981 (paper in possession of the author). Gibbins finds regional alienation in Canada threatening the survival of the national government. For the more extended argument, see Gibbins, *Regionalism: Territorial Politics in Canada and the United States* (Toronto: University of Toronto Press, 1981).

52. Harold A. Innis, *The Fur Trade in Canada: An Introduction to Canadian Economic History* (New Haven, Conn.: Yale University Press, 1930), 385. Innis made the same argument in *Settlement and the Mining Frontier* (Toronto: Macmillan of Canada, 1936), and in *The Cod Fisheries: The History of An International Economy* (New Haven, Conn.: Yale University Press, 1940).

53. For the resurgence of the staples theory, see Mel Watkins, "A Staples Theory of Economic Growth," *Canadian Journal of Economics and Political Science* 29 (May 1963): 141–58; Watkins, "The Staples Theory Revisited," *Journal of Canadian Studies* 12 (Winter 1977): 83–95; Kari Levitt, *Silent Surrender* (Toronto: Macmillan of Canada, 1970); and Daniel Drache, "Rediscovering Canadian Political Economy," in *A Practical Guide to Canadian Political Economy*, comp. Wallace Clement

and Daniel Drache (Toronto: James Lorimer, 1978). For a study that posits a staples-theory tradition for British Columbia, see Martin Robin, *The Rush for Spoils: The Company Province, 1871–1933* (Toronto: McClelland and Stuart, 1972).

54. Allan Smith, "The Writing of British Columbia History," in *British Columbia: Historical Readings,* ed. W. Peter Ward and Robert A. J. McDonald (Vancouver: Doublas and McIntyre, 1981), 6–7, 22–23, 25.

55. Robin Fisher, *Contact and Conflict: Indian-European Relations in British Columbia, 1774–1890* (Vancouver: University of British Columbia, 1977), xi–xiv. With the settlers' domination of British Columbia, Fisher concludes, Indian people had been effectively reduced to "a peripheral role in British Columbia's economy" (p. 210).

56. I have addressed this issue in chapter 2 (see also William G. Robbins, "Laying Siege to Western History: The Emergence of New Paradigms," in *Trails: Toward a New Western History,* ed. Patricia N. Limerick, Clyde Milner II, and Charles Rankin (Lawrence: University Press of Kansas, 1991).

57. For only a small sampling of the revisionist works on the northern West, see Richard White, *Land Use, Environment, and Social Change: The Shaping of Island County, Washington* (Seattle: University of Washington Press, 1980); Paula M. Nelson, *After the West Was Won: Homesteaders and Townbuilders in Western South Dakota, 1900–1917* (Iowa City: University of Iowa Press, 1986); Barbara Allen, *Homesteading the High Desert* (Salt Lake City: University of Utah Press, 1987); Michael P. Malone, *The Battle for Butte: Mining and Politics on the Northern Frontier, 1846–1906* (Seattle: University of Washington Press, 1981); David M. Emmons, *The Butte Irish: Class and Ethnicity in an American Mining Town, 1875–1925* (Urbana: University of Illinois Press, 1989); and William G. Robbins, *Hard Times in Paradise: Coos Bay, Oregon, 1850–1986* (Seattle: University of Washington Press, 1988). The classic noncelebratory study of a community in the northern West is Norman Clark, *Mill Town: A Social History of Everett, Washington* (Seattle: University of Washington Press, 1970).

58. Bob Roseth, "How the West Was Won: Historian Rides High on Specialty's Popularity," *University Week,* April 18, 1991.

59. Donald W. Meinig, "Continental America, 1800–1915: The View of an Historical Geographer," 201.

60. This is not to suggest that Canadian historians have not considered the Turner thesis. See the essays in Harrison, ed., *Crossing Frontiers,* see also Barry M. Gough, "The Character of the British Columbia Frontier," in Ward and McDonald, eds., *British Columbia,* 232–44.

CHAPTER FOUR: IN PURSUIT OF PRIVATE GAIN

1. E. J. Hobsbawm, *The Age of Capital, 1848–1875* (1975; New York: New American Library, 1984), 157.

2. Eric R. Wolf, *Europe and the People without History* (Berkeley: University of California Press, 1982), 5–6; David Montejano, *Anglos and Mexicans in the Making of Texas, 1836–1939* (Austin: University of Texas Press, 1987), 1–2; and Richard Oestreicher, "Urban Working-Class Political Behavior and Theories of American Electoral Politics, 1870–1940," *Journal of American History* 74 (1988): 1257–86.

3. The most immediate and successful effort is Richard White's *"It's Your Misfortune and None of My Own": A New History of the American West* (Norman: University of Oklahoma Press, 1991).

4. Arrell Morgan Gibson, *The West in the Life of the Nation* (Lexington, Mass.:

D. C. Heath, 1976), ix. For similar historiographical approaches, see Richard A. Bartlett, *The New Country: A Social History of the American Frontier, 1776–1880* (New York: Oxford University Press, 1974); Kent Ladd Steckmesser, *The Westward Movement: A Short History* (New York: Macmillan, 1969); and Ray Allen Billington, *Westward Expansion: A History of the American Frontier,* 3d ed. (New York: Macmillan, 1967). An older synthesis that largely avoids the ahistorical issues of national purpose and design is Robert V. Hine, *The American West: An Interpretive History,* 2d ed. (Boston: Little, Brown, 1984).

5. Gibson, *West in the Life of the Nation,* 3.

6. Rodman W. Paul, *The Far West and the Great Plains in Transition, 1859–1900* (New York: Harper and Row, 1988), 299, and Robert G. Athearn, *High Country Empire: The High Plains and the Rockies* (1960; Lincoln: University of Nebraska Press, 1965), vii–viii. Also see Montejano, *Anglos and Mexicans in the Making of Texas,* 1, and William G. Robbins, "The Indian Question in Western Oregon: The Making of a Colonial People," in *Experiences in a Promised Land: Essays in Pacific Northwest History,* ed. G. Thomas Edwards and Carlos A. Schwantes (Seattle: University of Washington Press, 1986), 51–67.

7. For further elaboration of this argument, see Leften S. Stavrianos, *The Promise of the Coming Dark Age* (San Francisco: W. H. Freeman, 1976), 168–69.

8. Douglas C. North, "International Capital Flows and the Development of the American West," *Journal of Economic History* 16 (1965): 494, and Hobsbawm, *Age of Capital,* 45. See also Walter Prescott Webb, *Divided We Stand: The Crisis of a Frontierless Democracy* (New York: Farrar and Rinehart, 1937), 90–110.

9. The following sources have shaped my thinking on these issues: Peter Berger, *The Capitalist Revolution: Fifty Propositions about Property, Equality, and Liberty* (New York: Basic Books, 1986), 3–31; Donald Worster, *Dust Bowl: The Southern Plains in the 1930s* (New York: Oxford University Press, 1979), 3–8; and Wolf, *Europe and the People without History,* 3–23.

10. Emile Boutmy is quoted in William Cronon, *Nature's Metropolis: Chicago and the Great West* (New York: W. W. Norton, 1991), 53–54.

11. North, "International Capital Flows and the Development of the West," 495, 500; Hobsbawm, *Age of Capital,* 27–28; Wolf, *Europe and the People without History,* 312; and Oscar O. Winther, "Promoting the American West in England, 1865–1890," *Journal of Economic History* 16 (1956): 513. For surplus British capital investment in the western United States, see Clark C. Spence, *British Investments and the American Mining Frontier, 1860–1901* (Ithaca, N.Y.: Cornell University Press, 1958), 2, 238–39; Larry A. McFarlane, "British Agricultural Investment in the Dakotas, 1877–1953," in *Business and Economic History,* 2d ser. vol. 5 (Papers presented at the Twenty-Second Annual Meeting of the Business History Conference, March 12–13, 1976, pp. 113–14); and McFarlane, "British Investment in Midwestern Farm Mortgages and Land, 1875–1900: A Comparison of Iowa and Kansas," *Agricultural History* 48 (January 1974): 182, 196–97.

12. Patricia Nelson Limerick, *A Legacy of Conquest: The Unbroken Past of the American West* (New York: W. W. Norton, 1987), 82–83; and Steve Talbot, *Roots of Oppression: The American Indian Question* (New York: International Publishers, 1981), 34–35.

13. John Opie, *The Law of the Land: Two Hundred Years of American Farmland Policy* (Lincoln: University of Nebraska Press, 1987), 25–27, and Alan Trachtenberg, *The Incorporation of America: Culture and Society in the Gilded Age* (New York: Hill and Wang, 1982), 22.

14. Malcolm J. Rohrbough, *The Land Office Business: The Settlement and Administration of American Public Lands. 1789–1837* (New York: Oxford University

Press, 1968), xi–xii, 299–301. See also Gerald D. Nash, "Bureaucracy and Reform in the West: Notes on the Influence of a Neglected Interest Group," *Western Historical Quarterly* 2 (1971): 293–304. Elsewhere Nash observed that the carrying out of land policy in California "was vitiated by corruption" and loosely drafted legislation (Nash, "The California State Land Office, 1858–1898," *Huntington Library Quarterly* 27 [August 1964]: 347).

15. William H. Goetzmann, *Army Exploration in the American West: 1803–1863* (1959; Austin: Texas State Historical Society, 1991), 65, 261–62, 295, 305, and Goetzmann, *Exploration and Empire: The Explorer and the Scientist in the Winning of the West* (New York: W. W. Norton, 1966), 281, 316–17. Richard White brilliantly captures the function and influence of the federal government in the American West in *"It's Your Misfortune and None of My Own,"* 57–59.

16. Henry Nash Smith, *Virgin Land: The American West as Symbol and Myth* (New York: Alfred A. Knopf, 1950), 23–24, 31–34. Benton's speech is printed in *Congressional Globe*, 30th Cong., 2d sess., February 7, 1849, 473.

17. Trachtenberg, *Incorporation of America*, 20; and John Agnew, *The United States in the World Economy: A Regional Geography* (New York: Cambridge University Press, 1987), 3. For the point about land and resources as qualitative productive factors, see North, "International Capital Flows and the Development of the American West," 493.

18. Walter Nugent, *Crossings: The Great Transatlantic Migrations, 1870–1914* (Bloomington: Indiana University Press, 1992), 3.

19. Richard A. Bartlett, *Great Surveys of the American West* (Norman: University of Oklahoma Press, 1962), xiii–xiv; Goetzmann, *Exploration and Empire*, 391–92, 485–90, 530–31; and Trachtenberg, *Incorporation of America*, 19–20.

20. Bartlett, *Great Surveys of the American West*, 373–75.

21. Thomas G. Manning, *Government in Science: The United States Geological Survey, 1867–1894* (Lexington: University of Kentucky Press, 1967), xi–xiii, 2–4; David F. Noble, *America by Design: Science, Technology, and the Rise of Corporate Capitalism* (New York: Oxford University Press, 1977), 3; and White, *"It's Your Misfortune and None of My Own,"* 126.

22. Hobsbawm, *Age of Capital*, 149; Anthony Giddens, *A Contemporary Critique of Historical Materialism* (Berkeley: University of California Press, 1981), 121–22; Agnew, *United States in the World Economy*, 49–50; and North, "International Capital Flows and the Development of the American West," 495.

23. Agnew, *United States in the World Economy*, 49.

24. For a discussion of this phenomenon, see Nugent, *Crossings*, xv, 3, and Hobsbawm, *Age of Capital*, 70, 192–93.

25. Limerick, *Legacy of Conquest*, 82; Paul, *Far West and Great Plains in Transition*, 198–99; Gene M. Gressley, *Bankers and Cattlemen* (New York: Alfred A. Knopf, 1966), ix; and Athearn, *High Country Empire*, 141.

26. Paul, *Far West and Great Plains in Transition*, 200–202; and Athearn, *High Country Empire*, 142–44.

27. Athearn, *High Country Empire*, 144–45, and Gressley, *Bankers and Cattlemen*, 298.

28. Paul, *Far West and Great Plains in Transition*, 203–5; and Carl Abbott, Stephen J. Leonard, and David McComb, *Colorado: History of the Centennial State* (Boulder: Colorado Associated University Press, 1982), 168–69.

29. For an elaboration of this point, see Worster, *Dust Bowl*, 83, and Barrington Moore, Jr., *Social Origins of Dictatorship and Democracy: Lord and Peasant in the Making of the Modern World* (Boston: Beacon Press, 1966), 133.

30. For a discussion of changes in capitalism and the question of inevitabil-

ity, see Martin J. Sklar, *The Corporate Reconstruction of American Capitalism, 1890–1916* (New York: Cambridge University Press, 1988), 11–13.

31. These ideas are adapted from ibid., 1–19.

32. Hobsbawm, *Age of Capital*, 192.

33. See Albro Martin, *James J. Hill and the Opening of the Northwest* (New York: Oxford University Press, 1976).

34. Elwin B. Robinson, *History of South Dakota* (Lincoln: University of Nebraska Press, 1966), 137–43; Robert P. Wilkins and Wynoma Huchette Wilkins, *North Dakota: A Bicentennial History* (New York: W. W. Norton, 1977), 50–51; and Gilbert C. Fite, *The Farmers' Frontier, 1865–1900* (New York: Holt, Rinehart, and Winston, 1966), 76–90.

35. Robinson, *History of North Dakota*, 141–42; and Michael P. Malone and Richard B. Roeder, *Montana: A History of Two Centuries* (Seattle: University of Washington Press, 1976), 133–36.

36. Joseph Kinsey Howard, *Montana: High, Wide, and Handsome* (1943; Lincoln: University of Nebraska Press, 1983), 196.

37. Fite, *Farmers' Frontier*, 75–81; and Robinson, *History of North Dakota*, 137–39.

38. William Appleman Williams, *The Roots of the Modern American Empire: A Study in the Growth and Shaping of Social Consciousness in a Marketplace Society* (New York: Random House, 1969), 180–82; Fite, *Farmers' Frontier*, 81–84; and Robinson, *History of North Dakota*, 139.

39. Fite, *Farmers' Frontier*, 87–90.

40. Gilbert C. Fite, "Failure on the Last Frontier: A Family Chronicle," *Western Historical Quarterly* 18 (1987): 5–14.

41. Kathleen Norris, *Dakota: A Spiritual Geography* (New York: Ticknor and Fields, 1993), 6.

42. Wright Morris, *Will's Boy: A Memoir* (New York: Harper and Row, 1981), 1.

43. Robert W. Richmond, *Kansas: A Land of Contrasts* (Arlington Heights, Ill.: Forum Press, 1980), 104–43; Howard Ottoson et al., *Lands and People in the Northern Plains Transition Area* (Lincoln: University of Nebraska Press, 1966), 35–38; and Keith L. Bryant, Jr., *History of the Atchison, Topeka and Santa Fe Railway* (Lincoln: University of Nebraska Press, 1974), 15–63.

44. Bryant, *History of the Atchison, Topeka and Santa Fe*, 64–65, and Ottoson et al., *Lands and People in the Northern Plains Transition Area*, 35.

45. James C. Malin, "The Turnover of Farm Population in Kansas," *Kansas Historical Quarterly* 4 (1935): 339–72.

46. Worster, *Dust Bowl*, 83–84.

47. William Kittredge, "White People in Paradise," *Esquire*, December 1991: 152–62, 193–95.

48. For emphasis on the significance of land and resources to economic expansion, see Agnew, *United States in the World Economy*, 48–49, and Trachtenberg, *Incorporation of America*, 20–22.

49. Donald Worster draws attention to that pervasive world, the collective frame of reference, the "economic culture" that moved settlers to act as they did (Worster, *Dust Bowl*, 4–6).

50. Nugent, *Crossings*, 34.

51. James MacGregor Burns, *The American Experiment*, vol. 2 of *The Workshop of Democracy* (New York: Alfred A. Knopf, 1985), 127–30.

52. Lance E. Davis, "The Investment Market, 1870–1914: The Evolution of a National Market," *Journal of Economic History* 25 (1965): 385–86, and Allan Bogue,

Money at Interest (Ithaca, N.Y.: Cornell University Press, 1955). For the general sense that farmers were losing their autonomy, see Russell B. Nye, *Midwestern Progressive Politics* (East Lansing: Michigan State University Press, 1959), 7–12.

53. Paul, *Far West and Great Plains in Transition*, 232–33; John Thompson, *Closing the Frontier: Radical Response in Oklahoma, 1889–1923* (Norman: University of Oklahoma Press, 1986), 5–8; Opie, *Law of the Land*, 101; Ottoson et al., *Lands and People in the Northern Plains Transition Area*, 37; Marshall Sprague, *Colorado: A Bicentennial History* (New York: W. W. Norton, 1976), 108–9; and Goetzmann, *Exploration and Empire*, 168–69.

54. Ottoson et al., *Lands and People in the Northern Plains Transition Area*, 43–45; Fite, *Farmers' Frontier*, 125–32; and Opie, *Law of the Land*, 102.

55. Wolf, *Europe and the People without History*, 311–15; Agnew, *United States in the World Economy*, 55–56; and Trachtenberg, *Incorporation of America*, 39. Gerald Nash has argued that in the United States, railroads were major instruments of economic growth until 1914. See Nash, *The American West in the Twentieth Century: A Short History of an Urban Oasis* (1973; Albuquerque: University of New Mexico Press, 1984), 19.

56. For a summary view of those developments, see Nugent, *Crossings*, 3, 11; Gilbert C. Fite, "The Great Plains: Promises, Problems, Prospects," in *The Great Plains: Environment and Culture*, ed. Brian W. Blouet and Frederick C. Luebke (Lincoln: University of Nebraska Press, 1979), 187–88; and especially Wolf, *Europe and the People without History*, 312–13, 318–19.

57. Nugent, *Crossings*, 34.

58. On the uniqueness of the development of California agriculture, especially its tradition of large units of production, see Carey McWilliams, *California, The Great Exception* (1949; Santa Barbara: Peregrine Smith, 1979), 93–100. Gerald Nash points out that California reached self-sufficiency in supplying its own food needs by 1856 (Nash, *State Government and Economic Development: A History of Administrative Policies in California, 1849–1933* [Berkeley: University of California Press, 1964], 64).

59. Josiah Royce, *California: From the Conquest in 1846 to the Second Vigilance Committee in San Francisco* (1886; Santa Barbara, Calif.: Peregrine Publishers, 1970), 37–38, and Hubert Howe Bancroft, *History of California*, 7 vols. (San Francisco: History Company, 1890), 7: 3–5. Dana is quoted in Kevin Starr, *Americans and the California Dream, 1850–1915* (New York: Oxford University Press, 1973), 41.

60. McWilliams, *California, The Great Exception*, 89–90; Donald Worster, *Rivers of Empire: Water, Aridity, and the Growth of the American West* (New York: Pantheon, 1985), 98–99; and Nash, "The California State Land Office," 348, 356.

61. Raymond F. Dasmann, *The Destruction of California* (New York: Macmillan, 1965), 61–69, 120–22; Worster, *Rivers of Empire*, 99–100; McWilliams, *California, The Great Exception*, 99–100; and Donald Pisani, *From Family Farm to Agribusiness: The Irrigation Crusade in California and the West, 1850–1931* (Berkeley: University of California Press, 1984), 442. Henry George is quoted in McWilliams.

CHAPTER FIVE: THE INDUSTRIAL WEST

1. William L. Lang, "You Have to Start with the Work," *Northern Lights* 4:1 (January 1988): 26.

2. *Denver Post*, October 17, 1991.

3. Carlos A. Schwantes, "The Concept of the Wageworker's Frontier: A Framework for Future Research," *Western Historical Quarterly* 18 (January 1987): 41. For a brief overview of ethnicity and early industrialism in the West, see David M. Emmons, "Social Myth and Social Reality," *Montana: Magazine of Western History* 39 (Autumn 1989): 2-9. In a delightfully provocative essay, Richard Maxwell Brown draws a distinction between the classic and counterclassic in western history and culture. The classic West was infused with Indians, mountain men, cowboys, and the like; the counterclassic embraced its antithesis—urbanization, industrialization, and technological advances (Brown, "The New Regionalism in America, 1970-1981," in *Regionalism and the Pacific Northwest*, ed. William G. Robbins, Robert J. Frank, and Richard E. Ross [Corvallis: Oregon State University Press, 1983], 71).

4. Bernard DeVoto, "The West: A Plundered Province," *Harper's Magazine*, August 1934, 355-64, and Walter Prescott Webb, *Divided We Stand: The Crises of a Frontierless Democracy* (New York: Farrar and Rinehart, 1937).

5. For special reference to the industrialization of the West during World War II, see Earl Pomeroy, *The Pacific Slope: A History of California, Oregon, Washington, Idaho, Utah, and Nevada* (New York: Alfred Knopf, 1965), and Gerald D. Nash, *The American West in the Twentieth Century: A Short History of an Urban Oasis* (Englewood Cliffs, N.J.: Prentice Hall, 1973), 233-34, 300. Michael Malone and Richard Etulain argue that "Uncle Sam remade the regional economy" during the years of the New Deal and World War II with infusions of investment that propelled "the West's industrialization and urbanization." The consequence was an economy that shifted from reliance on natural-resource extraction and agriculture to a more diversified infrastructure (Malone and Etulain, *The American West: A Twentieth-Century History* [Lincoln: University of Nebraska Press, 1989], 6-7). For a discussion of colonialism in the West, see William G. Robbins, "The 'Plundered Province' Thesis and the Recent Historiography of the American West," *Pacific Historical Review* 55 (November 1986): 577-97.

6. Pomeroy, *Pacific Slope*, 297-98 (emphasis added).

7. Gerald D. Nash, *The American West Transformed: The Impact of the Second World War* (Bloomington: Indiana University Press, 1985), 17-18, 201.

8. For the transformation of the Canadian West during World War II, see Jean Barman, *The West beyond the West: A History of British Columbia* (Toronto: University of Toronto Press, 1991), 261-69.

9. Patricia Nelson Limerick, *The Legacy of Conquest: The Unbroken Past of the American West* (New York: W. W. Norton, 1986), 99, 108, 124, and Michael Malone, "The Collapse of Western Metal Mining: An Historical Epitaph," *Pacific Historical Review* 55 (1986): 455. Ralph Mann believes that post-Indian western American history is largely an urban story and that the early mining towns established that urban character (Mann, *After the Gold Rush: Society in Grass Valley and Nevada City, California, 1849-1870* [Stanford: Stanford University Press, 1982], vii).

10. Ellen Meloy, "Urban Miner," *Northern Lights* 4:1 (January 1988): 16.

11. Richard E. Lingenfelter, *The Hardrock Miners: A History of the Mining Labor Movement in the American West, 1863-1893* (Berkeley: University of California Press, 1974), 31-32; Lawrence H. Larson, *The Urban West at the End of the Frontier* (Lawrence: University Press of Kansas, 1978), 14; and Mann, *After the Gold Rush*, 1.

12. Lingenfelter, *Hardrock Miners*, 32, 64-65, 106. For a general commentary on the development of western mining beyond the Comstock, see Rodman W.

Paul, *The Far West and the Great Plains in Transition, 1859–1900* (New York: Harper and Row, 1988), 254, 264–65.

13. For a discussion of the capitalist appropriation and incorporation of the West, see Alan Trachtenberg, *The Incorporation of America: Culture and Society in the Gilded Age* (New York: Hill and Wang, 1982), 11–37.

14. William Issel and Robert W. Cherny, *San Francisco, 1865–1932: Politics, Power, and Urban Development* (Berkeley: University of California Press, 1986), 24–25, and Paul, *Far West and Great Plains in Transition*, 72, 84.

15. Carlos A. Schwantes, "The Concept of the Wageworkers' Frontier: A Framework for Future Research," *Western Historical Quarterly* 18 (January 1987): 39–56, and Emmons, "Social Myth and Social Reality," 4.

16. John Agnew, *The United States in the World Economy: A Regional Geography* (New York: Cambridge University Press, 1987), 52–53.

17. Larry A. McFarlane, "British Agricultural Investment in the Dakotas, 1877–1953," in *Business and Economic History*, ed. Paul Uselding, 2d ser., vol. 5 (Papers presented at the Twenty-Second *Annual Meeting of the Business History Conference*, 113–14).

18. Matthew Simon, "The Pattern of New British Portfolio Foreign Investment, 1865–1914," 15, 23–27, and Brinley Thomas, "Migration and International Investment," 53, both in *The Export of Capital from Britain, 1870–1914*, ed. A. R. Hall, (London: Methuen, 1968).

19. Clark C. Spence, *British Investments and the American Mining Frontier, 1860–1901* (Ithaca, N.Y.: Cornell University Press, 1958), 2–3.

20. Mark Wyman, *Hard Rock Epic: Western Miners and the Industrial Revolution, 1860–1910* (Berkeley: University of California Press, 1979), 18–19; Robert L. Spude, "Mineral Frontier in Transition: Copper Mining in Arizona, 1880–1885," *New Mexico Historical Review* 51 (1976): 22; and Spence, *British Investments and the American Mining Frontier*, 238–39.

21. See the inventory to the Samuel T. Hauser Papers in the Montana Historical Society, Helena, Montana. See also K. Ross Toole, "When Big Money Came to Butte: The Migration of Eastern Capital to Montana," *Pacific Northwest Quarterly* 44 (1953): 24.

22. Robert A. Chadwick, "Montana's Silver Mining Era: Great Boom and Great Bust," *Montana: Magazine of Western History* 32 (Spring 1982): 20–21, and Richard H. Peterson, *The Bonanza Kings: The Social Origins and Business Behavior of Western Mining Entrepreneurs, 1870–1900* (1971; Lincoln: University of Nebraska Press, 1977), 115.

23. The influence of railroads in the expansion of copper mining, especially the reduction in transportation costs, is emphasized in Spude, "Mineral Frontier in Transition," 20.

24. Agnew, *United States in the World Economy*, 111–12, and B. J. L. Berry and F. E. Horton, *Geographic Perspectives on Urban Systems* (Englewood Cliffs, N.J.: Prentice-Hall, 1970), 35.

25. Martin Sklar argues that we should think of the emergence of corporate capitalism in the late nineteenth century "as something that people are making happen" (Sklar, *The Corporate Reconstruction of American Capitalism, 1890–1916* [New York: Cambridge University Press, 1988], 11–12).

26. Spude, "Mineral Frontier in Transition," 20, 25–29; and Marc Simmons, *New Mexico: An Interpretive History* (1977; reprint, Albuquerque: University of New Mexico Press, 1988), 160. For the role of foreign capital in southern and southwestern railroad construction, see Dorothy Adler, *British Investment in*

American Railways, 1834–1898 (Charlottesville: University Press of Virginia, 1970), 192.

27. *Phelps-Dodge Corporation, 1881–1981: Standing with Arizona for 100 Years* (Bisbee, Ariz.: Copper Queen Publishing Company, 1981), 4, 7, and Paul, *Far West and Great Plains in Transition*, 275–77. For a scholar who eulogizes Phelps-Dodge, see Robert Glass Cleland, *A History of Phelps-Dodge, 1834–1950* (New York: Alfred A. Knopf, 1952).

28. Paul, *Far West and Great Plains in Transition*, 276–79.

29. W. Eugene Hollon, *The Southwest: Old and New* (1961; Lincoln: University of Nebraska Press, 1968), 337, and Carlos A. Schwantes, ed., *Bisbee: Urban Outpost on the Frontier* (Tucson: University of Arizona Press, 1992), 1–5.

30. For the standard textbook version, see Mary Beth Norton et al., *A People and A Nation: A History of the United States*, 3d ed. (Boston: Houghton Mifflin, 1990), 593–99.

31. Chadwick, "Montana's Silver Mining Era," 19.

32. Malcolm J. Rohrbough, *Aspen: The History of a Silver Mining Town, 1879–1893* (New York: Oxford University Press, 1986), 219.

33. A brief but descriptive account of the fallout from the House report is in James E. Fell, Jr., *Ores to Metals: The Rocky Mountain Smelting Industry* (Lincoln: University of Nebraska Press, 1979), 201–2. See also Chadwick, "Montana's Silver Mining Era," 28, and Stanley Dempsey and James E. Fell, Jr., *Mining the Summit: Colorado's Ten Mile District, 1860–1960* (Norman: University of Oklahoma Press, 1986), 229–30.

34. Rohrbough, *Aspen*, 219–20, and Fell, *Ores to Metals*, 202–3.

35. Chadwick, "Montana's Silver Mining Era," 16–17, 31.

36. Quoted in Muriel S. Wolle, *Montana Pay Dirt* (Denver: Sage Books, 1963), 250, 252.

37. Michael P. Malone, *The Battle for Butte: Mining and Politics on the Northern Frontier, 1864–1906* (Seattle: University of Washington Press, 1981), 54–55, and Fell, *Ores to Metals*, 202.

38. Malone, "Collapse of Western Metal Mining," 457–58.

39. For these impressions of Butte, see the following sources: Mark Ciabattari, "The Fall and Rise of Butte, Montana," *New York Times Magazine*, March 1, 1992, 48–61; Lang, "You Have to Start with the Work," 25–29; Emmons, "Social Myth and Social Reality"; Malone, *Battle for Butte*; and Joseph Kinsey Howard, "What Happened in Butte," *Harper's Magazine*, August 1948, 89–96.

40. For an assessment of these trends, see Mann, *After the Gold Rush*, 214–18.

41. For the formation of the copper trust, see Malone, *Battle for Butte*, 131–40.

42. Carl Abbott, Stephen J. Leonard, and David McComb, *Colorado: A History of the Centennial State* (Boulder: Colorado Associated University Press, 1982), 133, and H. Lee Scamehorn, *Pioneer Steelmaker in the West: The Colorado Fuel and Iron Company, 1872–1903* (Boulder: Pruett Publishing Company, 1976), 4.

43. H. Lee Scamehorn, *Mill and Mine: The CF&I in the Twentieth Century* (Lincoln: University of Nebraska Press, 1992), 1, 7.

44. Scamehorn, *Pioneer Steelmaker*, v, 4–5; Abbott et al., *Colorado*, 135; and H. A. Brassert to Carl H. Behr, September 1, 1943, Report on the Colorado Fuel and Iron Company, box 19, Business Interests, Papers of the Rockefeller Family, Rockefeller Archive Center, North Tarrytown, New York.

45. This discussion parallels the argument in William Cronon, "Kennecott Journey: The Paths out of Town," in *Under An Open Sky: Rethinking America's*

Western Past, ed. William Cronon, George Miles, and Jay Gitlin (New York: W. W. Norton, 1992), 28–51.

46. Duane A. Smith, *When Coal Was King: A History of Crested Butte, Colorado, 1880–1952* (Golden: Colorado School of Mines, 1984), x, 51–53, 57, 123, and James B. Allen, *The Company Town in the American West* (Norman: University of Oklahoma Press, 1966), 157.

47. Abbott et al., *Colorado,* 135–36, and Scamehorn, *Pioneer Steelmaker,* 4–5.

48. For the disruption of Hispanic communities in northern New Mexico, see Richard L. Nostrand, *The Hispano Homeland* (Norman: University of Oklahoma Press, 1992), 169, 190–91.

49. The analysis and the quotation are from Sarah Deutsch, *No Separate Refuge: Culture, Class, and Gender on an Anglo-Hispanic Frontier in the American Southwest, 1880–1940* (New York: Oxford University Press, 1987).

50. George S. McGovern and Leonard F. Guttridge, *The Great Coalfield War* (Boston: Houghton Mifflin, 1972), 6–11.

51. Ibid., 12–15.

52. For a listing of the board of directors shortly after the Rockefellers gained controlling interest in CF&I, see Annual Report, Colorado Fuel and Iron Company, October 17, 1904, box 25, Business Interests, Rockefeller Family Papers. For John D. Rockefeller, Jr's., position on labor unions, see George P. West, United States Commission on Industrial Relations, *Report on the Colorado Strike* (Washington, D.C.: 1915).

53. Scamehorn, *Pioneer Steelmaker,* 5, and Philip F. Keebler to Henry James, January 2, 1945, box 84, Business Interests, Rockefeller Family Papers. See also McGovern and Guttridge, *Great Coalfield War,* 98.

54. Gates to John D. Rockefeller, Jr., May 3, 1907, and Gates to Bowers, November 12, 1907, both in box 21, Business Interests, Rockefeller Family Papers.

55. Gates to Bowers, November 19, 1907, ibid.

56. McGovern and Guttridge, *Great Coalfield War,* 59–63.

57. Bowers to John D. Rockefeller, Jr., November 4, 1912, box 21, Business Interests, Rockefeller Family Papers.

58. Rockefeller, Jr., to Bowers, November 25 and December 2, 1912, ibid.; and McGovern and Guttridge, *Great Coalfield War,* 78–79.

59. McGovern and Guttridge, *Great Coalfield War,* 63–69; and Bowers to John D. Rockefeller, Jr., February 21, 1912, box 21, Business Interests, Rockefeller Family Papers. The McNamara reference is to John and James McNamara who confessed to dynamiting the *Los Angeles Times* building in 1910 in retribution for the newspaper's vitriolic antiunion policy. See Sidney Lens, *The Labor Wars: From the Molly Maguires to the Sitdowns* (New York: Doubleday, 1973), 218–19.

60. McGovern and Guttridge, *Great Coalfield War,* 80–81, and Bowers to John D. Rockefeller, Jr., February 24, 1912, box 21, Business Interests, Rockefeller Family Papers.

61. Quoted in McGovern and Guttridge, *Great Coalfield War,* 111.

62. West, *Report on the Colorado Strike,* 15.

63. Scamehorn, *Mill and Mine,* 38–55.

64. Deutsch, *No Separate Refuge,* 203.

65. The Industrial Representation Plan (or Rockefeller Plan) was a company-sponsored arrangement for channeling employee grievances and other points of dispute between management and labor. Employee representatives, however, had no decisionmaking powers; the plan was dropped in 1933 when employees opted for an independent union. See McGovern and Guttridge, *Great Coalfield War,* 335–42.

66. Welborn to Rockefeller, December 17, and Rockefeller to Welborn, December 23, 1920, both in box 15, Business Interests, Rockefeller Family Papers. See also Scamehorn, *Mill and Mine,* 4.

67. Scamehorn, *Mill and Mine,* 5. A brief financial history of CF&I is in a communication from H. A. Brassert to Dillon Read and Company, September 1, 1945, box 19, Business Interests, Rockefeller Family Papers.

68. Duane A. Smith, *Mining America: The Industry and the Environment, 1800-1980* (Lawrence: University Press of Kansas, 1987), 30; and Malone, "Collapse of Western Metal Mining," 464.

69. Jeremy Bernstein, "Report from Aspen," *New Yorker,* November 25, 1991, 121-23, and Rohrbough, *Aspen,* 122-23.

70. Julia Welsh, "Letter to the Editor, *Northern Lights,* vol. 5, no. 1 (January 1989).

CHAPTER SIX: FROM CAPITALIST PATRIARCHY TO
CORPORATE MONOPOLY

1. This statement, made in 1912, is quoted in William Appleman Williams, *The Contours of American History* (1961; Chicago: Quadrangle Books, 1966), 390.

2. The dinner scene is described in Edwin O. Holter to Anton M. Holter, December 10, 1913, box 29, Anton M. Holter Papers, Montana Historical Society. For an excellent personal portrait of John D. Ryan, see Carrie Johnson, "Electrical Power, Copper, and John D. Ryan," *Montana: Magazine of Western History* 38 (Autumn 1988): 24-37.

3. The argument here is adapted from Spencer C. Olin, "Free Markets and Corporate America," *Radical History Review* 50 (1991): 213-20 (quotation on 216).

4. Alfred D. Chandler, *The Visible Hand: The Managerial Revolution in American Business* (Cambridge, Mass.: Harvard University Press, 1977), 286, 334, 338.

5. David F. Noble, *America by Design: Science, Technology, and the Rise of Corporate Capitalism* (New York: Oxford University Press, 1977), 70.

6. Williams, *Contours of American History,* 350-54.

7. Martin J. Sklar, *The Corporate Reconstruction of American Capitalism, 1890-1916* (New York: Cambridge University Press, 1988), 1-10. Sklar argues that the historical development of capitalism in the United States was characterized in the late nineteenth century by its transformation from competitive to corporate operations.

8. Ibid., 3-4; Williams, *Contours of American History,* 354; and Louis Galambos and Joseph Pratt, *The Rise of the Corporate Commonwealth: United States Business and Public Policy in the Twentieth Century* (New York: Basic Books, 1988), 71.

9. For a general discussion of capitalism as a transforming, dynamic, even cataclysmic force, see Williams, *Contours of American History*; Robert Heilbroner, *The Nature and Logic of Capitalism* (New York: W. W. Norton, 1985); Peter Berger, *The Capitalist Revolution: Fifty Propositions about Prosperity, Equality, and Liberty* (New York: Basic Books, 1986); and Peter F. Drucker, *The New Realities: In Government and Politics, in Economics and Business, in Society and World View* (New York: Harper and Row, 1989). For the influence of capitalism as an agency of change in rural hinterland areas, see Steven Hahn and Jonathan Prude, eds., *The Countryside in the Age of Capitalist Transformation: Essays in the Social History of Rural America* (Chapel Hill: University of North Carolina Press, 1985). For special reference to the American West, see Alan Trachtenberg, *The Incorporation of America: Culture and Society in the Gilded Age* (New York: Hill and Wang, 1982); Michael P. Ma-

lone, "Beyond the Last Frontier: Toward a New Approach to Western American History," *Western Historical Quarterly* 20 (November 1989): 409–28; and William G. Robbins, "Western History: A Dialectic on the Modern Condition," *Western Historical Quarterly* 20 (November 1989): 429–49.

10. For a discussion of the issues of external control and persisting change for the northern West, see William G. Robbins, "'At the End of the Cracked Whip': The Northern West, 1880–1920," *Montana: Magazine of Western History* 38 (Autumn 1988): 2–11, and Robbins, "The Northern Tier States as 'Plundered Provinces,' 1900–1940," *Centennial West: Essays on the Northern Tier States*, ed. William L. Lang (Seattle: University of Washington Press, 1991), 11–38. For a few select sources that address external control over Montana, see Joseph Kinsey Howard, *Montana: High, Wide, and Handsome* (1943; Lincoln: University of Nebraska Press, 1983); K. Ross Toole, *Twentieth-Century Montana: A Land of Extremes* (Norman: University of Oklahoma Press, 1972); Clark G. Spence, *Montana: A Bicentennial History* (New York: W. W. Norton, 1977); Arnon Gutfeld, *Montana's Agony: Years of War and Years of Hysteria, 1917–1921* (Gainesville: University Presses of Florida, 1979); and Michael P. Malone, *The Battle for Butte: Mining and Politics on the Northern Frontier, 1864–1906* (Seattle: University of Washington Press, 1981).

11. Quoted in typescript notes in box 14, Philip R. Barbour Papers, Montana Historical Society.

12. This brief sketch is based on the guide to the Samuel T. Hauser Papers. This rich collection, especially useful for the years 1864 to 1914, provides valuable insights into the influence of external investment capital and the speculative character of economic activity in the northern West. For a study of Hauser's business career until the silver bust of 1893, see John W. Hakola, "Samuel T. Hauser and the Economic Development of Montana: A Case Study in Nineteenth-Century Frontier Capitalism" (Ph.D. diss., Indiana University, 1961). For a review of Hauser's later efforts in power development, see Alan S. Newell, "A Victim of Monopoly: Samuel T. Hauser and Hydroelectric Development on the Missouri River, 1898–1912" (Master's thesis, University of Montana, 1979).

13. For an assessment of Clark's career, see Malone, *Battle for Butte*, and Malone, "Midas of the West: The Incredible Career of William Andrews Clark," *Montana: Magazine of Western History* 33 (1983): 2–17.

14. General information about Hauser's life can be found in Michael Leeson, comp., *History of Montana, 1739–1885* (Chicago: Warner, Beers, 1885), 1217; Joaquin Miller, *An Illustrated History of the State of Montana* (Chicago: Lewis Publishing Company, 1894), 126–27; *Progressive Men of Montana* (Chicago: A. W. Bowen, 1900), 202–3; and William L. Lang and Rex C. Myers, *Montana: Our Land and People* (Boulder, Colo.: Westview Press, 1979), 45–48.

15. Paul C. Phillips, ed., *Forty Years on the Frontier as seen in the Journals and Reminiscences of Granville Stuart* (Glendale, Calif.: Arthur H. Clark, 1957), 265. See also William S. Reese, "Granville Stuart of the DHS Ranch, 1879–1887," *Montana: Magazine of Western History* 31 (July 1981): 14–27.

16. Circular letter to F. Billings et al., July 11, 1889, box 32, Hauser Papers.

17. Hauser to J. D. Cameron, May 29, 1891, box 35, ibid. (emphasis added).

18. Hauser to E. O. Holter, July 1, 1902, box 36, ibid.

19. Howard, *Montana: High, Wide, and Handsome*; Malone, "Midas of the West," 2–17; and Malone, *Battle for Butte*, 12–15, 82–83, 160–62.

20. Clark to Hauser, January 18, 1911, box 30, and Hauser to Clark, August 30, 1910, box 33, Hauser Papers.

21. John W. Hakola suggests that Hauser made several errors of judgment, including the decision to concentrate his investments in silver mining and smelt-

ing in the area to the south of Helena in lieu of copper mining in Butte. See Hakola, "Hauser and Economic Development of Montana," 311.

22. Hauser to Martin Maginnis, October 28, 1877, box 20, Hauser Papers.

23. Hauser to S. T. Hauser, Jr., June 5, 1907, box 33, ibid.

24. Hauser to Clark, August 1, 1906, box 36; Hauser to Robert Harris, January 16, 1886, box 32; and Hauser to John S. M. Neil, April 15, 1908, box 33, ibid.

25. I use the term silver bust to describe the effects of the national depression on the Montana economy. The refusal of the federal government to sustain the price of silver and the consequent glut on the market brought on the collapse of the world price for silver in summer 1893. The resulting depression was particularly harsh for Montana's large industrial work force. See Robert A. Chadwick, "Montana's Silver Mining Era: Great Boom and Great Bust," *Montana: Magazine of Western History* 32 (Spring 1982): 16–31.

26. Guide to Samuel T. Hauser Papers, Montana Historical Society, Helena.

27. Sklar, *Corporate Reconstruction of American Capitalism*, 4n.

28. Hakola, "Hauser and Economic Development of Montana," 152–54; and Robert Harris to George C. Coe, president, American Exchange National Bank, June 23, 1887, box 15, Hauser Papers.

29. Hauser to Robert Harris, January 16, and Harris to Hauser, January 18, 1886, box 32, Hauser Papers. For further evidence of Hauser's initiatives in railroad matters, see Albro Martin, *James J. Hill and the Opening of the Northwest* (New York: Oxford University Press, 1976), 339–40.

30. Returning from a trip over the Missoula Road in late 1887, Hauser telegrammed Robert Harris extolling the agricultural potential of the Missoula Valley and the abundance of "magnificent timber" on the adjacent hillsides, commenting that "mines so far as developed looks splendid." There would be "no doubt as to the future of the road, track laid thirty six miles. Valley settled and continues good for about fifty miles beyond end of track." See Hauser to Robert Harris, December 16, 1887, box 32, Hauser Papers.

31. Hakola, "Hauser and Economic Development of Montana," 158–59.

32. Thomas F. Oakes to Hauser, February 28, 1884, box 10, Hauser Papers.

33. T. F. Oakes to Hauser, January 2, 1885, box 12, ibid.

34. Oakes to Hauser, April 19, 1887, box 15, ibid. Even in the face of such denunciations, Hauser continued to stroke the Northern Pacific leadership. When Oakes planned a trip through Montana in fall 1888, Hauser telegrammed his Helena office advising local business leaders that it would "be a good idea to serenade Oakes on his arrival." Because "others have honored him, Helena ought to" (Hauser to Hervey Barbour, October 8, 1888, box 32, ibid.).

35. J. A. Barker to Hauser, November 4, 1887, box 15; J. M. Hannaford to Hauser, June 7, 1889, box 19; and Hannaford to Hauser, January 15, 1900, box 26, ibid.

36. For studies that focus in part on the industrial character of the depression, see Malcolm J. Rohrbough, *Aspen: The History of a Silver Mining Town, 1879–1893* (New York: Oxford University Press, 1986); James E. Fells, Jr., *Ores to Metals: The Rocky Mountain Smelting Industry* (Lincoln: University of Nebraska Press, 1979); Mark Wyman, *Hard Rock Epic: Western Miners and the Industrial Revolution, 1860–1910* (Berkeley: University of California Press, 1979); Ronald C. Brown, *Hard-Rock Miners: The Intermountain West, 1860–1920* (College Station: Texas A&M University Press, 1979); and Malone, *Battle For Butte.*

37. Guide to First National Bank of Helena Records, 1865–1903, Montana Historical Society, and Bill Skidmore, *Treasure State Treasury: Montana Banks, Bankers and Banking, 1864–1984* (Helena: n.p., 1985), 28.

38. V. P. Snyder to Hauser, February 23, 1886, box 14, and Hauser to W. L. Trenholm, October 19, 1886, box 34, Hauser Papers (emphasis added).

39. Hauser to comptroller of the currency, March 31, 1892, box 35, and deputy comptroller to Hauser, March 7, 1893, box 6, ibid.

40. The source of this phrase is Skidmore, *Treasure State Treasury*, 39.

41. Chadwick, "Montana's Silver Mining Era," 16–17, 28–31.

42. Andrew B. Hammond to Hauser, June 10 and 12, July 1, 11, and 19, and August 8, 1893, box 23, Hauser Papers.

43. Hauser to Hammond, December 2, and Hammond to Hauser, December 7, 1893, ibid.

44. For information on Hammond's career, see Dale L. Johnson, "Andrew B. Hammond: Education of a Capitalist on the Montana Frontier" (Ph.D. diss., University of Montana, 1976); Gage McKinney, "A. B. Hammond, West Coast Lumberman," *Journal of Forest History* 28 (October 1984): 196–203; and Daniel Cornford, *Workers and Dissent in the Redwood Empire* (Philadelphia: Temple University Press, 1987), 153–54.

45. Hammond to Hauser, December 7, 1893, box 23, Hauser Papers.

46. Hauser to Seligman, January 15, 1895, and Hauser to Francis J. Kennett, June 17, 1895, box 36, ibid. In an earlier letter demanding payment on an overdue note, the Seligman banking house expressed surprise: "We cannot see what use there is in making agreements between business men if they are to be broken" (J. & W. Seligman to Hauser, October 18, 1894, box 23, ibid.).

47. Hauser to E. H. Pullin, August 15, 1896, box 36, ibid.

48. J. Sam Brown to James H. Eckels, March 18, 1897, box 41, Records of the First National Bank of Helena, Montana Historical Society. Brown's statement parallels an authorial assessment of both W. A. Clark and Hauser as men who grasped the wisdom of frontier success: "It is good to be shifty in a new country." See Michael P. Malone and Richard B. Roeder, *Montana: A History of Two Centuries* (Seattle: University of Washington Press, 1976), 66.

49. Norman B. Holter to Anton M. Holter, March 27 and April 2, 1899, box 29, Holter Papers. On one occasion involving a question of Holter lands that were to be flooded by the construction of Hauser's Missouri River dams, the elder Holter took exception to the practices of his old business associate: "I feel that I deserve different treatment from you. I do not wish to enter into any arguments, but I could refer to many past transactions that have hardly been just to me" (Anton Holter to Hauser, November 16, 1908, ibid.).

50. Edwin B. Holter to Anton M. Holter, February 8, 1897, box 27, ibid.

51. Sklar, *Corporate Reconstruction of American Capitalism*, 26. For the rise of professional white-collar office personnel, see Oliver Zunz, *Making America Corporate, 1870–1920* (Chicago: University of Chicago Press, 1990), 124–26.

52. Hauser to John S. M. Neil, January 8, 1906; Hauser to Clark, November 5, 1906, October 12, 1907, and June 12, 1908, box 33, Hauser Papers.

53. Hauser to Norman Holter, April 15, 1905, ibid. (emphasis in original).

54. Hauser to Rogers, November 15, 1905, and February 17, 1906, ibid. For Rogers's declining influence and Ryan's emergence as the leading figure in Amalgamated's Montana enterprise, see Johnson, "Electrical Power, Copper, and John D. Ryan," 27–29.

55. Johnson, "Electrical Power, Copper, and John D. Ryan," 28, and Hauser to S. T. Hauser, Jr., May 14, 1910, box 33, Hauser Papers.

56. Hauser to John S. M. Neil, July 2, and Hauser to W. A. Clark, November 1, 1910, Hauser Papers.

57. William B. Gower to Albert Strauss, April 24, 1913, box 62, ibid. Strauss

chaired the reorganization committee of the United Missouri River Power Company.

58. Edwin Holter to Norman Holter, January 7, 1913, box 151, Holter Papers.

59. Johnson, "Electrical Power, Copper, and John D. Ryan," 33.

60. For two of the better book-length accounts, see Jerre C. Murphey, *The Comical History of Montana: A Serious Story for a Free People* (San Diego, Calif.: E. L. Scofield, 1912), and Howard, *Montana, High, Wide, and Handsome.*

61. Sklar, *Corporate Reconstruction of American Capitalism,* 3–4; Thomas R. Navin, *Copper Mining and Management* (Tucson: University of Arizona Press, 1978), 118, 213; and Malone, *Battle for Butte,* 202.

62. The metaphor is borrowed from Patricia Nelson Limerick, *The Legacy of Conquest: The Unbroken Past of the American West* (New York: W. W. Norton, 1987), 36–37.

CHAPTER SEVEN: AN "EQUILIBRIUM OF CHAOS"

1. Wallace Stegner, *Angle of Repose* (New York: Doubleday, 1971), 133.

2. This discussion is based on Norman Best's memoir, *A Celebration of Work,* ed. William G. Robbins (Lincoln: University of Nebraska Press, 1990).

3. Lewis Mumford, *Technics and Civilization* (New York: Harcourt, Brace and Company, 1934), 431.

4. Joseph Kinsey Howard, *Montana: High, Wide, and Handsome* (1943; Lincoln: University of Nebraska Press, 1983).

5. For a select few authors other than Howard who address the colonialism issue in the northern West, see Bernard DeVoto, "The West: A Plundered Province," *Harper's Magazine,* August 1934: 355–64; Carl Frederick Kraenzel, *The Great Plains in Transition* (Norman: University of Oklahoma Press, 1955); Robert G. Athearn, *High Country Empire: The High Plains and the Rockies* (1960; Lincoln: University of Nebraska Press, 1965); Wallace Stegner and Page Stegner, "Rocky Mountain Country," *Atlantic Monthly,* April 1978: 45–91; and Rodman W. Paul, *The Far West and the Great Plains in Transition, 1859–1900* (New York: Harper and Row, 1988).

6. This point is made in Oliver Zunz, *Making America Corporate, 1870–1920* (Chicago: University of Chicago Press, 1990), 39–40.

7. Lancaster Pollard, "The Pacific Northwest: A National Epitome," in *Northwest Harvest,* ed. V. L. O. Chittick (New York: Macmillan, 1948), and Carlos A. Schwantes, "The Concept of the Wageworkers' Frontier: A Framework for Future Research," *Western Historical Quarterly* 18 (1987): 43.

8. DeVoto, "West: Plundered Province," 358.

9. For select studies of regional protest, see Carlos A. Schwantes, *Radical Heritage: Labor, Socialism, Reform in Washington and British Columbia, 1885–1917* (Seattle: University of Washington Press, 1979); Normal Clark, *Mill Town: A Social History of Everett, Washington* (Seattle: University of Washington Press, 1970); Michael P. Malone, *The Battle for Butte: Mining and Politics on the Northern Frontier, 1864–1906* (Seattle: University of Washington Press, 1981); and K. Ross Toole, *Twentieth-Century Montana: A State of Extremes* (Norman: University of Oklahoma Press, 1972).

10. For an interesting discussion of the issue of use of federal troops, see Bruce A. Keizer, "Military Violence Effectively Solved 'the Indian Problem,'" *Seattle Times,* February 10, 1991.

11. Howard, *Montana*, 3.

12. For excellent insight into the problems faced by wage laborers in mining and agriculture in the northern West, see Schwantes, "Concept of Wageworkers' Frontier," 39–43.

13. William Bevis, "Nannie Alderson's Frontier—And Ours," *Montana: Magazine of Western History* 39 (Spring 1989): 33.

14. Porter was a relatively obscure federal employee at the time he wrote his famous assessment of the Census of 1890. See Gerald D. Nash, "Mirror for the Future: The Historical Past of the Twentieth-Century West," in *The Twentieth Century American West: Contributions to an Understanding*, ed. Thomas G. Alexander and John F. Bluth, (Provo, Utah: Charles Redd Monographs in Western History, 1983), no. 12, 4.

15. The *Settler's Guide* is quoted in John Fahey, *The Inland Empire: Unfolding Years, 1879–1929* (Seattle: University of Washington Press, 1986), 24.

16. The standard biography of Hill is Albro Martin, *James J. Hill and the Opening of the Northwest* (New York: Oxford University Press, 1976). For Hill's influence at the highest levels of government, see W. Thomas White, "A Gilded-Age Businessman in Politics: James J. Hill, the Northwest and the American Presidency, 1884–1912," *Pacific Historical Review* 57 (1988): 439–56.

17. Martin, *James J. Hill*, 430, 455–59, 464; White, "A Gilded-Age Businessman in Politics," 454; and Carroll Van West, *Capitalism on the Frontier: Billings and the Yellowstone Valley in the Nineteenth Century* (Lincoln: University of Nebraska Press, 1993), 202–7. A recent history of the Great Northern argues that the 1896 agreement left real control of the reorganized Northern Pacific with the Morgan interests and the Deutsche Bank (see Ralph W. Hidy, Muriel E. Hidy, and Roy V. Scott, with Don L. Hofsommer, *The Great Northern Railway: A History* [Boston: Harvard Business School Press, 1988], 90–92).

18. Memorandum of a conference held in London, April (?), 1896, in General Correspondence, James J. Hill Papers, James Jerome Hill Reference Library, St. Paul, Minnesota, and White, "Gilded-Age Businessman in Politics," 448. The epithet "Empire Wrecker" is from Bruce Nelson, *Land of the Dacotahs* (Minneapolis: University of Minnesota Press, 1946), cited in Athearn, *High Country Empire*, 173. For a favorable view of Hill, see Martin, *James J. Hill*, and Hidy et al., *Great Northern Railway*. More critical assessments are Howard, *Montana*; W. Thomas White, "The War of the Railroad Kings: Great Northern–Northern Pacific Rivalry in Montana, 1881–1896," in *Montana and the West: Essays in Honor of K. Ross Toole*, ed. Rex C. Myers and Harry W. Fritz (Boulder, Colo.: Pruett Publishing Company, 1984), 37–54; and *Inland Empire*, 36–37.

19. For John S. Kennedy and George Stephen, see biographical sketches in card file, Hill Library. See also Martin, *James J. Hill*, 135–38, 146–61, 159–61, and Heather Gilbert, *The Life of Lord Mount Stephen*, vol. 2, *The End of the Road, 1891–1921* (Aberdeen, Scotland: Aberdeen University Press, 1977).

20. James J. Hill to George Stephen, September 27, 1898, General Correspondence, Hill Papers.

21. Hill to Stephen, October 9, 1898, Hill to William C. Van Horne, November 27, 1898, Hill to T. G. Shaughnessy, June 24, 1899, General Correspondence, Hill Papers. See also Hidy et al., *Great Northern Railway*, 86–87, 92.

22. Gordon B. Dodds, *The American Northwest: A History of Oregon and Washington* (Arlington Heights, Ill.: Forum Press, 1986), 140; C. H. Coster to James J. Hill, November 26, 1898, General Correspondence, Hill Papers. For an account of the financial health of the Hill-controlled lines shortly after the turn of the century, see Hill to Charles Ellis, May 19, 1902, General Correspondence, Hill Pa-

pers. On the Hill and Harriman fight, see Hidy et al., *Great Northern Railway,* 92–93.

23. For this assessment of Hill's influence, see White, "Gilded-Age Businessman in Politics," 451–56. See also Fahey, *Inland Empire,* 178–80, 194; Richard B. Roeder, "A Settlement on the Plains: Paris Gibson and the Building of Great Falls," *Montana: Magazine of Western History* 42 (Autumn 1992): 4–19; William L. Lang, "Corporate Point Men and the Creation of the Montana Central Railroad, 1882–87," *Great Plains Quarterly* 10 (Summer 1990): 152–66; and W. Thomas White, "Paris Gibson, James J. Hill and the 'New Minneapolis': The Great Falls Water Power and Townsite Company, 1882–1908," *Montana: Magazine of Western History* (Summer 1983): 60–69.

24. For a select few studies that address the various forms of economic exploitation in the northern West, see Clark, *Mill Town;* Malone, *Battle for Butte;* Donald W. Meinig, *The Great Columbia Plain: A Historical Geography, 1805–1910* (Seattle: University of Washington Press, 1968); Arnon Gutfeld, *Montana's Agony: Years of War and Hysteria, 1917–1921* (Gainesville: University Presses of Florida, 1979); Schwantes, *Radical Heritage;* and William G. Robbins, *Hard Times in Paradise: Coos Bay, Oregon, 1850–1986* (Seattle: University of Washington Press, 1988). See also Fahey, *Inland Empire,* and Howard, *Montana.*

25. For the general outline of these developments, see Thomas R. Cox, *Mills and Markets: A History of the Pacific Coast Lumber Industry to 1900* (Seattle: University of Washington Press, 1974); Robert E. Ficken, "Weyerhaeuser and the Pacific Northwest Timber Industry, 1899–1903," *Pacific Northwest Quarterly* 70 (October 1979): 146–54; William G. Robbins, "The Social Context of Forestry: The Pacific Northwest in the Twentieth Century," *Western Historical Quarterly* 16 (1985): 413–15; and Robbins, "The Western Lumber Industry: A Twentieth-Century Perspective," in *The Twentieth-Century West: Historical Interpretations,* ed. Gerald D. Nash and Richard W. Etulain (Albuquerque: University of New Mexico Press, 1989), 233–36.

26. Murray Morgan, *The Mill on the Boot: The Story of the St. Paul and Tacoma Lumber Company* (Seattle: University of Washington Press, 1982), 8–54; Ficken, "Weyerhaeuser and the Pacific Northwest Timber Industry," 146–54.

27. The best summary of these conditions is in Robert E. Ficken, *The Forested Land: A History of Lumbering in Western Washington* (Seattle: University of Washington Press, 1987). The quotation is from Clark, *Mill Town,* 234.

28. The suggestion that Everett might serve as a prototype for an extractive industrial town is based on my reading of Clark's classic study, *Mill Town* (see especially pp. 30–33.

29. The phrase is from a book of that title: C. B. Glasscock, *The War of the Copper Kings* (New York: Grosset and Dunlap, 1935).

30. Robbins, "Social Context of Forestry," 414; and Clark, *Mill Town,* 233.

31. William G. Robbins, *Lumberjacks and Legislatures: Political Economy of the U.S. Lumber Industry, 1890–1941* (College Station: Texas A&M University Press, 1982), 242–48; and Robbins, "Social Context of Forestry," 415–20. See also Robbins, *Hard Times in Paradise,* 122–37.

32. Robbins, *Lumberjacks and Legislatures,* 133–71, and Ficken, *Forested Land,* 176; Long is quoted in Ficken.

33. For a summary of the sequence and the most dramatic periods of the timber harvests in the modern West, see Robbins, "The Western Lumber Industry," 233–56.

34. I. J. Mason, "Grays Harbor Study," April 4, 1935, in S Plans, Timber

Management, Olympic, 1927–35, box 54139, Federal Records Center, Seattle, Washington, and Robbins, "Social Context of Forestry," 417–18.

35. Clark, *Mill Town*, 235–38.

36. For the more general accounts, see Malone, *Battle for Butte;* Fahey, *Inland Empire;* Carlos A. Schwantes, *In Mountain Shadows: A History of Idaho* (Lincoln: University of Nebraska Press, 1991); Joseph Cash, *Working the Homestake* (Ames: Iowa State University Press, 1973); Thomas R. Navin, *Copper Mining and Management* (Tucson: University of Arizona Press, 1978); and Isaac F. Marcosson, *Metal Magic: The Story of the American Smelting and Refining Company* (New York: Farrar, Straus and Company, 1949).

37. Michael Malone, "The Collapse of Western Metal Mining: An Historical Epitaph," *Pacific Historical Review* 55 (1986): 455, and William L. Lang, "You Have to Start with the Work," *Northern Lights* 4 (January 1988): 25–26.

38. Stephen Voynick, "The Birth of the New Frontier," *Northern Lights* 4 (January 1988): 9, and Patricia Nelson Limerick, *The Legacy of Conquest: The Unbroken Past of the American West,* (New York: W. W. Norton, 1987), 124.

39. Marcus Daly to James J. Hill, January 29, 1893, General Correspondence, Hill Papers. For a discussion of Hill's representatives in Montana and the northern West—Paris Gibson and Martin Maginnis—see Martin, *James J. Hill,* 333–35; Hidy et al., *The Great Northern Railway,* 56–57; and White, "Paris Gibson, James J. Hill and the 'New Minneapolis,'" 60–69.

40. Malone, *Battle for Butte,* 217.

41. Gutfeld, *Montana's Agony,* 1; K. Ross Toole, "When Big Money Came to Butte: The Migration of Eastern Capital to Montana," *Pacific Northwest Quarterly* 44 (1953): 29; Howard, *Montana,* 83. For an appraisal of Howard's career, see Gerald Diettert, "Montana's Conscience," *Northern Lights* 3 (1987): 35.

42. Malone, "Collapse of Western Metal Mining," 459.

43. Herbert S. Schell, *History of South Dakota,* 3d ed., rev. (Lincoln: University of Nebraska Press, 1975), 146–47, and John Milton, *South Dakota: A Bicentennial History* (New York: W. W. Norton, 1977), 116–17.

44. Cash, *Working the Homestake,* 27, 55, 67, and Milton, *South Dakota,* 117.

45. Fahey, *Inland Empire,* 174–75; William G. Robbins, "'At the End of the Cracked Whip': The Northern West, 1880–1920," *Montana: Magazine of Western History* 38 (Autumn 1988): 10; *Portland Oregonian,* November 2, 1981.

46. Fahey, *Inland Empire,* 181–82, and Navin, *Copper Mining and Management,* 117.

47. Fahey, *Inland Empire,* 185–87.

48. Meinig, *Great Columbia Plain,* 365.

49. Although the origins of the term are obscure, it apparently derived from Slavic immigrants who were referred to contemptuously as "hunyaks," and subsequently on the high plains it became a generic reference to all foreigners. See Howard, *Montana,* 180–81.

50. Robert C. Athearn, *The Mythic West in Twentieth-Century America* (Lawrence: University Press of Kansas, 1986), 26.

51. Mary Wilma Hargreaves, *Dry Land Farming in the Northern Great Plains, 1900–1925* (Cambridge, Mass.: Harvard University Press, 1957), 83–84, and Meinig, *Great Columbia Plain,* 411.

52. See Kraenzel, *Great Plains in Transition,* 137–40.

53. Gilbert C. Fite, "The Great Plains: Promises, Prospects," in *The Great Plains: Environment and Culture,* 187–88; Walter Prescott Webb, *The Great Plains* (1931; reprint, New York: Grosset and Dunlap, n.d.), 17–26; Hargreaves, *Dry Land Farming,* 85–97.

54. Hargreaves, *Dry Land Farming*, 109, 158, 179. For dry farming in eastern Oregon, see Barbara Allen, *Homesteading the High Desert* (Salt Lake City: University of Utah Press, 1987). Thomas Shaw's pamphlet, *Dry Farming in America* (St. Paul: Great Northern Railway, n.d.), carried the following directive on its cover: "Some fundamental principles which should be followed by the farmer who is cultivating land where the rainfall runs from 12 to 20 inches a year."

55. Hargreaves, *Dry Land Farming*, 442, 449; Allen, *Homesteading the High Desert*, 116–21, 129–33; Gerald Friesen, *The Canadian Prairies* (Toronto: University of Toronto Press, 1984); Paula M. Nelson, *After the West Was Won: Homesteaders and Town-Builders in Western South Dakota, 1900–1917* (Iowa City: University of Iowa Press, 1986), xiv–xv.

56. Howard, *Montana*, 196.

57. The USDA report is printed in Hargreaves, *Dry Land Farming*, 115.

58. Howard, *Montana*, 183; Hargreaves, *Dry Land Farming*, 442, 447; Fite, "Great Plains," 189.

59. Allen, *Homesteading the High Desert*, 97–102, and Nelson, *After the West Was Won*, xiv–xv.

60. Robert P. Wilkins and Wynoma H. Wilkins, *North Dakota: A Bicentennial History* (New York: W. W. Norton, 1977), 88–89; David B. Danbom, "North Dakota: The Most Midwestern State," in *Heartland: Comparative Histories of the Midwestern States*, ed. James H. Madison (Bloomington: Indiana University Press, 1988), 115–16; Michael P. Malone and Richard B. Roeder, *Montana: A History of Two Centuries* (Seattle: University of Washington Press, 1976), 216; Kraenzel, *Great Plains in Transition*, 160; and Herbert T. Hoover, "South Dakota: An Expression of Regional Heritage," in Madison, ed., *Heartland*, 199.

61. Howard, *Montana*, 285, and Danbom, "North Dakota," 115. For an account that brilliantly captures the essence of the depression on the Canadian plains, see James Gray, *The Winter Years: The Depression on the Prairies* (Toronto: Macmillan, 1966). See also Friesen, *Canadian Prairies*, 382–417.

62. Kraenzel, *Great Plains in Transition*, 151; Malone and Roeder, *Montana*, 255–58; Danbom, "North Dakota," 116, 123; Fite, "Great Plains," 200.

63. Fahey, *Inland Empire*, 87–90, and W. Thomas White, "Main Street on the Irrigation Frontier: Sub-Urban Community Building in the Yakima Valley, 1900–1910," *Pacific Northwest Quarterly* 77 (1986): 95.

64. Fahey, *Inland Empire*, 94–96.

65. Ibid., 100–103, 118–20.

66. Hugh T. Lovin, " 'Duty of Water' in Idaho: A 'New West' Irrigation Controversy, 1890–1920," *Arizona and the West* 23 (1981): 6, and F. Ross Peterson, *Idaho: A Bicentennial History* (New York: W. W. Norton, 1977), 123. Wallace Stegner has captured the entrepreneurial spirit of the place and the time in *Angle of Repose*, a novel based on the writings of Mary Hallock Foote.

67. Hugh T. Lovin, "A 'New West' Reclamation Tragedy: The Twin Falls–Oakley Project in Idaho, 1908–1931," *Arizona and the West* 20 (1978): 7, and Peterson, *Idaho*, 125–28.

68. Peterson, *Idaho*, 134–38. For an overview of reclamation activity in Arizona and California, see Donald Worster, *Rivers of Empire: Water, Aridity, and the Growth of the American West* (New York: Pantheon, 1985), and Donald J. Pisani, *From the Family Farm to Agribusinesss: The Irrigation Crusade in California and the West, 1850–1931* (Berkeley: University of California Press, 1984). For the Arkansas River Valley, see James Sherow, *Watering the Valley: Development along the Plains Arkansas River, 1870–1950* (Lawrence: University Press of Kansas, 1990).

69. Peterson, *Idaho*, 140.

70. Kittredge is quoted in the *Oregonian*, April 29, 1984.

71. Toole, *Twentieth-Century Montana*, 281, and Clark Spence, *Montana: A Bicentennial History* (New York: W. W. Norton, 1977), 196.

CHAPTER EIGHT: THE SOUTH AND THE WEST

1. Douglas F. Dowd, "A Comparative Analysis of Economic Development in the American West and South," *Journal of Economic History* 16 (1956): 559.

2. Kevin Starr, "A Response: Moving beyond the Turner Thesis," *Proceedings of the American Antiquarian Society* 101, pt. 1 (1991): 125. For general references to the mythical West of natural abundance, see Donald Worster, *Under Western Skies: Nature and History in the American West* (New York: Oxford University Press, 1992), and Wallace Stegner, *Where the Bluebird Sings to the Lemonade Springs* (New York: Random House, 1992).

3. Stegner, *Where the Bluebird Sings*, xxi.

4. Jack Temple Kirby, *Rural Worlds Lost: The American South, 1920–1960* (Baton Rouge: Louisiana State University Press, 1987), 20.

5. Gavin Wright, *Old South, New South: Revolutions in the Southern Economy since the Civil War* (New York: Basic Books, 1986), vii.

6. Joel Garreau, *The Nine Nations of North America* (Boston: Houghton Mifflin, 1981), 131, and Dewey W. Grantham, *The Regional Imagination: The South and Recent American History* (Nashville, Tenn.: Vanderbilt University Press, 1979), ix. For the classic source on southern agrarianism, see Twelve Southerners, *I'll Take My Stand: The South and the Agrarian Tradition* (New York: Harper and Brothers, 1930).

7. Donald Meinig, "American Wests: Preface to a Geographical Interpretation," *Annals of the Association of American Geographers* 62 (June 1972): 160, 170–75. For scholars who underscore the rapidity of change in the West, see Arrell Morgan Gibson, *The West in the Life of the Nation* (Lexington, Mass.: D. C. Heath, 1976), ix, 3–9, and William Appleman Williams, *The Contours of American History* (Chicago: Quadrangle Books, 1961), 227.

8. Alan Trachtenberg argues that the West served both as "myth and as economic entity"; it provided resources essential to economic development, and it proved "indispensable to the formation of a national society" (Trachtenberg, *The Incorporation of America: Culture and Society in the Gilded Age* [New York: Hill and Wang, 1982], 17). The reference to redesigning human geography is paraphrased from Donald Meinig, "Continental America, 1800–1915" (Paper presented at the annual meeting of the Organization of American Historians, Reno, Nevada, March 26, 1988, 17; copy in the author's possession).

9. Dowd, "Comparative Analysis of Economic Development in the West and South," 559–64.

10. It should be added that Dowd saw many similarities between the South and the West: primary production economies, development directed from outside, unfavorable terms of trade with the North, and a lower per capita income. Yet for the West those hallmarks of underdevelopment were not institutional (Dowd, "A Comparative Analysis of Economic Development in the American West and South," 560–61).

11. Jonathan M. Wiener, "Class Structure and Economic Development in the American South, 1865–1955," *American Historical Review* 84 (1979): 970, 981, 985.

12. Wiener, following the earlier suggestion of Barrington Moore, Jr., ar-

gued that the old planter elite maintained control of the political and economic apparatus and eventually ushered the South into the modern industrial world as a nonunion, low-tax, cheap-labor place to do business (see ibid., 985–86). For an elaboration of the Prussion Road argument, see Eugene D. Genovese, *The Political Economy of Slavery: Studies in the Economy and Society of the Slave South* (New York: Random House, 1961), 206–7, and Barrington Moore, Jr., *The Social Origins of Dictatorship and Democracy: Lord and Peasant in the Making of the Modern World* (Boston: Houghton Mifflin, 1966), chap. 8. For a recent assessment of the Prussian Road thesis, see James C. Cobb, "Beyond Planters and Industrialists: A New Perspective on the New South," *Journal of Southern History* 54 (1988): 48–49.

13. Steven Hahn, "Class and State in Postemancipation Societies: Southern Planters in Comparative Perspective," *American Historical Review* 95 (1990): 92–96.

14. E. J. Hobsbawm, *The Age of Capital, 1848–1875* (1975; New York: New American Library, 1984), 198–99, 205–6.

15. John Agnew, *The United States in the World Economy* (New York: Cambridge University Press, 1987), 112. See also Steven Hahn, *The Roots of Southern Populism: Yeomen Farmers and the Transformation of the Georgia Upcountry, 1850–1890* (New York: Oxford University Press, 1983).

16. This summary is from Gilbert C. Fite, *Cotton Fields No More: Southern Agriculture, 1865–1980* (Lexington: University Press of Kentucky, 1984), 28, 47, 230–31. See also Edward L. Ayers, *The Promise of the New South: Life after Reconstruction* (New York: Oxford University Press, 1992), vii.

17. For the peculiarities of western economic conditions and the free movement of labor, see Carlos A. Schwantes, "The Concept of the Wageworkers' Frontier: A Framework for Future Research," *Western Historical Quarterly* 18 (1987): 39–56.

18. Melvyn Dubofsky, *We Shall Be All: A History of the Industrial Workers of the World* (Chicago: Quadrangle Books, 1969), 19–20.

19. Ibid., 54–55, and William G. Robbins, *Hard Times in Paradise: Coos Bay, Oregon, 1859–1986,* (Seattle: University of Washington Press, 1988), chap. 10.

20. Mark Wyman, *Hard Rock Epic: Western Miners and the Industrial Revolution, 1860–1910* (Berkeley: University of California Press, 1979), 33–34, 59.

21. William Allen White, *The Changing West: An Economic Theory about Our Golden Age* (New York: Macmillan, 1939), 123; Wyman, *Hard Rock Epic,* 59–60, 252–53; and Melvyn Dubofsky, *Industrialism and the American Worker, 1865–1920* (Arlington Heights, Ill.: Harlan Davidson, 1985), 16.

22. Jack Temple Kirby, "Capitalism and Southern History: The Twentieth Century" (Paper presented at the annual meeting of the Organization of American Historians, Saint Louis, Missouri, April 7, 1989, 3; copy in the author's possession), and Wright, *Old South, New South,* 124.

23. Wright, *Old South, New South,* 124–25; and David L. Carlton, *Mill and Town in South Carolina, 1880–1920* (Baton Rouge: Louisiana State University Press, 1982), 7.

24. Wright, *Old South, New South,* 130, 138–40; Carlton, *Mill and Town in South Carolina,* 8–11; and Jacquelyn Dowd Hall et al., *Like a Family: The Making of a Southern Cotton Mill World* (Chapel Hill: University of North Carolina Press, 1987), 114.

25. David L. Carlton, "The Revolution from Above: The National Market and the Beginning of Industrialization in North Carolina," *Journal of American History* 77 (1990): 448–49, 473.

26. Jack Temple Kirby indicates that the southern work force held a "pecu-

liar place" within the capitalist order with its persisting reliance on an isolated and unskilled labor pool (Kirby, "Capitalism and Southern History," 3–4).

27. Tannenbaum is quoted in Wright, *Old South, New South*, 146.

28. Ibid., 146. Ronald Eller points out that company towns in the Appalachian South acted as a barrier to new forms of enterprise and to economic diversification. Moreover, because absentee ownership was the norm in Appalachia, only the wages stayed in the community, and "under the closed company town system, these too flowed largely out of the mountains" (Eller, *Miners, Millhands, and Mountaineers: Industrialization of the Appalachian South, 1880–1930* [Knoxville: University of Tennessee Press, 1982], 198, 228).

29. Ibid., 140, 147.

30. Carlton, "Revolution from Above," 447; and Wright, *Old South, New South*, 156, 174. The lack of an indigenous technology in the South should be contrasted to the expansiveness of the technology in mining that developed in San Francisco in the aftermath of the California gold rush. See Rodman Paul, *The Far West and the Great Plains in Transition, 1859–1900* (New York: Harper and Row, 1988), 72, 84, 93, 264.

31. Earl Black and Merle Black, *Politics and Society in the South* (Cambridge, Mass.: Harvard University Press, 1987), 24. David Carlton contends that even southern industrial society was different; its manufacturing sectors did not lead to the building of great cities (Carlton, "Revolution from Above," 446). Edward Ayers points out that for the first fifty years of the twentieth century, "railroads, textile mills, coal mines, sawmills, cotton fields, and small towns still dominated the landscape" (Ayers, *The Promise of the New South*, 438).

32. Black and Black, *Politics and Society in the South*, 24, 34, 37, and Kirby, *Rural Worlds Lost*, xiii, 3.

33. Kirby, *Rural Worlds Lost*, xv, 1, 8–9. See also Donald J. Pisani, *From the Family Farm to Agribusiness: The Irrigation Crusade in California and the West, 1850–1931* (Berkeley: University of California Press, 1984). The development of large-scale corporate agriculture in California brought with it the early alienation of labor. Whereas small farming enterprises muted the tendency toward rigid class lines, "the social and psychological climate on the large-scale commercial farm promoted impenetrable class and caste lines that admitted of not the slightest ambiguity" (Cletus Daniel, *Bitter Harvest: A History of California Farmworkers, 1870–1941* [Berkeley: University of California Press, 1981], 17).

34. Carey McWilliams, *Factories in the Field: The Story of Migratory Farm Labor in California* (1935; Santa Barbara, Calif.: Peregrine Publishers, 1971), 5.

35. Cobb, "Beyond Planters and Industrialists," 55–65, and Kirby, *Rural Worlds Lost*, 14. For the influence of government-sponsored science in promoting agriculture and the mining industry in California, see Gerald D. Nash, *State Government and Economic Development: A History of Administrative Policies in California, 1849–1933* (Berkeley: University of California Press, 1964), 104–5.

36. Kirby, *Rural Worlds Lost*, 10–12; Moses S. Musoke and Alan L. Olmstead, "The Rise of the Cotton Industry in California: A Comparative Perspective," *Journal of Economic History* 42 (1982): 385–412; William J. Briggs and Henry Cauthen, *The Cotton Man: Notes on the Life and Times of Wofford B. ("Bill") Camp* (Columbia, S.C.: University of South Carolina Press, 1983), 35, 52, 108; and McWilliams, *Factories in the Field*, 5.

37. Briggs and Cauthen, *Cotton Man*, 110–11, 147–51, 201–4.

38. McWilliams, *Factories in the Field*, 5; Pisani, *From the Family Farm to Agribusiness*, 441–43; and Kirby, *Rural Worlds Lost*, 16.

39. Richard Lowitt, *The New Deal and the West* (Bloomington: Indiana University Press, 1984), 218, 225–26.

40. On the West the seminal work is Gerald D. Nash, *The American West in the Twentieth Century: A Short History of an Urban Oasis* (Englewood Cliffs, N.J.: Prentice-Hall, 1973). See also Nash, *The American West Transformed: The Impact of the Second World War* (Bloomington: Indiana University Press, 1985), and Nash, *World War II and the West: Reshaping the Economy* (Lincoln: University of Nebraska Press, 1990); and James N. Gregory, *American Exodus: The Dust Bowl Migration and Okie Culture in California* (New York: Oxford University Press, 1989).

41. Nash, *American West Transformed*, vii, and Nash, *World War II and the West*, xii.

42. Pete Daniel, *Breaking the Land: The Transformation of Cotton, Tobacco, and Rice Cultures since 1880* (Urbana: University of Illinois, 1985), 239.

43. Kirby, *Rural Worlds Lost*, 51, 276.

44. This assessment is paraphrased from Jon C. Teaford, "The Twentieth-Century's Great Migration," *Reviews in American History* 18 (1990): 222.

45. Two writers who address the issue of the rural exodus in the South both employ this term; see Kirby, *Rural Worlds Lost*, 276, and Daniel, *Breaking the Land*, 168–183, 293.

46. Daniel, *Breaking the Land*, 168, and Kirby, *Rural Worlds Lost*, 276.

47. Daniel, *Breaking the Land*, 65, 240–41. Due to mechanization and crop diversification, the southern farm population declined by more than 20 percent during World War II alone. See David R. Goldfield, *Promised Land: The South Since 1945* (Arlington Heights, Ill.: Harlan Davidson, 1987), 7. For an excellent source of statistical information on this period, see Bruce J. Shulman, *From Cotton Belt to Sun Belt: Federal Economic Policy and the Transformation of the South, 1938–1980* (New York: Oxford University Press, 1991).

48. Goldfield, *Promised Land*, 1–2; Wright, *Old South, New South*, 270; and Kirby, *Rural Worlds Lost*, 321, 353.

49. James C. Cobb, *Industrialization and Southern Society, 1877–1984* (Lexington: University Press of Kentucky, 1984), 136–39. From the mid-1960s to the present, many western trendsetting metropolitan areas have increasingly exhibited social, economic, and racial characteristics similar to those in Atlanta.

50. Cobb, "Beyond Planters and Industrialists," 66.

51. Ibid., 46, 67; Kirby, *Rural Worlds Lost*, 360; Eller, *Miners, Millhands, and Mountaineers*, 228; and John Gaventa, *Power and Powerlessness: Quiescence and Rebellion in an Appalachian Valley* (Chicago: University of Chicago Press, 1980), 35.

52. Gilbert Fite, *American Farmers: The New Minority* (Bloomington: Indiana University Press, 1981), 243.

53. Linda Majka and Theo Majka, *Farm Workers, Agribusiness, and the State* (Philadelphia: Temple University Press, 1982), 5, 7, 9, 11–14.

54. Stephen Hahn, "Capitalism and Southern History: The Nineteenth Century" (Paper presented at the annual meeting of the Organization of American Historians, St. Louis, Missouri, April 9, 1989, p. 17; copy in the author's possession).

CHAPTER NINE: OF COUNTRY AND CITY

1. Elizabeth Fox-Genovese and Eugene Genovese, *Fruits of Merchant Capital: Slavery and Bourgeois Property in the Rise and Expansion of Capitalism* (New York: Oxford University Press, 1983), 211–12.

2. Ian Frazier, *Great Plains* (New York: Farrar, Straus, Giroux, 1989), 91; Kathleen Norris, *Dakota: A Spiritual Geography* (New York: Ticknor and Fields, 1993), 9, 31; Glenn V. Fuguitt, "City and Village Population Trends in the United States," in *The Great Plains: Environment and Culture*, ed. Brian Blouet and Frederick C. Leubke (Lincoln: University of Nebraska Press, 1979), 225–26; and Gilbert C. Fite, "The Great Plains: Promises, Problems, Prospects," in Blouet and Leubke, eds., *Great Plains*, 200. For an excellent portrait of the prairie West, see William Least Heat-Moon, *Prairy Erth* (Boston: Houghton Mifflin, 1991).

3. Joel Garreau, *The Nine Nations of North America* (Boston: Houghton Mifflin, 1981), 287–327; Carey McWilliams, *California: The Great Exception* (1949; Santa Barbara, Calif.: Peregrine Smith, 1979), 82; and Richard Rhodes, "A Plundered Province Revisited: The Colonial Status—Past and Present—of the Great American West," *American Heritage* 29 (August/September 1978): 6.

4. Some of these ideas were expressed in "What's Wrong and What's Right in Western History: A Panel Discussion," Annual Meeting of the Western History Association, Tacoma, Washington, October 13, 1989. The panelists were William Cronon, Carol O'Connor, Richard White, and Donald Worster.

5. For example, see Gerald Nash, *The American West in the Twentieth Century: A Short History* (Englewood Cliffs, N.J.: Prentice Hall, 1973); Earl Pomeroy, *The Pacific Slope: A History of California, Oregon, Washington, Idaho, Utah, and Nevada* (New York: Alfred A. Knopf, 1965); and Carl Abbott, *The New Urban America: Growth and Politics in Sunbelt Cities* (Chapel Hill: University of North Carolina Press, 1981).

6. *New York Times*, July 13, 1989. For the decision by the multinational firm, Gulf Resources, to close Kellogg's famous Bunker Hill mining and smelting facility, see *Portland Oregonian*, November 2, 1981.

7. Stanley Aronowitz, "The End of Political Economy," *Social Text: Theory, Culture, and Ideology* 1:2 (1979): 18; Andre Gorz, *Socialism and Revolution*, trans. Norman Denny (New York: Doubleday, 1973), 219–21; and Donald W. Meinig, "American Wests: Preface to a Geographical Interpretation," *Annals of the Association of American Geographers* 62 (1972): 179.

8. Harold Chorney, "Amnesia, Integration, and Repression: The Roots of Canadian Urban Political Culture," *Urbanization and Urban Planning in Capitalist Society*, ed. Michael Dear and Allan J. Scott (New York: Methuen, 1982), 535, 539; Patricia Marchak, *In Whose Interests: An Essay on Multinational Corporations in a Canadian Context* (Toronto: McClelland and Stuart, 1979), 100; Ken Drushka, *Stumped: The Forest Industry in Transition* (Vancouver: Douglas and McIntyre, 1985), 137; and Carlos Schwantes, "Protest in a Promised Land: Employment, Disinheritance, and the Origin of Labor Militancy in the Pacific Northwest, 1885–1886," *Western Historical Quarterly* 13 (1982): 373–90.

9. Anthony Giddens, *A Contemporary Critique of Historical Materialism* (Berkeley: University of California Press, 1981), 201; David Harvey, "Urban Process," in Dear and Scott, eds., *Urbanization and Urban Planning in Capitalist Society*, 104; and Fernand Braudel, *Afterthoughts on Material Civilization and Capitalism*, trans. Patricia M. Ranum (Baltimore: Johns Hopkins University Press, 1977), 82–85. Ann Markusen points out that struggle occurs when most owners of transport and finance live in one area and the bulk of the producers live in another (Markusen, *Regions: The Economics and Politics of Territory* [Totowa, N.J.: Rowan and Littlefield, 1987], 4).

10. Ivan T. Berend and Gyorgy Ranki, *The European Periphery and Industrialization, 1780–1914* (Cambridge: Cambridge University Press, 1982), 9, and

Thomas J. McCormick, "World Systems," *Journal of American History* 76 (June 1990): 125–27.

11. For the early seminal works of core/periphery relations, see Immanuel Wallerstein, *The Capitalist World Economy* (New York: Cambridge University Press, 1979); Wallerstein, *The Politics of the World Economy: The States, the Movements, and the Civilizations* (Cambridge: Cambridge University Press, 1984); Braudel, *Afterthoughts on Material Civilization and Capitalism;* Leften S. Stavrianos, *The Promise of the Coming Dark Age* (San Francisco: W. H. Freeman, 1976); Gorz, *Socialism and Revolution;* and Andre Gunder Frank, *Capitalism and Underdevelopment in Latin America: Historical Studies of Chile and Brazil,* rev. ed. (New York: Monthly Review Press, 1976). For critical reviews that touch on metropolitan/hinterland relations, see Steve J. Stern, "Feudalism, Capitalism, and the World System in the Perspective of Latin America and the Caribbean," *American Historical Review* 93 (October 1988): 829–72, and Thomas F. O'Brien, "Dependency Revisited: A Review Essay," *Business History Review* 59 (Winter 1985): 663–69. William Cronon has suggested the potential for studying core and periphery relations as a means to understanding the dynamics of American capitalism (Cronon, "Revisiting the Vanishing Frontier: The Legacy of Frederick Jackson Turner," *Western Historical Quarterly* 18 [1987]: 174–75). See also Richard White, *Roots of Dependency: Subsistence, Environment, and Social Change among the Choctaws, Pawnees, and Navajos* (Lincoln: University of Nebraska Press, 1983); John Thompson, *Closing the Frontier: Radical Response in Oklahoma, 1889–1923* (Norman: University of Oklahoma Press, 1986); Thomas D. Hall, *Social Change in the Southwest, 1350–1880* (Lawrence: University Press of Kansas, 1989); and Sarah Deutsch, *No Separate Refuge: Culture, Class, and Gender on an Anglo-Hispanic Frontier in the American Southwest, 1880–1940* (New York: Oxford University Press, 1987).

12. William Cronon, *Nature's Metropolis: Chicago and the Great West* (New York: W. W. Norton, 1991), xiii, 7–8.

13. Michael P. Conzen, "The Maturing Urban System in the United States, 1840–1910," *Annals of the Association of American Geographers* 67 (March 1977): 89.

14. White, *Roots of Dependency,* xvii. In his striking study of Appalachia, John Gaventa employs the term "structured inequalities" (see Gaventa, *Power and Powerlessness: Quiescence and Rebellion in an Appalachian Valley* [Urbana: University of Illinois Press, 1980], 55–58).

15. David Harvey, *The Urbanization of Capital: Studies in the History and Theory of Capitalist Urbanization* (Baltimore: Johns Hopkins University Press, 1985), 190, 205, 216. See also Harvey, *Consciousness and the Urban Experience: Studies in the History and Theory of Capitalist Urbanization* (Baltimore: Johns Hopkins University Press, 1985), 3. For Alan Trachtenberg, the term metropolis implies "a commanding position within a region which included hinterland." See Trachtenberg, *The Incorporation of America: Culture and Society in the Gilded Age* [New York: Hill and Wang, 1982], 113.

16. Markusen, *Regions,* 2.

17. For the most cogent articulation of this argument, see Donald C. Meinig, *Atlantic America, 1492–1800,* vol. 1, *The Shaping of America: A Geographical Perspective of 500 Years of History* (New Haven, Conn.: Yale University Press, 1986).

18. Carl Abbott, "The Urban West and the Twenty-First Century," *Montana: Magazine of Western History* 43 (Spring 1993): 68.

19. Eric C. Monkkonen, *America Becomes Urban: The Development of U.S. Cities and Towns, 1780–1980* (Berkeley: University of California Press, 1988), 85, 92, 207; Carl Abbott, "The Metropolitan Region: Western Cities in the New Urban Era," in *The Twentieth-Century West: Historical Interpretations,* ed. Gerald D. Nash

and Richard W. Etulain (Albuquerque: University of New Mexico Press, 1989), 71–98; and Abbott, "Urban West and Twenty-First Century," 63. The phrase "metropolitan mode" is from Walter Nugent, *Structures of American Social History* (Bloomington: Indiana University Press, 1981), 31.

20. Wasson's essay is cited in Trachtenberg, *Incorporation of America*, 113.

21. Adna Ferrin Weber, *The Growth of Cities in the Nineteenth Century* (1899; reprint, New York: Cornell University Press, 1963), 187, 211–12.

22. Walter Prescott Webb, "Ended: 400 Year Boom, Reflections on the Age of the Frontier," *Harper's Magazine*, October 1951: 27–29; Webb, "Windfalls of the Frontier," *Harper's Magazine*, November 1951: 71–75; and Webb, *Divided We Stand: The Crisis of a Frontierless Democracy* (New York: Farrar and Rinehart, 1937).

23. Henry Nash Smith, *Virgin Land: The American West as Symbol and Myth* (New York: Vintage Books, 1950), 214–15, 223, 303.

24. Pomeroy, *Pacific Slope*, 120–21.

25. John M. Findlay, "Far Western Cityscapes and American Culture since 1940," *Western Historical Quarterly* 22 (February 1991): 22, and Findlay, *Magic Lands: Western Cityscapes and American Culture after 1940* (Berkeley: University of California Press, 1992), 1–2.

26. Weber, *Growth of the Cities in the Nineteenth Century*, 223, and Trachtenberg, *Incorporation of America*, 115. For a study of rural New England, see Hal S. Barron, *Those Who Stayed Behind: Rural Society in Nineteenth-Century New England* (Cambridge and New York: Cambridge University Press, 1984).

27. The argument that the capitalist class often works in concert similar to other social movements is argued in Martin J. Sklar, *The Incorporation of American Capitalism, 1890–1916* (New York: Cambridge University Press, 1988); and Joe R. Feagin, *Free Enterprise City: Houston in Political and Economic Perspective* (New Brunswick, N.J.: Rutgers University Press, 1988), 18.

28. Feagin, *Free Enterprise City*, 25–28; Pomeroy, *Pacific Slope*, 121; and Norbert MacDonald, "Population Growth and Change in Seattle and Vancouver, 1880–1960," *Pacific Historical Review* 39 (1970): 321.

29. See the discussion in Giddens, *Contemporary Critique of Historical Materialism*, 210.

30. Gaventa, *Power and Powerlessness*, 80.

31. For use of "thickened" to describe urban growth in the West, see Trachtenberg, *Incorporation of America*, 113.

32. Cronon, *Nature's Metropolis*, 68.

33. Ibid., Monkkonnen, *America Becomes Urban*, 79, 81; John Agnew, *The United States in the World Economy* (New York: Cambridge University Press, 1987), 3; Meinig, "American Wests," 170; and Weber, *Growth of Cities in the Nineteenth Century*, 228. Carl Abbott put Weber's remark in a slightly different context: "Virtually every observer thinks that the rich get richer when it comes to headquarters activity" (Abbott, "Urban West and Twenty-First Century," 65). On the relationship between capitalism and technological innovation, see Giddens, *Contemporary Critique of Historical Materialism*, 121–22.

34. Duane A. Smith, *Rocky Mountain West: Colorado, Wyoming, and Montana* (Albuquerque: University of New Mexico Press, 1992), 98–104.

35. Monkkonnen, *America Becomes Urban*, 79; Trachtenberg, *Incorporation of America*, 57; Cronon, *Nature's Metropolis*, 325, 374; and Pomeroy, *Pacific Slope*, 99.

36. Donald W. Meinig, *Imperial Texas: An Interpretive Essay in Cultural Geography* (Austin: University of Texas Press, 1969), 75–77.

37. Hunsaker is quoted in Norman Clark, *Mill Town: A Social History of Everett Washington* (Seattle: University of Washington Press, 1970), 41.

38. Lawrence H. Larsen and Roger T. Johnson, "A Story That Never Was: North Dakota's Urban Development," *North Dakota History* 47 (Fall 1980): 8–10.

39. Feagin, *Free Enterprise City*, 31; Harvey, *Urbanization of Capital*, 136; and Pomeroy, *Pacific Slope*, 124.

40. McWilliams, *California: The Great Exception*, 26; and Wallace Stegner, "A Little Bit of Heaven with Good P. R.," *New York Times Book Review*, February 24, 1985, 1. See also William G. Robbins, *Hard Times in Paradise: Coos Bay, Oregon, 1850–1986* (Seattle: University of Washington Press, 1988), 12.

41. Agnew, *United States in the World Economy*, 111, and William Issel and Robert W. Cherny, *San Francisco, 1865–1932: Politics, Power, and Urban Development* (Berkeley: University of California Press, 1986), 14, 23. For the reference to San Francisco as a city-state, see Pomeroy, *Pacific Slope*, 123.

42. Issel and Cherny, *San Francisco*, 15–16.

43. Peter Wiley and Robert Gottlieb, *Empires in the Sun: The Rise of the New American West* (New York: G. P. Putnam's Sons, 1982), 92–93; Issel and Cherny, *San Francisco*, 203, 212; and Abbott, "Urban West and Twenty-First Century," 65.

44. Wiley and Gottlieb, *Empires in the Sun*, 104; and R. B. Cohen, "The NEW Industrial Division of Labor, Multinational Corporations and Urban Hierarchy," in Dear and Scott, eds., *Urbanization and Urban Planning*, 300–301.

45. See Lawrence H. Larsen, *The Urban West at the End of the Frontier* (Lawrence: University Press of Kansas, 1978); John W. Fahey, *The Inland Empire: The Unfolding Years, 1879–1929* (Seattle: University of Washington Press, 1986); Bradford Luckingham, *The Urban Southwest: A Profile History of Albuquerque, El Paso, Phoenix, Tucson* (El Paso: Texas Western University Press, 1982); Lyle W. Dorsett, *The Queen City: A History of Denver* (Boulder: University of Colorado Press, 1977); John W. Reps, *Cities of the American West: A History of Urban Planning* (Princeton, N.J.: Princeton University Press, 1979); and Gunther Barth, *Instant Cities: Urbanization and the Rise of San Francisco and Denver* (New York: Oxford University Press, 1965).

46. See Wiley and Gottlieb, *Empires in the Sun*, 121; Barth, *Instant Cities*; and William Gilpin, *Notes on Colorado and Its Inscription in the Physical Geography of the North American Continent* (London, 1870), 32–33.

47. Larsen, *Urban West at End of Frontier*, 17; Wiley and Gottlieb, *Empires in the Sun*, 121; Carl J. Abbott, Stephen J. Leonard, and David McComb, *Colorado: A History of the Centennial State* (Boulder: Colorado Associated University Press, 1982), 2.

48. Dorsett, *Queen City*, 127–29, and Wiley and Gottlieb, *Empires in the Sun*, 122–23.

49. Dorsett, *Queen City*, 261–62, and Wiley and Gottlieb, *Empires in the Sun*, 139.

50. For El Paso's unique historical development, see Mario T. Garcia, *Desert Immigrants: The Mexicans of El Paso, 1880–1920* (New Haven, Conn.: Yale University Press, 1981), 2–5; Oscar J. Martinez, *Border Boom Town: Ciudad Juarez since 1848* (Austin: University of Texas Press, 1978), 3–22; and W. Eugene Hollon, *The Southwest: Old and New* (Lincoln: University of Nebraska Press, 1961), 460–61.

51. Garcia, *Desert Immigrants*, 15; Bradford Luckingham, "The American Southwest: An Urban View," *Western Historical Quarterly* 15 (1984): 263–68; and Luckingham, *Urban Southwest*, 33–35.

52. Thomas R. Navin, *Copper Mining and Management* (Tucson: University of Arizona Press, 1978), 241–50, and Garcia, *Desert Immigrants*, 19–20.

53. Linda B. Hall and Don M. Coerver, *Revolution on the Border: The United States and Mexico, 1910–1920* (Albuquerque: University of New Mexico Press, 1988), 18, 50, 57–64; Meinig, *Imperial Texas*, 102; and David Montejano, *Anglos and Mexicans in the Making of Texas, 1836–1986* (Austin: University of Texas Press, 1987), 94.

54. Cronon, *Nature's Metropolis*, 54 and 91. The term Inland Empire first appeared as a euphemism in promotional tracts: early newspapers, railroad booster pamphlets, and eventually in Spokane newspapers and chamber of commerce publications. See Fahey, *Inland Empire*, xi; and Herman J. Deutsch, "Geographic Setting for the Recent History of the Inland Empire," *Pacific Northwest Quarterly* 49 (1958): 152.

55. W. Hudson Kensel, "Inland Empire Mining and the Growth of Spokane, 1883–1905," *Pacific Northwest Quarterly* 60 (1969): 84–97; Fahey, *Inland Empire*, 176–81; and the author's interview with Fahey, July 1978. See also William Greever, *Bonanza West: The Story of the Western Mining Rushes, 1848–1900* (Moscow: University of Idaho Press, 1963). Donald Meinig sketches a more limited regional influence for Spokane in *The Great Columbia Plain: A Historical Geography, 1805–1910* (Seattle: University of Washington Press, 1968), 459–65.

56. William G. Robbins, " 'At the End of the Cracked Whip': The Northern West, 1880–1920," *Montana: Magazine of Western History* 38 (Autumn 1988): 9–11; Fahey, *Inland Empire*, 178–82, 216–20; Carlos Schwantes, *The Pacific Northwest: An Interpretation* (Lincoln: University of Nebraska Press, 1989), 171–75; and Kensel, "Inland Empire Mining," 97.

57. Carlos A. Schwantes, "The Concept of the Wageworkers' Frontier: A Framework for Future Research," *Western Historical Quarterly* 18 (1987): 41–42.

58. Schwantes, *Pacific Northwest*   173, 239–45, 251–65; Melvyn Dubofsky, *We Shall Be All: A History of the Industrial Workers of the World* (Chicago: Quadrangle Books, 1969), 175–84; and Schwantes, "Concept of the Wageworkers' Frontier," 39–55.

59. W. Thomas White, "Railroad Labor Protests, 1894–1917," *Pacific Northwest Quarterly* 75 (1984): 13–14.

60. Dubofsky, *We Shall Be All*, 175–84. For a personal insight into labor activity in the Spokane area during and after World War II, see Norman Best, *A Celebration of Work*, edited and with an introduction by William G. Robbins (Lincoln: University of Nebraska Press, 1990).

61. Garcia, *Desert Immigrants*, 85. David Montejano contends that ethnic relations in El Paso and other border cities were more flexible and pragmatic, "more a matter of class than of race," than in cities further removed from the international boundary (Montejano, *Anglos and Mexicans in the Making of Texas*, 265).

62. Feagin, *Free Enterprise City*, 43–54; Markusen, *Regions*, 100; and Fahey, *Inland Empire*, 228. For public subsidies to mining enterprises, see William K. Wyant, *Westward in Eden: The Public Lands and the Conservation Movement* (Berkeley: University of California Press, 1982), 160–93.

63. The references to the Spokane area are based on the author's lecture notes from a variety of sources. For El Paso, see Luckingham, *Urban Southwest*, 75–76; Luckingham, "American Southwest," 272–77; Niles Hansen, *The Border Economy: Regional Development in the Southwest* (Austin: University of Texas Press, 1981), 45; and Hollon, *Southwest*, 460.

64. Stephen Hahn and Jonathan Prude, eds., *The Countryside in the Age of*

Capitalist Transformation: Essays in the Social History of Rural America (Chapel Hill: University of North Carolina Press, 1985), 1, and Monkkonen, *America Becomes Urban*, 1.

CHAPTER TEN: EPILOGUE

1. The Lakewood story is in Joan Didion, "Letter from California: Trouble in Lakewood," *New Yorker*, July 26, 1993, 46–47 (emphasis added).
2. Ibid.
3. Gerald D. Nash, *The American West in the Twentieth Century: A Short History of an Urban Oasis* (Englewood Cliffs, N.J.: Prentice-Hall, 1973), 6, and Neil Morgan, *Westward Tilt: The American West Today* (New York: Random House, 1961), 6.
4. Nash, *American West in the Twentieth Century*, 290–99.
5. The phrase is that of Jerry Phillips, an Oregon forester, who was describing the destabilizing influence that timber-dependent communities experience when making the conversion from dependence on old-growth timber to a tree-farming regime (author's interview with Phillips, April 6, 1984).
6. Didion, "Letter from California," 65.
7. On the rumor, see ibid., 65. The expression "unbroken past" is the subtitle to Patricia N. Limerick's *Legacy of Conquest: The Unbroken Past of the American West* (New York: W. W. Norton, 1987).
8. Foster Church, "The California Exodus," *Portland Oregonian*, October 20, 1991.
9. Ibid.
10. Ibid.
11. Raye C. Ringholz, *Little Town Blues: Voices from the Changing West* (Layton, Utah: Gibbs Smith, 1992), 13–15.
12. Ibid., 106–7.
13. *Oregonian*, May 16, 1990, and October 20, 1991.
14. These percentages are printed in the *Oregonian*, October 20, 1991.
15. For a gloomy assessment of California's future, a requiem of sorts, see Neal R. Peirce, "Economists Prepare Requiem for a Heavyweight State," *Oregonian*, September 14, 1992. See also Bill Bradley, "California's Social Experiment May Set National Tone," *Oregonian*, May 24, 1990.
16. See *High Country News*, August 23, 1993.
17. Kittredge is quoted in *Time*, September 6, 1993, 27.
18. For the comments of Larry Eastland, a prominent Idaho Republican consultant, see *Oregonian*, December 15, 1991.
19. For a discussion of the tiered societies that are developing, see Ringholz, *Little Town Blues*, and *Oregonian*, November 24, 1991. For references to the new breed of "telecommuters" and "modem cowboys," see *Time*, September 6, 1993, 23.
20. *Oregonian*, November 24, 1991.
21. Ibid.
22. Ibid., January 26, 1992.
23. Ibid. (emphasis added).
24. Ibid., January 31, 1992.
25. Spencer C. Olin, "The View from the Top: Orange County's Political Elites since World War II" (Paper presented at the annual meeting of the Pacific

Coast Branch of the American Historical Association, Seattle, Washington, August 21, 1984, 4–8; copy in the author's possession).

26. Ibid., 19–21.

27. Carl Abbott to the author, November 5, 1993.

INDEX